FORWARD WITH THE FIFTH

The Author's thanks are due to the Australian War Museum for permission to publish photographs, and to Miss Enid Derham, M.A., for permission to publish her two poems—"Gallipoli" and "The Return." Also to Messrs. J. Sears, T. Humphrey and Co., Colograph Art. Co., and J. Wallace Ross, Esq., for photographs acknowledged under their names.

[Photo., T. Humphrey & Co.]

Colonel D. S. Wanliss, C.M.G.
"The Father of the Regiment."

FORWARD
WITH THE FIFTH

The Story of Five Years' War Service
Fifth Inf. Battalion, A.I.F.

(Published by Authority of
5th Battalion (A.I.F.) Regimental Association.)

BY
A. W. KEOWN
Late 571 Pte. 5th Batt.

The Naval & Military Press Ltd

Published by
The Naval & Military Press Ltd
5 Riverside, Brambleside, Bellbrook
Industrial Estate, Uckfield, East Sussex,
TN22 1QQ England
Tel: +44 (0) 1825 749494
Fax: +44 (0) 1825 765701
www.naval-military-press.com
www.military-genealogy.com
www.militarymaproom.com

CPI Antony Rowe, Chippenham and Eastbourne
*In reprinting in facsimile from the original, any imperfections are inevitably reproduced
and the quality may fall short of modern type and cartographic standards.*

FOREWORD

By

COLONEL D. S. WANLISS, C.M.G.

(Chief Justice, New Guinea.)

The First Commanding Officer of the 5th Battalion A.I.F.

August, 1914—July, 1915.

It is just seven years ago that the Fifth embarked on board the *Orvieto*—H.M.A.T. 3—which formed one of the great convoy that carried the 1st Division of the Australian Imperial Force, bound for The Great Adventure. The Battalion, like the whole of that force, was then an untried body, but no one that had seen it, still less those who had watched it during those first few months of its existence, could fail to feel confident of its value.

The physique and the intelligence, the self-reliance and *esprit-de-corps*, were sufficient to gladden the heart of any leader. And though that splendid thousand men who formed the original Battalion dwindled away through the hard long years of war, their places were filled by others who maintained the same spirit and dash to the very end.

Now, after the lapse of those seven years, the Battalion has ceased to be, and has taken its place in history. The story of its share in the making of that history is told in the book to which this is the Foreword; and it is fitting that it should be written

5

by one who was among the first to join the Regiment, who fought with it from the beginning, and whose heart is bound up in it.

It is perhaps hard to write a Foreword to a book one has not seen—and I have not seen this. It would be hard in this case, were the object of the book other than what it is. But that object is to record the deeds of a very gallant corps—deeds which, however deserving of fame, must be lost in the immensity of the war, if not preserved in this way. And with this object, too, is the further one of strengthening the ties that bind the comrades who lived and fought and died in the ranks of the Fifth.

May this History help to perpetuate the memory of deeds nobly done, of gallant men; of their bravery, their endurance, their cheerfulness; of Death bravely met and sufferings bravely endured.; and may it enable those who sent their husbands, sons and brothers to realise what manner of men they proved to be.

And now, as a last word, may I take this opportunity of sending a greeting to all my comrades of the old Fifth—to those, too, who joined it after my time with it had passed—to all those gallant souls who made the Fifth what it was, who lived and died *Sans Regrets?*

D. S. WANLISS.

Rabaul,
    New Guinea.
        1st Nov., 1921.

THE AUTHOR'S INTRODUCTION

Every book needs an introduction, and this one will not be different from others in this regard. The author begs the consideration of his readers on several points. Firstly, it may seem strange that the making of it has taken so long, but if the difficulties of gathering and collating the necessary information were known, then he is sure of your generous indulgence. The lack of literary experience must be so obvious as to disarm the higher criticism, while any historical inaccuracies must be ascribed to the varied sources, written and oral, from whence the material came. The absence of an official record (which was in the hands of Captain Bean, the war historian, at the time this was written) made the work a long and difficult one, and to those who lent their aid the author's best thanks are tendered. Those who lent their diaries; the little band who gathered regularly during the latter part of the writing to pad with anecdote and reminiscence, (some of it, alas! unprintable) facts's dry bones; the friends whose hospitality made these weekly yarns a delight to the writer—all have their share in whatever merit the story deserves.

If it appears uninteresting in parts, you will remind yourself that the men who figure in these pages also found the time stale and unprofitable. If it seems exaggerated, you will know from your reading or experience that this is impossible.

The writer's reward has been in the writing. Should the reading of it bring to you a hundredth part of the pleasure that has been his in these past months, then it has not failed.

Once a year, on the 25th of July, anniversary of the Battle of Pozieres, the Regimental Association gathers to renew old friendships. As memories grow dim with the passing of the years, perhaps this book will stimulate the recollection of the strange places and strange times, here perforce only lightly touched upon.

Here's hoping we may never forget the good comrades who marched in the dust of Egypt or the mud of France with us; some of them gone with Death, or scattered over the earth in their peaceful pursuits.

Here's wishing they may look back on their services with the Fifth "without regret."

CONTENTS

BOOK I.
AUSTRALA—EGYPT.

BOOK II.
GALLIPOLI—EGYPT.

9

BOOK III.

FRANCE AND FLANDERS.

Chapter   Page

LIST OF ILLUSTRATIONS

BOOK 1.
AUSTRALIA—EGYPT

Chapter I.

THE BIRTH OF A BATTALION.

NO one place can be designated as the birthplace of the regiment. Men were enlisted at Ripponlea, at Prahran, at Albert Park and Victoria Barracks, for service with the Fifth Battalion, in those early days of August, 1914. That we chose to regard the regiment as an entity—something that had soul and being, is not strange. The reader, if he has been a member of the unit, will have felt something of this conviction stirring in his mind at times, however faintly. Those of you whom sex or age or physique debarred from service in the Great Adventure will perhaps feel at the end of the story that some intangible, but strong and potent force, held these few hundred men together; bound them tightly with comradeship, pride, and no little discipline, to achieve what they did in spite of fear and misery, both of mind and body.

Many things perforce remain unrecorded. The friendships, strong and clean as new steel, forged in the desert sand or the Somme mud, that will savour life for us to the very end; the happy days of furlough or convalescence in the Home Country, where our kinsmen's warm kindness made lonely men take fresh heart for the dangers to be faced again; incident and humour that made the monotony of camp life or the distastefulness of fatigue work more bearable—these are still unwritten.

It has been difficult to keep the matter herein of
general interest. Some of the incident recorded has
barely rippled the surface of the company life, or
reached the next platoon; some of it may be uninteresting to everyone but the few who participated.
Be that as it may, it is as veracious and impartial a
chronicle as the circumstances will allow.

Excepting the few men who were attested at the
Victoria Barracks, the remainder of the first enlistments were medically examined and sworn in at
one or other of the Drill Halls mentioned, buildings
familiar to every Australian; iron or weather-
boarded sides, iron roof and high wired windows;
inside, a canopy of naked roof principals with tawdry
shreds of decoration from some long-ago regimental
ball hanging drearily; a vista of doors and hat racks
in serried rows, of rifle racks, and an indecently bare
oasis of wooden floor, with a few tables and chairs
at one end. Here it was that the patriot, with no
little trepidation, badly concealed beneath the
bluster of a D'Artagnan, advanced on the table
where a staff sergeant-major sat behind a trim heap
of blue papers. And here it was that each one
acknowledged previous military service, some of it
in apocryphal regiments, and divulged sacred details
of family history that the covers of the family Bible
had hitherto held inviolate. Passed on to the waiting
medicos (most infernally particular about teeth in
those days) and if satisfactory, on to another table
where he swore to "faithfully serve His Majesty the
King . . . for the duration of the war or four
months thereafter." Lightly and blithely the average recruit took that mighty oath, and little recked
in most cases that the sacred vows of matrimony
could more easily be cast aside than this pledge of
fealty to the Empire. It is an axiom that it is

The New-Born Regiment Marching to Camp, 19th August, 1914.

[By courtesy Sears.]

easier to desert your wife and offspring than to abscond from His Majesty's Forces. This ceremony over, the newly-made soldier, with an exaggerated military bearing, swaggered out into the sunshine of 17th August, 1914, a member of the Fifth Infantry Battalion, Second Brigade, First Australian Imperial Expeditionary Force, as it was then called.

Two days later, on the 19th, the Prahran men assembled in the road in front of their military birthplace, piled their diverse collection of kits on to the baggage waggons, were pushed and led and bullied into some semblance of order, and moved off down Commercial Road into St. Kilda Road, and thence to Victoria Barracks, where other recruits were assembling in the barrack square.

The fearsome array of officers of every grade of rank, every variety of uniform, and of most astounding diversity in words of command, duly impressed the recruits, and one unfortunate who scratched his ear whilst standing at attention, drew down on his luckless head the objurgations of at least four commanding voices, which threw the whole battalion into a state of nervous expectancy. No one was led out for execution, however, and the men breathed freely again.

As many of the Second Brigade as had been recruited in Melbourne, now being assembled, Lt.-Col. J. W. McCay, V.D., made a stirring patriotic speech, and then to the music of a Citizen Force Band the column swung out of the barracks gate through an avenue of admiring and already tearful womenfolk, along St. Kilda Road and through the city towards Broadmeadows. What a motley crowd they were, to be sure! A mingling of uniform and mufti that would have been highly humorous had it not been for the enthusiasm that kindled in each man's face.

Here were the Garibaldi shirts and khaki Glengarry
cap of citizen force regiments; there the dark tar-
tan kilts and red-checked cap of the Victorian Scottish Regiment; but the majority in every conceiv-
able type of civilian garb.   Some in their very best
clothes, caring little whether they would ever use
them again; other more cautious, in their very oldest
suits.   Tweed caps and felt hats; straw hats and
boxers; leggings, golf stockings and putties. Despite
the variety of clothing, the whole were actuated by
common impulses of patriotism or adventure, and
permeated with an infectious good cheer and
camaraderie.

Of the dusty, foot-wearying trudge to Broadmeadows—through the northern suburbs, past Fawkner
Cemetery, and along Sydney Road to the gates of
their new home—no one who took part in it will
need reminding. Most of the men were untrained to
this form of exercise, and as others had regaled
themselves upon pastry, sweets, aerated water or
beer, the march of 11 miles seemed a long one indeed.
The veterans of two days who formed the advance
guard of the battalion clustered round the entrance
to the Camp and grinned insolently at the dragging
fours.   *They* had come out by train or waggon,
and could appreciate the humour of it.

The camp was situated in a large paddock, part
of the demesne of Major Wilson.   Formerly it had
been under cultivation, and on the south and west
sides, and round the homestead itself, it was fringed
with well-grown pine trees.   The site was, roughly
speaking, rectangular, being bounded on the north
by paddocks under cultivation, on the south by the
road that ran between Sydney Road and Broadmeadows railway station, on the east by the disused
Melbourne-Campbelltown railway that ended here-

about, and on the west by fields dotted with stony outcrop, a description which might aptly include the cemetery in the S.W. corner. The land sloped from the centre eastward and westward. Water was being hastily laid on at this period—as it proved, with a remarkably poor pressure, of which everyone has poignant memories. Previously water was supplied to the stock by waterholes, and it was alongside one of these that the last halt was made. The weary column of men passed through the gibing crowd at the main gate, and through an interested and critical group of Imperial Reservists who had been responsible for the work of laying out the camp. They were then unaccountably halted alongside one of the muddy waterholes, and ordered to bathe their feet. This was their first experience of military hygiene, and it was not kindly received by the majority, whose feet were tolerably clean before the enforced ablution.

This over, the battalions were marched a little further till they were abreast of the lines they were to occupy, and in the failing light were addressed by one of their new officers. The theme of his remarks was "Discipline," and the listeners were bluntly informed that the path of the young soldier who conformed to the rules laid down by a beneficent government was strewn with roses, but otherwise—then Heaven protect them, for the officers had the thick end of the stick, and would not scruple to use it. Which naturally determined this particular officer's nickname as "The Thick End" until such time as a more euphonious and descriptive cognomen usurped its place.

Then the company lines were pointed out, eight of them in those days of eight-company battalion organisation, and a rush ensued for tents, little

groups of old friends and new acquaintances having
been formed already.   Large hessian sacks, when
filled with straw and tied at the ends make a reasonably comfortable mattress, and by the time these
were issued and filled, tea was served. From the
mostly unskilled hands of the temporary cooks, it was
an unappetising repast, but hunger overbore the
meticulous qualms of those used to restaurant dining or the niceties of home fare. Food disposed of,
came the search for baggage among the hopeless
mountains at the end of each line, and by the light
of candles, men endeavoured to make themselves
comfortable with the aid of two blankets and the
straw palliass, supplemented by all their spare
clothes. New-found chums swapped confidences and
arranged their kits next each other, and already dif-
ferences of opinion arose as to the amount of tent
space allotted to each man.   The pessimist openly
derided the possibility of sixteen men sleeping in
one tent, even if they did arrange themselves spoke-
like, feet to the centre, as it was explained all the
best soldiers did.   The optimist cheerily suggested
that they should sleep with their heads outside the
flap, to enlarge the circle. So with half serious and half
good-natured grumble, lights went out gradually,
though official ''Lights out'' had sounded long ago.
The mumble of conversation made pleasant company
for the new sentry, who half expected an enemy
attack during his period of duty, and, keenly alert
for the slightest sound, heard names, occupations,
birthplaces and cigarettes freely exchanged.   The
orderly officer's gruff order to go to sleep made no
appreciable difference to the undercurrent of conversation, which did not abate till long after midnight.

Chapter II.

EARLY TRAINING DAYS, BROADMEADOWS.

THE days that followed were much the same that all soldiers, whether in the Dominions or in England, were experiencing, and that every citizen soldier has seen. The issue of arms and equipment, then, after a short time, of uniforms; the gradual absorption of discipline; the acquisition of the knowledge that it was not good form to address your officer as "Bill"—even if he had been courting your sister in the days of peace; the knowledge that untidiness and dirt were abhorrent and dangerous in a closely crowded community; these and many other things were slowly and ofttimes painfully imparted to willing learners by patient and earnest instructors. The mysteries of leave, the system of issuing beer at the Brigade canteen, the correct method of puttee winding, the proper way of assembling web equipment, (there was nothing in taking it apart) these were quickly learnt by a Brigade that, despite their attested "previous military experience" were, to the extent of about sixty per cent., ignorant of the correct military methods.

So was created that wonderful thing, *esprit de corps*. No word in English seems to express quite the same shade of meaning, or possibly the word would not have persisted in our language. Men of the Fifth began to boast in the canteen and in the Y.M.C.A. of what *their* battalion had done, was

doing, and intended to do. Of the beautiful
trenches they had dug that day; of how the battalion had marched from the "Red House" back to
the main gate in so many minutes; of the super-
excellence of their band; of how their particular
platoon commander was "one of the best," and so
on, ad infinitum. All of which was good. Thus the
Battalion's soul was being evolved, its personality
was slowly taking shape, mainly through the in-
fluence of its commander and officers; its individuality
being moulded from the formless, heterogeneous mass
of humanity that had been promiscuously thrust into
it. Remember, it had no tradition to look back to;
no glorious record of past battles to thrill the new
recruits; no tattered standards or faded colours. It
was soulless. What work lay in front of everyone
in authority, from the Colonel to the newest lance-
corporal!

It has been noted that many of the Victorian Scottish Regiment had joined the Fifth. Lieutenant-
Colonel Wanliss, the C.O., Captain Stewart, the
Adjutant, and many more of the officers came from
that regiment. Nearly the whole of "A" company
and part of "B" were old Scottish men, and the
skirl of bagpipes was heard in the lines. Hopes
ran high indeed among the enthusiasts of making it
another Scottish regiment, and of adorning the men
with kilts, hopes which were not dissipated till
Egypt was left behind.

Not only was the battalion unique for this strong
Scottish element, but from the fact that "F" company was a Public School unit. Every man in this
company claimed connection with a Public School or
College, and never has Public School rivalry been so
splendidly combined to a common end. In the beginning the other companies held somewhat aloof,

crediting them with a certain amount of "swank," but later mingling with them and finding that quality non-existent. The idea at this time was to keep the company purely as a Public School one, and to divert a similar class of reinforcements to it; but with the advent of the "double company" system, this plan was abandoned. Then "F" was blended with "H," and the Public School spirit, instead of being kept a lump, leavened a larger mass.

One incident of training days deserves mention for its unusualness. A man of the regiment was punished for some ordinary breach of discipline, but evidently took to heart the old adage "as well be hanged for a sheep as a lamb," and with the fancied enormity of his punishment rankling in his mind, began to look for more trouble, which is a bad thing in the army. It was comparatively easy to run foul of constituted authority again, to be duly brought to righteous account, to assume a wholly imaginary vindictiveness on the part of the individuals who had inflicted the punishment, and, within a brief period of time, to become the black sheep, sullenly indifferent to cumulative punishment and common-sense exhortations not to be a damfool. There could be only one ending to such wilful disregard of the common law, and that followed quickly on the heels of one particularly bad break—Field Punishment No. 1. This consisted of stretching the victim on the earthen floor of the guard tent on his back, with arms and legs outstretched. Tent pegs, one on each side of wrists and ankles, made the posture an awkward and painful one, from which the ropes made escape impossible.

The incident created a ripple on the placid surface of the Battalion's life, and the curious walked past the guard tent many times in the day in an unsuccessful endeavour to see the prisoner. Neighbouring regiments generated more excitement than did the Fifth, and when work was over for the day, the guard tent became the centre of interest for the camp. Generally the opinion seemed to be that this punishment of "crucifixion" was degrading; and so perhaps it would have been to the men who so judged it, but under the circumstances it was authorised and defensible.

In the wet canteens that evening the talk rose hot and loud—oddly enough, loudest and hottest among those of other regiments who knew little or nothing of the case. A crowd, mostly curious, but very restless and slightly menacing, had gathered round the guard tent, and the Orderly Company fell in as a precaution against a rescue, such as was by this time being openly advised by some few orators, discreetly stationed at the rear of the gathering. Swelled by a number from the Fourteenth Battalion, not long in camp, the mob had assumed alarming proportions, and, to avoid trouble, the prisoner was released after about four hours spent in his cramped position, and the crowd raised an exultant cheer and moved away. The prisoner proved to be not at all improved or even impressed by the severity of the punishment, and between then and the battalion's going into action, the guard tent knew his presence almost continually.

The battalion had now assumed an entity. The Colonel rode at the head of the column on the march, no longer looking uneasily behind at the broken, winding procession which had pained his gaze a few weeks ago, but looking ahead, proudly conscious that behind him marched a compact body, moving with the swing that comes only with constant training; a living column, with the flexibility of spring steel in each man's step.   Not quite perfect as judged by the regular soldier's standard, for it takes many weeks to turn the sedentary worker into muscularity.   Still, the change wrought in the men as a whole was a remarkable one.   They were distinctly browner, heavier and healthier, and, best sign of all, they were asking when they would be leaving for the Front.

By this time the men had become less inexpert in the handling and wearing of the "web equipment"—that ingenious tangle of canvas straps and bags with which the British Infantryman envelops himself.   Displayed deftly before the recruit by an instructor who probably has spent years of his life mastering its intricacies, it looks sublimely simple. Later, the innocent "rookie" is handed some fourteen or fifteen pieces, told that is his equipment, and ordered to put it together.   The average platoon could have the whole Sahara desert to lay the "web" out on, but would later emerge, a sweating, swearing mass, to find that besides having assembled it altogether wrongly, each one had either taken some of the next man's parts; or in some devilish, inexplicable way buckled their kits on to his.

The inventor probably died insane while endeavouring to work out new combinations and complexities of this ingenious equipment.   Every infantryman devoutly hopes so.

After having arrived home late from leave, no one can plumb the depths of misery more quickly than an infantryman who, a quarter of an hour before "fall in" next morning, endeavours to restore his "stripped belt" back to "marching order."   Inevitably he gets it wrong, and probably begins the march feeling like a camel with loose parcels tied all over it, nothing being more uncomfortable than ill-fitting ''web.''

Sport was not neglected in camp, and a championship meeting had been arranged to take place on a certain Saturday afternoon. A rough running track had been laid out at the expense of several sweating fatigue parties, on the ground that lay between the camp and Broadmeadows station, and units held their eliminative competitions on the preceding Sunday. At this meeting the Fifth worthily established their prowess, ''F'' Company not unnaturally contributing some fine athletes. The high jump, relay race, hundred yards and platoon marching contest were won, and numerous places filled in the other events by the Fifth, and it was a joyous regiment that serenaded the officers' mess that night.

There were many aspirants for non-commissioned rank, and the examinations which took place a few weeks after the formation of the camp were not without their humorous side. From the gallant and courteous candidate who said, ''Gentlemen! Attention!'' to the rougher, but no less earnest one, who gave the order, ''Fall in! Two thick!'', everyone was a trier and a goodly lot were eventually chosen.

Meanwhile events in Europe chased each other with alarming significance. The Battle of the Marne and the British retreat, the overwhelming advance of the German army and the Belgian outrages, these events were the main topics of the camp. Would they get to Europe in time to see fighting? This question worried the men greatly. The visitors who came in their tens of thousands on Sunday afternoons all talked of this. The womenfolk, of course, hoped it would be over before the soldiers had time to leave Australia. The fathers were jolly pleased that the boys had enlisted, but still they thought it would be only a pleasure trip. "You'll get there just in time to see the end, old chap!" "Wait till the British Navy gets at 'em, but I hope you'll get to the Old Country," and so on.

How the men felt in regard to fighting is hard to describe. Had they enlisted for a pleasure trip, or was there hard and bloody fighting in front of them? Later they would be called "Six-bob-a-day tourists," and though that phrase had not then been coined, the vast majority of people at this time regarded the war as being both far distant and short-lived. The armchair critic, secure in his estimate of Britain's sea-power, saw nothing but an imminent naval battle of such magnitude as to smash Germany utterly on sea, and thus leave the French army to complete their discomfiture and defeat on land.

The reasons for enlistment were of great diversity, but underlying each one was the feeling that fighting lay ahead. As one glances now over letters from men in camp at this period, one finds this thought repeatedly expressed. One lad asks his friend to come down from the country if possible and see him before they sail. "We will be leaving soon, if rumours are true," he writes, "and I feel that there are some of us who will never return. Do try and come." And there are others which voice the same conviction. This to them was a serious adventure.

Leave from the camp was meagre, especially for country men, who had but one week-end, in most cases, to bid farewell to home. Week-night leave was one night in four, conditions which contrasted strongly with those surrounding later contingents. Not only in this respect, but in many others, were the men of the First Division pioneers. Broadmeadows camp at this time did not possess one permanent building. Administrative offices, canteens, troops,—all were under canvas. The tents were minus floors, and in the wet weather, which was fairly frequent at this season, they covered a circle of mud only slightly less thick than that outside. Water ran through and soaked the bedding, and mud was everywhere. Cooks toiled in the open with damp wood and smoky fires, but all these discomforts were endured almost cheerfully. Who that has slept in the confines of a bell tent in wet weather, with twelve to fifteen men his inescapable companions in discomfort, can ever forget the misery of it all? Was it only a "furphy" that some of the men who came after grumbled at the deficiencies of wooden huts with spring mattresses in the bunks? Shades of the First Division!

That part of the First Division now quartered in Broadmeadows Camp was by this time deemed fit for inspection, and the desire of the public in this regard was satisfied by a street march. This took place on 25th September, the infantry and other dismounted arms being conveyed to Spencer Street Railway Station by train, where they massed with the mounted services who had come by road. Proceeding up Collins Street, the column passed the saluting base in Spring Street, and moved via Bourke and Elizabeth Streets to Royal Park, where the infantry lunched and rested. The Second Brigade had marched with fixed bayonets "at the slope" for the whole of this distance; no light test. Their reward came in the form of the applause of adoring and excited crowds, and appreciative press references the next day. The march was remarkable for the discipline shown by these new troops, a result of the men being exhorted by their officers not to recognise friends or relations in the crowd. It was with the aplomb of veterans and the steadiness of regulars that they passed through their people, and many a mother was sad when she failed to attract the attention of her boy as he marched past with eyes fixed steadily in front.   After resting, the battalion took the same road to camp as they had trod some few weeks before   Then they had been a rabble; now they moved with the free confidence of trained men.

Then came a period of false alarms.   Just as a chance remark in a small country town spreads and amasses detail, so the idly conceived and uttered word goes through the battalion (which is very parochial in its way) like a scrub fire, but soon losing its original form and becoming a wondrous statement of fact, duly attested by the highest authority.   Next morning sees yesterday's story discarded and reviled, and a new rumour in full flight.   So, as will be explained, these rumours came to be known throughout the Victorian portion of the First Division as "furphies," the term being later adopted by the whole of the A.I.F. into its language.   An explanation of its origin may not be amiss, as showing how fame of a sort was thrust upon a country water-cart manufacturer.   These carts were originally designed for use in the country, and bore the maker's name "Furphy," on the side in large letters.   They were utilised by the authorities for sanitary purposes in connection with the latrines, and as it was at these institutions that rumour was most widely disseminated, the term "a furphy" came to be used for a baseless rumour; an untruth.

The Eighth Battalion were the first to be stirred by the false alarms.   Known as "The Dirty Eighth" from a stricture passed on the cleanliness of their surroundings by their C.O., they had been further humiliated by being marched through the lines of the other battalions so as to be taught how tents

should be kept.   Detractors of the Eighth com-
monly ascribe the nickname to a highly-coloured
romance, in which a female is concerned—but this is
perhaps a "furphy."

First the Eighth packed their tents and kits and
went—only to return, and undergo the weary process of unpacking and re-erecting.   Then the turn
of the Fifth came. Tents were struck, packed and
piled.   Kits were stacked at the end of company
lines, and the Battalion in full marching order moved
out to the parade ground, everyone agog with plea-
surable excitement.   "We're off!" declared all except a few pessimists, dismal as usual.   But rumour
had lied again, and after a long wait, during which
the men sat and smoked, and the more sentimental
surreptitiously scribbed farewell notes, the battalion
trooped back, to unpack bad-temperedly and begin
monotony anew.

They had streamed from the lines one bright Sunday morning to see the Light Horse leave, the
friendly cheers of the Infantry inciting fresh horses
to wondrous exhibitions of bucking and pig-rooting:
then the three other battalions and various units
in camp had left in quick succession; and another
false alarm had been endured before the Fifth were
really off.   They left on the morning of Wednesday, October 21, 1914.

The regiment was reassured when they reached
the Broadmeadows station and found a gaily decorated engine to draw their train.   The pessimists
thought still it might be part of the training, but the
last faint growls of the consistent grumblers were
drowned by the mighty cheer that rose and startled
the old grey horse of the soft-drink vendor who had
clung to the skirts of the battalion on all its journeyings, but was now left behind as the train steamed
out with its happy freight on adventure bound.

Chapter III.

FAREWELL, AUSTRALIA.

THE arrangements for the transport of the First Division to England meant the employment of a large fleet of transports, and the largest of the vessels in the various ports were commandeered and transformed into troop-carrying vessels, with scant regard for passenger fittings. Latrines, cookhouses, washhouses and other accommodations were built on deck where necessary; smoking and dining rooms were gutted, and mess tables and seats, hammock racks and rings, installed in their stead.

Of the many vessels comprising the fleet, the finest, if not the largest, was reserved for Headquarters Staff, Nurses, the Fifth, and the Second Field Company Engineers. This was the *Orvieto,* an Orient liner of twelve thousand odd tons.

An advance guard from "A" Company had reached the boat and were busy cleaning up the workmen's litter and generally preparing for the battalion's arrival. Some seven or eight horses, the chargers of the various "brass hats" aboard, were accommodated with boxes aft of the lower promenade deck, the Engineers were berthed up forward, and the various infantry companies were distributed between decks, amidships and aft. Lucky people, like the sergeants and the Postal Corps, had second-class cabins, while the abodes of the officers were popularly supposed to be replete with every comfort. "H" Company received the dregs of the accommodation, so to speak, and were immured in the bowels of the ship below the water line.

The *Orvieto* was naturally last to leave, and the secrecy which had veiled the movements of the rest of the fleet, and was so questioned by the armchair critics, slightly lifted now that the others had got safely away.

The wandering German sea-raiders were then scouring the seas, and this secrecy was not ill-judged, as later events proved.   At any rate, the departure of the *Orvieto* was the breaking-point of the steadily growing crowd of anxious relatives, strictly excluded from the wharf, who had watched the bustle of departure of other transports, uncertain as to which held their loved one, who was being mysteriously whisked off. It was so different from the orthodox way in which Britain had always sent her fighters forth.   Such sure signs of the departure of this last ship brought patience to the culminating point, at which mothers and sisters, bursting with stifled love and anxiety, overwhelmed the armed guard thrown across the pier entrance, and flowed up the wharf to the ship's side, thrusting impatiently away the impotent, wavering bayonets of the harassed citizen soldiery.   What a good-bye this last ship received!   The browned, cheerful men leaning over the rails, peering from portholes, and clinging to the rigging and deckhouses, saw few familiar faces among the crowd, and perhaps did not wholly realise the significance of this vicarious farewell from swelling hearts who had been denied the painful pleasure of seeing their own lads go.

So with breaking lines of coloured streamers that shone bravely in the sun, and the band blaring from an upper deck, the ropes were cast off and the fussy tugs edged the ship away from the wharf.   The

The "Orvieto" Leaving Port Melbourne, 21st October, 1914. [By courtesy Sears.]

widening space was whipped up to milky froth, the
last reluctant streamer broke, and the ship nosed her
careful way into the channel. Perhaps it was then
that some of the cheerful faces smiling towards the
shore grew suddenly grave; and who shall blame the
eyes of youth if the crowd seemed somewhat dim and
out of focus?

Soon the pier was like a dry stick that had by a
miracle bloomed at the end into coloured glory, as
the crowd clustered at the furthermost point, and
waved tirelessly, long after the *Orvieto* was hull down
on the horizon, and the men were busying themselves
about their first meal on the transport.

The familiar black canvas kit-bag had been packed
some days before, and in its place had appeared the
"sea kit bag," a white one of more flimsy material,
on which the owner's name and regimental particulars
appeared more or less legibly and artistically in indelible pencil.   Canvas hammocks, blankets, and
lifebelts (the latter doing duty as pillows), were
issued, and   messes   arranged.   Queenscliff was
reached in the rosy haze of sunset, the pilot was taken
on board, a string of flags on the look-out fluttered
good-bye, and on a smooth swell the ship turned into
the heart of the sunset and met the rough caress of
the Southern Ocean.   Insidious qualms now began
to attack some of the troops, not a curious thing when
one considers that a fair number had never before
seen the sea, and many had never been on a ship.
Surely excuses can be found for the man thus cir-
cumstanced who disdained the supper call, and remained dismally contemplating fast-vanishing Victoria from the rail.

Now came the swift realisation that life on a transport was confined to very narrow limits, despite the
comparative spaciousness of the ship.   Men came to

B

know others in the battalion, of whose existence they
had previously been unaware. If the battalion in
camp had possessed many of the peculiarities of a
small country town, here it became like one that was
cut off from the surrounding countryside by floods.
The wonder is that the men did not become bored
with each other, but it is axiomatic that one does not
have time to be bored with hard work. Fatigued,
yes; but not bored. The men soon learnt that certain parts of the ship were taboo. The boat deck
was reserved for officers; this naturally made the
bridge inaccessible, except to the fortunate signaller
on duty. The saloons were also forbidden ground to
the ranks, but in every other part of the ship they
pried and peered with lively curiosity. They invaded
the crew's quarters, engineroom and stokehold till
checked. Sleeping on deck became fashionable long
before the temperature made it comfortable, and
none but the sick or stodgy slept below. Deck space
became valuable, and when tea was over, everyone
grabbed their roll of blankets, hammock and lifebelt,
and rushed up to reserve their sleeping space. Plac-
ing the roll again the wall was not efficacious, unless
a careful watch was kept upon it, for one might return after a brief absence to find his bed in the
scupper and a look of bland innocence on the face of
the "claim jumper."

Albany was reached after five days, on the twenty-
fifth of October at half-past seven in the morning,
and here the remainder of the fleet awaited the rearguard. This very beautiful harbour showed to great
advantage from the deck of a large steamer, and when
the inner anchorage was reached, the immensity of
the fleet was revealed. Preparations were now complete for departure, the New Zealand portion of the
fleet having arrived, looking very warlike in battle-

ship grey, in contradistinction to the other ships, which wore their work-a-day colours, mostly dingy. In the early light of Sunday morning, the first of November, the *Orvieto* led the line through the winding channels and bays to the open sea again. Albany lay veiled in an opalescent shroud, the harbour unruffled beneath the windless dawn.   The smoke from scores of funnels drifted slowly upward and hung in canopies over each ship as she slowly moved into line and followed the flagship of this new Armada.   At perfect intervals they fell astern, and as the sun topped the hills, a faint breeze disturbed the mirrored reflections, and brisk wavelets lapped the bows of each craft in farewell benediction.   Now the smell of the land was succeeded by the brisk salt breeze, and the ruder buffets of the open sea saluted the plunging craft.   Good-bye, Australia! The green of the Australian hills merged gradually into purple and then imperceptibly into the blue of the horizon. Cape Leeuwin was the last of the coast visible.   For many of these men it was good-bye for the last time.

Chapter IV.

TROOPSHIP DAYS.

AS the fleet ploughed its way into more temperate climes, costumes became more scanty. The
issue suits of blue dungaree were grievously
maltreated. Many coats fell overboard or became
the perquisites of the crew, and the trousers were abbreviated to knickers. Uniform, boots and puttees
were discarded except for church parades, and the
ordinary working costume was white hat, singlet, and
short "blueys." The indigo dye in these, proved not
by any means "fast," took many strenuous washings
to dissipate wholly, and before this was effected, the
men stripped for their baths looking like woad-painted
Britons.

Physical training and lectures were the main events
of working hours, and work barely served at times
to keep monotony at bay. Reading matter was
scarce, and little was attempted in the way of amusement, though a few "sing-songs" were held on deck
with the aid of a harmonium. The band at this time
were going through little troubles peculiar to bands,
and for a short period it was silent until the disputed
matter of practising in working hours was satisfactorily settled. The pipers were active, however, six or
seven of them, and long and bitter were the arguments
between the two schools of thought represented on the
boat. With admirable zeal, the true Scottish-Aus-
tralian defended the pipes, striving manfully to con-

vince his opponent, and at the same time to remove any lingering doubts in his own mind as to the real musical value of the instrument. The Sassenachs, who greatly outnumbered their antagonists, sneered loudly at the idea of an Australian regiment tolerating such "blanky windbags," and were not averse to groaning like stricken souls when "On the Banks of Allan Water" droned out from the officers' deck after mess. Of this violent antipathy of the majority to good Scottish music, more anon.

The deadly monotony of troopship life, accentuated by the languor of the tropics, had now settled on the troops, and they grumbled mightily under the hard hand of discipline, which, had they only known it, was the only thing that kept them out of misery.

An amusing incident of shipboard life was the beer issue. A quantity of beer had been purchased out of regimental funds, and in order to eke it out it was sparingly issued at midday, one pint to a man. The price was threepence a pint, and its very rarity made it the more appreciated by the temperate ones. The malcontents, however, could not even through the medium of kind teetotal friends, obtain a sufficiency of the precious fluid, and accordingly they fathered the "furphy" that the beer had been a gift from the breweries, and that "some people" unnamed, but vaguely referred to as "The Heads," were basely selling to the troops their own property. Whereupon they argued that if the men refused to buy, then "they" would be brought to see the error of their ways. The boycott was loudly proclaimed to begin the next day, but, alas! for the weakness of human nature, at the usual time, instead of a disconsolate Q.M. wailing for customers that never came, behold the fearful spectacle of a lengthy, thirsty queue, differing no whit from that of yesterday, excepting for the absence of the few discontented ones. Even they succumbed to temptation the next day, and thenceforward uncomplainingly paid their threepences.

An incident occurring on the voyage was interesting in the light of later events. Two of the *Orvieto* stewards were desirous of joining the A.I.F., and accordingly they were sworn in, at once relinquishing their ship's duty for the irksome life of the soldier. In view of the fact that Australians in England, when conscription was there instituted, were not allowed to join the A.I.F., it is curious to reflect how this addition to the Fifth's strength was officially effected.

The fleet was now fairly in the tropics; the shoals of blue and silver flying fish, the smooth unbroken circle of intensely indigo sea, and the gorgeous sunset effects all proclaimed it. The equator was passed in a tropical downpour, which brought the men forth in a joyous, naked band, capering in wild enjoyment of their first and only freshwater shower of the voyage. The nights were perfect. Sleeping on deck was delightful, though smoking was forbidden, and the fear of being sent below meant keeping the blanket over heated bodies. To gaze over the rail at night was to see a fairyland of swirling phosphorescent lights that stretched ghostily behind, to where a faint blur of white marked the wave at the bow of the ship astern.

The story of the *Sydney-Emden* fight has been told so often and so well that a brief reference will suffice here, and that rather concerning the audience that waited for news a few miles away over the horizon, than the chief actors in that stirring sea-drama.

Keeping watch on the left of the convoy was H.M.A.S. *Sydney*, H.M.S. *Black Prince* and *Mont Calais*, with H.M.A.S. *Minotaur* in the van, the Japanese cruiser *Ibuki*, H.M.A.S. *Melbourne* and

Philomel on the right, and H.M.S. *Pioneer* forming the rearguard.

This formation was unbroken until the morning of the tenth of November, when the *Sydney*, simultaneously with others of the fleet, received the appeal for help from Cocos Island. The *Sydney* vanished quickly over the horizon in a blur of smoke; the *Ibuki* turned swiftly inward and crossed the *Orvieto's* bows at what seemed to be the distance of a biscuit toss, revealing to the wondering spectators on the troopship the bustling preparation for action that portended serious work. Her bows in a smother of foam, and with a dense plumage of smoke, the Japanese boat sped over to the Sydney's former position, guarding the left flank.

The excitement that possessed the whole ship was heightened by the wireless message that was soon made available, "Am in action. Enemy ship heading easterly;" and later reached its culminating point when the news came, "Enemy ship beached and damaged. Believed to be *Emden.*" The rejoicing that followed this auspicious news was untinged by any dread presentiment of what was bound up in this event for the Fifth; but the men were soon to heap maledictions on the heads of the Hun raiders. Just now, in blissful ignorance of the double guards— "ship" and "prisoners", that were soon to be theirs, they loudly cheered the feat of their comrades of the navy.

Some few days later, when nearing Colombo, the victorious *Sydney* passed up through the lines of the convoy with her prisoners, but as some of these were seriously wounded, instructions were issued to troops to refrain from cheering, so that their applause took the form of silent waving, when they had an overwhelming inclination to yell. On the sixteenth, at Colombo, four officers and forty-eight men of the *Emden* were transhipped to the *Orvieto*, provision having been made for their reception on the extreme end of the after well-deck. The officers refused parole, and were accommodated with a cabin with sentry attached. Captain von Mueller, for all his bravery, acted very cavalierly, and was discourteous enough to spit at the sentry one day for standing too near the porthole of his cabin. The presence of the Huns on board meant double guard as has been noted, and in addition all men were cleared from the lower promenade deck for two hours each morning while the prisoners exercised. Physically they were finer men than ours, and performed physical exercise under the commands of their petty officers in a smart and thorough manner. They were not averse to bartering hatbands, canteen tokens, and other trifles for tobacco or fancy biscuits, and one at least chatted to his guards in good English. This man had been in Melbourne for some years, and was on a trip to Germany when the military machine closed on him and allotted him to the navy.

Provided with the same bedding as the troops, they complained of discomfort, and were issued with mattresses and bed linen, dug up from the passengers' linen stores. Even a free issue of the beer that their guards had to purchase, did not appease the grumbling Boche, and "H" Company were deeply chagrined when they were ousted from their quarters below to make room for the Germans, and perforce had to occupy the rather breezy quarters on deck, to which the latter objected. This is to be recorded as a German outrage equal to any of those committed in Europe, if one were to judge by "H" Company's martyred outcries. When Captain von Mueller, together with a young sprig of the upas tree (a lieu-

5th Battalion Lines, Mena Camp. Officers' Tents in Foreground; Mess Huts in Rear.

tenant who was a nephew of the Kaiser) and the other Huns were transhipped to H.M.S. *Yarmouth* on reaching Suez, they left behind them a few mementoes of the famous sea fight, and a greatly relieved battalion of Australian infantry.

The only incident of note during the First Division's voyage, apart from the *Sydney-Emden* fight, was the collision at night of the *Ascanius* and the *Shropshire*. With only a masked stern-light on the ship ahead, navigation, in such close order as the convoy sailed in, was difficult on the dark nights. The *Ascanius* rammed the stern of the *Shropshire* late this night, glanced off and struck her again on the side. The collision alarm was given, lifeboat crews "stood to," and the troops mustered without alarm at their stations. So coolly did some of them take the incident, that on one of the boats men were afterwards "crimed" for refusal to leave their beds below when ordered. One of them excused himself at the subsequent orderly room proceedings by stating that he knew there was no danger below, "or the officer wouldn't have been there."

Both ships escaped with not very serious damage, but a recurrence of the mishap was to some extent obviated by an interesting, if not novel, means. A large empty cask was sealed, attached to some hundred feet of rope, and at night might be seen, a dim phosphorescent blotch, bobbing in the wake of each transport as a warning to the look-out of the ship astern.

Early one calm morning Ceylon glimmered on the horizon like a painted frieze, and by breakfast time a strip of yellow beach fringed with white wave lines against green palms was clearly to be seen. Far out to sea stood a scattered fleet of small craft with leg-of-mutton sails; seabirds flew over, and the water

was specked with driftwood, and the varied flotsam
of civilisation.

Later the fleet anchored off the breakwater in tur-
bid yellow water, foul with drifting weed, and the
men glued themselves to every vantage point to gaze
on the foreign shores.   The feathery fronded palms
that fringed red-roofed buildings, the catamarans
standing out to sea in a smother of foam, the far
glimpses of native life ashore, piqued the imagination to a confused recollection of all the tropical tales
that youth had known and loved. It brought a sparkle
to eyes jaded with ocean vistas of nothingness. A swarm
of butterflies fluttered through the rigging.   Copper-
coloured natives swarmed round the ship in their dugouts, wild with excitement at this unprecedented and
stupendous invasion of large craft, and duly performed the tricks that have charmed the heart of
the traveller since travel began.   They dived and
swam and fought sub-aqueously for coins, but soon
proved to be saturated with the sordor of com-
merce by refusing to dive for copper coins.   Sitting
on their wave-washed planks silently contemptuous of
pennies, they rolled their eyes ceaselessly in the search
for silver money, which the troops quickly learnt not
to throw.   The futility of fighting fiercely over half-
crowns which proved on capture to be pennies coated
with tinfoil eventually disgusted the divers, and they
paddled off from the *Orvieto* to seek a more
sympathetic audience who did not throw potatoes or
stale loaves of bread by way of encouragement.

All gazed longing at the tall building which they
were informed by a travelled one, was the *Galle Face*
Hotel, but, rightly enough, no leave was granted.
Purple evening fell.   The fruit barges and catamarans put into shore.   The breakwater light shone
out.   A carillon of ships' bells told eight o'clock;

lights twinkled from the shores where the privileged were undoubtedly drinking iced drinks; a gentle zephyr blew across the island and brought strange land scents on its wings; the troops sighed, and reluctantly turned their backs on the forbidden Eden.

In the forenoon of the 17th of November the fleet left Ceylon astern and headed for the Red Sea, pursuing an uneventful course until the *Hampshire* came alongside the *Orvieto* on the 22nd, both ships having forged ahead of the main body. A shortage of fresh meat on the warship was adjusted, and they "reformed ranks." The island of Socotra was sighted the next morning, a mist-crowned, purple jewel, in a setting of fawn, with steep ravines scoring the hillsides down to the foam-fretted sands. At evening the island had receded from sight, and was forgotten in the charm of the tropical sunset, or remembered only for the bets that were won or lost when a hot dispute as to the distance between the ship and the island had been settled by one of the ship's staff. Even the most reckless conjectures placed it at not more than ten miles, but the expert decision made it about twenty.

A common error present in the minds of the First Division, and one which still persists, is that the Australian and New Zealand Expeditionary Force was diverted to Egypt primarily because of Turkey's declaration of war on the third of November, 1914.

In Lieutenant Staniforth Smith's book, *Australian Campaigns in the Great War,* he states authoritatively that two officers and Sir George Reid, who was then in England, inspected the proposed Australian camp on Salisbury Plain, and found it a quagmire of mud. Not only were the huts unbuilt, but the material was not even available, and there was no chance of the buildings being ready before April or May, 1915.

Lord Kitchener suggested that the troops should be disembarked in Egypt, where the warmer climate more nearly approached that of Australia, and where there were excellent training grounds for all arms of the service; and this was done. . . .

It would seem, however, that Turkey's imminent aggression (which threatened to take the form of a land advance against Britain's sea artery, the Suez Canal), and the possibility of a Holy War occurring in Egypt, were more cogent reasons for this change of plan, and the presence of such a formidable contingent doubtless did prevent the latter contingency from becoming an actual fact.   The former event, as we know, did take place, but even the German spur did not produce the requisite dash or enthusiasm in the Turkish army, whose feeble thrust spent itself vainly on the Canal defences early in 1915, an operation in which the Australians did not take an active part.

The arid scenery of the Red Sea, rising abruptly from an azure blue, and dyed with the rich colours of purples, reds, ochres and browns, was the next sight of interest, and brought to mind the vividly coloured costumes of scriptural times.   Innocent ones looked eagerly for a change in the colour of the sea, and possibly expected the ship to pass through water of a sanguinary hue, which would justify the name.   The lighthouse of Perim was passed, and on the 1st of December, Suez was sighted, and by noon the *Orvieto* had brought to in the midst of a vortex of ever-changing colour.   The double-ended craft of fruit-sellers made a vivid artistic fringe to the ship, and baskets of oranges dwindled rapidly under the demands of fruit-starved men. The patched gowns of the natives, the opalescent hues of the distant hills, and the white buildings of Suez, framed in vivid green, made a typi-

cal picture of the East, not easily forgotten.   Just
before sunset, the tug made fast, and the canal was
entered.   Bands of roving Arabs had made the passage of the "Ditch" rather uncomfortable for
steamers, and for safeguard in case this kind of gauntlet had to be run, a guard was formed from "F"
Company, who paraded on the promenade deck with
loaded rifles.   Darkness fell, and the guard felt that
in this eagerly-accepted duty lay their first taste of
active service.   Though they were under instructions
to await orders before firing, it is terrible to reflect
what risks the goat-tenders and camel-herds along
the banks ran that night.   The flare of a match
would certainly have been followed by a burst of rifle
fire from those eager watchers.   Morning arrived
without incident, and the disappointed guard dispersed.

Further along the Nubian bank of the canal was occupied by English and Indian troops, and cheer and
counter-cheer came from these newly-met comrades
in arms.   Some speculation was rife among those on
shore, and an English officer cupped his hands and
shouted:—"Who are you?"   Before a hundred ready
lips could frame the answer, an Engineer in the bows
yelled:—"2nd Field Company Engineers, with a few
Infantry."   This palpable misrepresentation met
with so stormy a dissent that the officer may have imagined himself the innocent cause of disaffection among
His Majesty's troops.

So, after seemingly interminable stretches of canal
and desert, Port Said was reached, and the familiar
advertisement of the world's best known soap greeted
the eyes.   On the right were moored some French
warships, and the Fifth band struck up the "Marseillaise."   Their band retaliated with "God Save," and
both sides cheered vociferously.   With true Gallic

courtesy, a huge crowd gathered at the stern of one of the warships, and, directed by a handsome giant with a black beard, waved their caps and led off in a real British cheer on a rather high note, beginning "Heep-heep-heep."

Coal was bunkered here in the mediaeval fashion that prevails in places where labour is cheap. Lighters made fast alongside, and a diverse collection of natives who ran the whole gamut of life from eight to eighty, made their appearance. Carrying the coal in bags, they shuffled up the inclined planks to the yawning opening in the ship's side, then down on the other side and obtained a refill. The services of an omnipresent foreman were obviously necessary, and with a rope's end he manfully earned his salt.

Shore leave was forbidden, and though a few escaped down the mooring ropes to the buoys, and there chartered passing boats, the majority impotently watched the lights spring out on shore a few miserable yards away, heard strange sounds, and sniffed suspiciously at the East, whose mysterious, intangible fascination worked oddly on their senses.

Next day, "A" Company, under command of Major Saker, debarked and left by train for Cairo as advance guard, and the fleet also moved for Alexandria. Still led by the *Orvieto* they passed the giant statue of de Lesseps, the canal engineer, and against a fresh breeze met the white caps of the open sea again.

Chapter V.

EGYPT AND THE DESERT.

DECEMBER 3rd brought the *Orvieto*, which had increased her speed and left the remainder behind, to Alexandria, and in the early morning she neared her moorings at the wharf, and the Fifth gazed curiously down on the small detachment of helmeted Tommies who were mustered there to assist in debarkation. The men's feet itched to be on shore again, and they restlessly fingered their money belts, with the strong conviction that in this strange new land there were sights to be seen and money to be spent in a delightful variety of ways. Newly-formed "D" Company supplied a wharf guard that set the seal of doom on their aspirations, and between whiles of getting kits and equipment together, the men gazed longingly over the railway tracks and dock buildings to the enchanted city. Not all of them were content with gazing, and it is regretfully recorded that later the guard were somewhat remiss in their duty, as proven by the nocturnal arrivals who vainly attempted to regain the ship noiselessly. No. 14 Platoon, "D" Company were chosen as rearguard, this questionable favour being conferred on them by virtue of their having most men missing. So they watched the battalion move off next morning in full marching order, then turned somewhat unwillingly to their task of cleaning troopdecks and horse-boxes, and clearing the hold of transport material and battalion

47

impedimenta, invoking the wrath of high heaven
meanwhile on the begetters of their misery. The
ship cleaned, they were placed on guard over a train
on the wharf nearby, which contained the transport
waggons and motor cars of the Automobile Corps,
and from that position they watched the *Orvieto* cast
off at about nine p.m. and resume her interrupted
voyage to England. This rearguard left Alexandria behind and followed the Battalion to Cairo
at 3 p.m. on the 5th of September. The men
sat on the steps of the third-class corridor carriages,
peculiar in construction and unique in smell, clambered on the roof, and looked eagerly on the scenes
of Egyptian suburban and rural life that rolled past.
The clusters of date palms, the unbelievably dirty
children, the goats and camels; the distorted architec-
ture of the flat-roofed mud-brick houses, all burst on
the eye so suddenly and changefully, so kaleidoscopi-
cally coloured, that it seemed as though a stage had
been set and the curtain drawn on the first act of a
Biblical play. Wayside stations served the wits well
for a display of humour on the names; orange vendors
and other pedlars aired their scanty stock of English
and asked exorbitant prices, doubtless giving thanks
to Allah that such men as these had come, who would
pay excessive demands without haggling. More
panoramas of green hills; strangely assorted teams, as
an ox and a camel drawing a quaint wooden plough;
narrow canals with strings of donkeys on the dusty
paths; black-robed and veiled women with enormous
loads on their heads; more groves of palms, more incredibly dirty children, and then the sight of the
Pyramids of Mena, hazily blue in the distance.

Cairo reached, the battalion formed up in the station yard, passed canteen tables smartly served by
Tommies, each man receiving a cup of excellent

cocoa, a small roll of bread, and a segment of a globular red-skinned and delicious cheese. Troops arriving later were taken on to the newly-made military station at Kasr-el-Nil. Then followed a brief march through crowds of curious natives and highly interested Tommies, over Kasr-el-Nil bridge, and so on to the Mena road for the hard eight-mile march. The men walked still with their sea legs, and envied eloquently the details who had stayed to load baggage and fodder on the tram cars, and now whizzed past, shouting ill-timed appreciation of their good fortune. No one was in the mood to dilate on the near view of the Pyramids, or the picturesqueness of Mena House, set in the midst of sturdy Australian eucalypts; and when the battalion had finished the last trying stretch of yielding sand which surrounded the whole camp, most men would not have walked ten yards to see a dog fight, and certainly would not have gone more than half a mile for a beer. That night, tents not being available, they slept in the open; a cold, dewy night, with the unclouded stars looking frostily down on the advance guard of this young nation, sleeping in the shadow of the tombs of the Pharoahs, that had withstood Time for thousands of years, and had seen countless legions pass, and repass, and die. "We'll go over and see the Pyramids to-morrow, Bill," murmured someone to his pal. "—— the Pyramids," testily retorted Bill, and shivered. "I thought this was a damn tropical country!"

Other battalions followed fast on the heels of the Fifth, and the camp began to take shape. A steam roller crushed a road of limestone through the centre of the sandy waste, tents arose like mushrooms, fatigue parties carried stone to form battalion boundaries, and the multifarious camp duties of the soldier were in full swing. Rush-matted canteens and stalls quickly appeared; the ubiquitous Y.M.C.A. erected a canvas marquee; and ere nightfall few troops remained untented.   Some did, however, owing to a tent shortage, and these built themselves rude gunyahs or "humpies" of sticks and native matting, which were allowed to remain, interspersed with the tents, during the whole time of the occupation of Mena.

Infantry Road, as the straight track through the camp was called, ended in the desert at 2nd Brigade Headquarters.   From there, looking toward the city, were placed the Second and First Brigades, beginning with the Eighth Battalion, next to B.H.Q., and ending with the First Battalion, next to the Engineers. On the other side, but in the same order, were the Y.M.C.A. hut, boxing stadium, Y.M. marquee, canteens "dry" and "wet," Cinema "Palace," and then Light Horse and Third Brigade Infantry Battalions.

From *Infantry Road* another road ran at right angles, and led to the main entrance at Mena House now staffed as a hospital) running oppositely through the habitations of the other, and—to the Fifth —less important, arms of the service.

The camp lay under the scarp of a rocky plateau that stretched eastward for some hundreds of yards from the foot of the Pyramids.   Southward lay the verdant green of the cultivated zone; northward and eastward the rolling, pink-tinged, endless billows of the Desert, that for the next four months was to be the mimic battle ground of these untried soldiers. It was not a "happy hunting ground" for the infantry. Its deadly monotony of sand-dune and valley, rocky plateaus and dry gullies, or *wadies,* made the always uninteresting training of the foot soldier an irksome duty.   The digging of trenches in sand that insidiously streamed back at the rate of two spadesful for every two and a half taken out, made the stock pastime disheartening; the futility of doubling over the yielding sand in the burning sun, throwing oneself down on sharp stones, and rising panting, to dash wildly on the invisible enemy, became more and more apparent to the average private as the days wore on. The battalions, leaving the firmness of Infantry Road, which perished abruptly in the desert, were like lost souls on their journey to Hades. Handkerchiefs wrapped round faces, heads bent, shuffling feet raising a column of dust that hung in the still, early air, a rosy canopy—the battalion's morning desert march to *Aeroplane Wady* or *Tiger's Tooth* was a daily terror. Practice engendered the habit of drinking sparingly, but the Powers that be cynically doubted their own good advice when they prescribed the diet of bread-rolls and tinned sardines for the troops' midday meal.

Late afternoon saw the battalions, bronzed and dust enshrouded, trudging homeward; silent, irritable, sagging at the knees, and filled with silent curses against the work, the food, the whole damned war. The outskirts of camp reached, the band awaiting their arrival struck up a lively march, and the miracle came. The feel of the good, hard road beneath, the bloodstirring blare of the music, the consciousness of a hard day's work well done, stirred life through the whole column. Rifles went to the "slope" before the order was given, and with heads up, feet lifted high, and snappy step, the battalion came home. A brief word of appreciation by the Colonel, "Private Parades, Gentlemen," and a volley of orders rose from all companies together. First dismissed, first to the wet canteen, and it was a wise Company Commander who got his men away to the lines and dismissed smartly.

Some people thought, and many still think, that

the officers were mounted.   So some of them were—
at times—but every man in the Fifth noticed and
appreciated the C.O.'s habit of marching with the
men.   It was this tacit acceptance of the fact that
they were all to work and endure and suffer together
—irrespective of rank—that made Colonel Wanliss
the best-beloved of commanders.   Even the modest,
newspaper-wrapped lunch that he carried in his own
haversack did not escape the keen critics.   His nickname of "Dad" was not bestowed in a spirit of levity.
The fatherly interest he took in individuals accounted
for that, and he knew and loved the battalion as a
village priest knows and loves his parishioners.   Even
the black sheep admitted that "the old man gives a
fair deal."

It must not be supposed that the whole of the
troops' working time was spent in the desert.   As a
variant to their sand diet, the men were "spelled" by
being engaged in route marches through the villages
which lay within the cultivated belt terminating at
the fringe of Mena Camp.   The delight of marching
on solid ground, and the eye-comfort of the vivid
green of herbage and trees never palled, although the
pack seemed to weigh just as heavily.

The line of demarcation between the green irrigated
belt separating Mena from Cairo and the illimitable
desert, of which the camp bordered the inner edge,
was as sharply defined as if painted.   One could
stand astride the blazing aridity of the desert and the
vivid fertility of the young crops intersected by in-
numerable runnels of water.

These marches along the canal banks were full
of interest always.   Here might be seen a patient fella-
heen on his endless task of baling water onto the
fields with a futile little bucket tip-tilted on a pivotal
beam counterbalanced with a stone; there the equiva-

lent of our "cocky" farmer, scratching the age-old field with his primitive wooden plough drawn by an ill-assorted team of camel and ox, even as did his ancestors, centuries far down the corridors of time.

Countless villages, so alike as to bewilder, sprawled untidily at every twist of the tortuous path. Veiled women in hot rusty black gowns and veils paused in their work of moulding dung fuel cakes to gaze curiously at the bare-armed, bronzed soldiers moving knee-deep in fine dust. Myriads of children lined the path and, unabashed, gave back Anglo-Arabic repartee—always vulgar.

Countless babies, borne on the backs of only slightly older infants, saw the "Inglezi" troops through a mist of flies that clustered in three black patches round eyes, nose and mouth. Where flies were a torment to the foreigners, they were entirely disregarded by the natives, and no one was ever foolish enough to disturb them from the place where they bred and lived.

The impudence of the small boys was no worse than that of the Paris gamin, the London urchin, or the Australian larrikin in embryo. Their language may have been a little obscure in meaning, but their actions were quite clear. The European gesture of contempt and scorn, as indicated by outstretched finger and thumb applied to the nose was delightfully surpassed by the small Gyppos' habit of lifting up their single garment in an ineffable and shameless motion of disdain, skipping nimbly out of reach of the dirt clods which inevitably followed.

Sometimes the battalions passed on opposite sides of a canal, and a running fire of personal comment and humour of the moment passed down the line, and was bandied across the intervening water.

In common with all other foot regiments, the Fifth had their band. Formed in the early Broadmeadows days, it progressed satisfactorily enough until the voyage over, when trouble manifested itself. Some misunderstanding occurred when the bandsmen were asked to practise outside their ordinary training hours, and as a bandsman can claim the privilege of returning to his job in the ranks, for some little time the troops missed their evening music. The trouble was soon adjusted, and the musical standard reached a very high level in Egypt.

As a quick-step was impossible on the desert sand, the band either stayed behind to practise, or—as was more often the case—they donned their armbands with the letters ''S.B.,'' and accompanied the battalion as stretcher-bearers to their daily work on the desert. The unfortunate man who fell ill during the day received the unmitigated contempt of the sweating bandsmen, who transported him to camp by stretcher with many and frequent rests by the way. Of course, none of the instruments left the ship at Gallipoli, and the bandsmen all did yeoman service with their stretchers.

Despite the men's fondness for music, there was comparatively little singing on the march, as contrasted with the practice of English regiments. In the first days of training in Australia, the strains of ''Tipperary'' always made the march easier, but its popularity soon waned, and not much later, it became a dire offence even to whistle it. Some of the evanescent popular ditties of the day had their brief season and were forgotten for ever. One of them was slightly altered to refer to the Brigadier, but this too disappeared before Egypt was reached.

More popular and certainly less transient was ''Parlez Vous?'' an old song which later in France changed its tune somewhat, had an extra verse added, and persisted under the guise of ''Mademoiselle from Armentieres.''   In Egypt it began with the verse, ''Oh, landlord, have you any good wine? Parlez vous,'' thrice repeated, and finished—as did each succeeding stanza, with:—

> ''That's fit for a soldier of the line,
> With his boots of calico, Yankee calico,
> Parlez vous.''

The song has a good swing, which served well for marching purposes, and many ribald verses told of the vicissitudes of the said landlord's daughter.

On reviewing the songs of the Australian Army, one must conclude that in a mass the Colonial is not given to singing. A Tommy regiment would pass marching at ease, always with their helmets cocked rakishly, the rifle balanced on the shoulders with the barrel forward, and some music hall triumph being lustily sung down the whole column.

A notable difference between the Australian troops and others that were on duty in Egypt—and one which could not fail to be observed—was in the clothing they wore.   While the Imperial troops had discarded the woollen tunic and trousers, and were garbed in light khaki drill and pith helmets, the Colonial troops still wore the heavyweight woollen tunics and thick corded breeches which had been deemed suitable for Europe.   Admitting that the Expeditionary Forces had not been equipped for tropical service, it must still be agreed that it was a very long time before steps were taken by the Australian Government to generally outfit the troops destined for Egypt with suitable clothing.   A concession was certainly made to the rigors of the climate, inasmuch as the Australians were allowed to purchase privately and wear the drill shorts and pith helmets that the Home troops wore as an issue. The majority of the Fifth did eventually wear shorts, while the wide-brimmed slouch hat was a fair substitute for the solar topee. Some regiments did make an ''issue'' of both these articles to the men, stopping the cost from their pay. Mostly, however, the regiments presented a motley appearance during training, owing to the men's individual choice of clothing, and from the C.O.'s efforts to make the battalion uniform in their parade appearance, rose the immortal incident of Colonel ''Pompey'' Elliott's hat.

The men's faces presented a strange appearance by this time. Even the fairest-skinned of them were tanned to a leather color, while those naturally more swarthy in complexion showed almost coffee-colored. To look round at a group of them with their hats off, was to be instantly struck by the livid line that extended round the chin, ran up either cheek, and faded away near the ears. This was the mark of the chin strap which protected a narrow strip of skin from the sun. It looked like the white line of a whip lash, so strongly marked it was on the darker ground of sunburnt skin.

The dietary was also unsuited to the climate, and still contained the large proportion of meat that the men desired, though much more than was necessary. An Imperial allowance for rations of sixpence half-penny per diem being expended by the Company Quartermasters as their wisdom dictated, tinned salmon, eggs and rice were welcome additions to the menus of the Fifth.

An average morning meal consisted of curried salmon, bread and jam or perhaps boiled eggs replacing the fish. The native jam, which in large tins dis-

[By courtesy J. Wallace Ross, Esq.]

Part of the 2nd Brigade Lines looking from Pyramids. 2nd Field Ambulance in Foreground. 5th Battalion Tents down for Airing.

graced the mess table, was a truly execrable mixture, being either so thin as to run off the knife, or so thickly tenacious as to refuse to leave it. Alarming rumours gained credence as to the method of making it, and as to its constituents; and comparatively little of it was eaten. The men often spoke regretfully of the good Australian jam, once so despised because superabundant.

For troops who were undergoing such remarkably strenuous training on an arid, scorching desert, the midday meal deserves more than passing notice. Tired with the long manœuvres over the yielding sand, parched with the fine rising dust and the heat of the day, men were not inclined to eat much, but could have wished for something less thirst-provoking than the tins of sardines which, accompanied by bread rolls, were provided by a thoughtful commissariat. When at the end of the long, hard day, camp was reached, a hot stew was almost always found awaiting the heated and fatigued men, a repast which was too often rejected by those who had a few piastres left with which to buy something more appetising at the nearby canteen.

The primitive open cooking trenches, which, from a military point of view, are never intended to do more than serve a temporary camp or bivouac, were never improved on in most of the regiments, and certainly not in the Fifth. The Engineers constructed for themselves a kind of long oven of mud, reinforced with wire netting, with holes on top into which the dixies fitted, and dignified with a chimney. However, the technical units were too busy throwing elaborate bridges across adjacent canals to bother about such trifles as cooking places, so that the cooks of the Fifth, in common with those of other Infantry battalions, continued to grope around in the smoke of

the open fires, with reddened streaming eyes, and
faces and hands that gave them the true local colour.
The cooks' lines were necessarily within easy distance
of their own and other regiments' horse lines, and
also of the latrines.   With every wind that blew,
sand and dust, and more minute, but none the less
injurious matter, were distributed amongst the food
in course of preparation or cooking, with the consequence that a very large proportion of Egypt was
consumed with every meal, the food receiving a further sprinkling through the agency of the open mess
huts.   It was quite common for the residual stew in
the bottom of the dixie to contain a tablespoonful of
sand, or more.

Regarding the health of the men, Lt.-Col. Spring-
thorpe, A.A.M.C., says, in an article in the *Age* on the
11th of December, 1920, *inter alia*:—''Either because
we (*i.e.*, the Australian medical staff) did not object,
or because our objections were overridden, our men
were trained only in sand, and monotonously overtaxed, their non-medical needs left to outside bodies,
exceptional vice and bad liquor unrestrained, and the
spread of infectious disease practically facilitated,
so that there was more disease in a world's sani-
torium like Mena, amongst picked troops, than in the
trenches of Flanders.''   The Fifth were perhaps
more fortunate—or better cared for than most others,
not many being evacuated ill, and only one death—
from pneumonia—occurring whilst the battalion was
at Mena.

The army canteens were conducted by Thomas
Lipton's successors, and though their charges could
scarcely be called moderate, still their wares filled a
want that the poor quality of the issue rations
created.   Bacon and eggs were regarded by the native
attendants as being the must succulent repast that
could be laid before a Britisher, and a meal of these,

finished off with a round, greasy kind of doughnut, formed a good foundation on which to lay the liquid refreshment which usually followed.

The "wet" canteen was also served by natives, but the traffic was necessarily controlled by a military picquet, drawn from the "duty" battalion.   A double queue was formed outside, no more than four pints were issued to one man at a time, and customers passed out by the other flap of the tent to sit on the sand and drink.   The length of the queue was generally so great that it was an impossibility to become intoxicated, though, of course, this happy state was sometimes achieved by pressing teetotal friends into service.   The beer was atrocious, after the light beers of the Colonies, being thick, and so murky that one could not see through a glass of it.   As a matter of statistics, it is placed on record that few could drink six pints, and remain sober.   The bottled beer which was surreptitiously sold by the natives under the labels of Greek firms was indescribably bad, and had probably been tampered with.   Spirits offered in the same way for sale were inevitably adulterated, so that little, if any, of the original fluid was left, and in its placed masqueraded a filthy decoction that only the native mind could have conceived and compounded. One such, offered for sale in a reputable firm's bottle, which had been skilfully bored through the bottom and thus emptied of its original contents, was proved to be constituted of methylated spirits and urine. The opponents of the "wet" canteen system would surely have conceded that there were worse things than the supply of wholesome Australian liquor under army supervision, the entire profits of which were enjoyed by the men, whether teetotallers or no, instead of swelling further the authorised brigandage of the British Army Canteen, or the pockets of the rascally natives.

Chapter VI.

DESERT DAYS.

"Sand, Sorrow, and Sore Eyes."

NONE of the food that remained uneaten by the troops was wasted. The surplus was sold, and the proceeds swelled the regimental fund. Some regiments let tenders for disposal of the rubbish to native contractors, and in consequence the scraps from the dixies and mess huts were carefully classified. Mess orderlies found their attention directed by large notices that "Tea Leaves Only" were to be put into this receptable, meat into that one, and so on. Where the system of tendering did not obtain, camp followers reaped the benefits, and in return for menial services, gained substantial crumbs from the tables. The one who attached himself to the Fifth was remarkably prominent among the host of natives infesting the camp. He had early been fitted out in a suit of blue dungarees and a white hat, and various humourists had succeeded in producing on him a startling effect. Badges of rank, and other distinctions, medals of tin and cardboard inscribed with records of unmentionable offences, were proudly worn, while across his back in large letters stared an unmistakable aspersion on his legitimacy. Achmed had an offsider, Kalihd, an old gentleman venerable in appearance, if not in moral worth and cleanliness. When not engaged on the cook's lines, they might have been observed together smoking a *hubble-bubble* pipe, rudely fashioned from a treacle tin, a bamboo stem and a tin tube with a funnel for tobacco at the top. When the mess orderlies had promiscuously emptied the scraps—despite the attempts of the two natives to imfuse some little system into the process—Achmed's work would begin, and the salving of pieces of meat and bread from the liquid slops, the careful picking therefrom of the tea leaves, and the subsequent wrapping in paper against the arrival of the buyer, was a regular occurrence. It was understood that the meat found its way into otherwise excellent meat pies which the next day made their appearance in various of the restaurants and canteens.

Besides these scavengers were the more thorough ones which eternally hovered over all Egyptian cities —the carrion hawk.. Large brown birds, not unlike our eagle-hawks in the air, they circled slowly at a great height, darting with incredible swiftness when food was seen. A piece of meat thrown in the air would be caught with a lightning swoop, and should it, as often happened, be seen by two or three birds at once, a fearful aerial battle would ensue, the progress of which could be estimated by the feathers that drifted slowly down from the combatants; but the meat was never lost.

Always one saw these unclean birds wheeling ceaselessly over the city, black against the stainless blue of the sky, or drooping satiated on the cornices of white-walled buildings. They and their rivals—the pariah dogs, lean of body and predatory in habits—effectively cleansed the city of what little refuse the native rejected as being unfit for consumption.

The coming of the Australians was unfortunate from the viewpoint of the Tommy. As the latter had necessarily to exist on the meagre pay that was his portion, prices had accommodated themselves to his financial stringency, and fruit and the like had hitherto been purchased at their market value.

With ample money and the disposition to expend it freely, the Colonial was responsible for immediate and monstrous increases in the prices of almost everything.   Oranges, which could before this be bought fifteen for a piastre, now became "five for one," and later half a piastre and a piastre each. This mattered but little to the easy-spending Australians, but it was a severe blow to the English soldier, who thus found his "cost of living" increased three and fourfold.

It is significant that not so very long after the First Division had landed in Egypt the principle of "Gibbit money first" was enunciated.   This shibboleth was soon universal with native and foreign shopkeepers, and the goods were not handed over till the money was safe in the dirty palm.   No one the world over, can descend to such unclean depths of rascality as the Egyptian native, and in low cunning he excels. Future tourists will no doubt benefit in some small degree by the many lessons the natives learnt from the Colonials.   The one thing that made any impression on their depraved minds, *i.e.*, violence, was the unfailing reward of their constant endeavours to cheat and defraud, and although the troops' money ran quickly through their fingers, they were not often deceived by the wily "Gyppo," and mostly got fair value.

It will certainly be aggravating to the future Cook's Tourist if the practice persists of demanding cab, taxi or donkey fares from the traveller before the journey is commenced, but at this time Egypt's national motto certainly was, "Gibbit money first."

Cairo was indeed a city of delight to the Australians.   The magic glamour of the East invested its

tree-lined streets with the coming of the sudden darkness.   The mystery of Arabian Nights tales gloomed
in every dimly lit doorway, or shone in chequered
rose-coloured light behind the *jalousies* of upper windows.   A city of violent contrasts, where modern
electric tramcars clanged furiously to clear the swaying camel from the track; where European sewerage
systems penetrated curiously insanitary, vile hovels,
patched and repaired against time's ravages; where
the twentieth-century courtesan in Paris modes jostled
the veiled women of the Egyptian harem in concrete
steel emporiums stocked with the latest eccentricities
of Fashion.

Next to the palatial, marble-colonnaded hotel, plate
glass-fronted and served with electric elevators, huddled the cave-like, low-ceilinged native shop where
proprietor and customer sat cross-legged and haggled
interminably in the manner of the East over the
hubble-bubble pipe between.

Taxi-cabs rounded corners perilously, and the two-
horsed   ''gharry,''   or   landaulette-cab,   galloped
through crowded streets with the warning ''mi-eend,
effendi—mi-eend!'' of the native drivers clearing the
way.

Vice here took its most appealing disguise, and
looked perilously like virtue. Public women of every
nationality (except English, thanks be!) plied their
ancient and sordid trade, with inevitable results.
Officially, vice did not exist, and despite the awful exhortations of the regimental medical officers and the
more awful examples that perforce seceded from
active service with the regiments each day, venereal
disease was alarmingly prevalent.

A huge barbed-wire compound disfigured the Mena
camp, but all the measures taken by the authorities
were remedial, and not preventive.   Before the re-

sulting conditions of things is judged too harshly, let
the reader remember the comparative innocence of our
Australian life, even in the larger cities, and attempt
to visualise some of the temptations that beset the
feet of our men in Engypt.

Physical fitness has its concomitant physical pas-
sions, and disregard it as we will in the native prudish-
ness and civilised prejudice of our minds, the result
must be faced without mock modesty.   Later—in
France and England—vice was officially recognised,
and prophylactics were issued with the leave passes,
but before then—witness, oh, high Heaven! the blindness of those in power, and have only pity for the
victim of impulse whose first departure from rectitude
so often wrote ''finis'' to his army career.

Restaurants were multitudinous, and it is to be wondered if most of them existed prior to the military invasion of Cairo.   Hotels that had been built to cater
for the wealthy tourist traffic were none too good for
the Colonials, and Shepheard's, probably the best
known hotel in the world, was besieged by the Australian and New Zealand private, N.C.O., subaltern, and
colonel.   Soon, however, the scandal of an English
captain failing to get a seat for dinner when whole
tables were reserved for Australian troops, and the
fearful impropriety of a full major being invited to
''have one with me'' by a slouch-hatted lance-corporal,
stirred the ''brass hats,'' and Shepheard's was taboo
to the ranker.

The Continental, further up the same street, then
increased in popularity, until this too became a place
where no officer could enter without being spoken to
chummily, and it speedily joined the long list of
''officer's hotels,'' and too obviously immoral boozing
dens, that were ''out of bounds'' to all troops.

Of the restaurants, the Cafe-Egyptien was easily

the most popular. The main room fronted the street, with long French windows, and at the end a dais accommodated a female orchestra, whose physical proportions excelled even the quality of the music. Scattered over the sawdusted floor were marble-topped tables, and an army of attendants made expert voyagings with loaded trays. It was understood that one could obtain eatables, but this was probably rumour, and possible no truer than the canard that the sawdust was swept up after each night and compressed for the sake of the beer that had soaked it.

The roar of voices, rattling of glasses and the faintly heard obligato of the orchestra apprised one of the position of the cafe, and coming suddenly through the door, one saw a sea of brown uniforms, brown faces and brown liquids, enshrouded in slowly drifting smoke. The music ceases and a roar of applause drives the haze apart. Deftly threading her way through the maze of tables and chairs and legs, comes the first violin, a maiden with an ivory-tinted, oval, Greek face, thickly braided black hair—and a plate. Smiling sweetly on all sides as the piastres rattle in, she catches from the roar of voices the oft-repeated cry for some particular tune, and the music begins anew.

The *Marseillaise* was never stale, and though no one knew the words, everyone hummed, ''la-la-la-ed,'' or whistled fortissimo the stirring French anthem.

None of the restaurants seemed ever to close, and long after the last electric car had left the city loaded precariously to the trolley pole, the brilliantly lit cafés disgorged those who could afford a taxi to camp.

Nearer Mena Camp, a mushroom city had sprung up that rivalled the township of Ballarat in gold-digging days. In a sandy valley between the foot

C

of the Great Pyramid and Mena House, rose the canvas and matchboarded, cafés and shops that served the wants of the men who could not, or would not, go to Cairo.

All kinds of antiques and curiosities ''one thousand years old, mistah!'' were taken straight from the Birmingham packing case and sold cheaply enough to the unsophisticated.   Gaudy native mats, postcards pictorial or purely indecent, and all the clutter of a pedlar's pack strewed the temporary shop fronts.

The humour of the Colonials found vent in the eagerly-sought advice they gave to the proprietor anent the naming of the shops.   The Egyptian mind quickly comprehended that native names meant nothing to the soldier, hence appeared in yard-high letters such touches from home as ''Young and Jackson's,'' ''Hotel Sydney,'' or such invitation to patriots as ''For the Allies Café,'' ''Fair Dinkum Restaurant,'' and so forth.

There were four or five cinema ''palaces'' erected within the confines of Mena Camp, at which the men were entertained with pictures and vaudeville, neither of a very high standard. Some of the latter, indeed, was very poor, and the Australian is not slow to express his disapprobation of anything he is not satisfied with. Many a performer in a volunteer camp concert party has found this to his cost. But here, the men were a little rougher than they had been at home.

During the progress of an unpopular item in a Mena vaudeville show, the front-row patrons might be observed filling cardboard cartons and paper bags with the damp sand that formed the floor of the ''theatre.'' To what end, the conclusion of the item soon explained.   A storm of catcalls, whistles, and profanity accompanied these "sand bombs," which, with oranges, hurtled round the luckless artist's head.

Looking from the rocky plateau that extended from the foot of the Pyramids and overlooked the sandy waste on which the camp was sited, one could see the nearby desert on the outskirts of the camp studded on Sunday mornings with divers symmetrical hollow squares, where the men were sitting down in the conventional church-parade formation. In the centre, the Union Jack fluttering over piled drums, and behind it, the white surplice of the chaplain made the only colour contrast to the drab monotony of the sand and the slightly darker khaki of the men.

Behind the chaplain stood the band, the sun coruscating from their newly furbished brass, and little flashes of white showing where the hymn cards were being passed down the ranks. Rising only for the singing, the lazy found the service an excellent opportunity for a snooze, while the irreverent betted on the chance of a particular hymn being chosen next or not. As there were only eight or ten hymns on the printed card, the "bookie" offered only short odds, and for the first hymn, "Onward, Christian Soldiers," as the favourite, could generally be backed only at "odds on." The officers being massed inside the hollow square, the N.C.O.'s mostly turned an unseeing eye to the money being passed, and at times may have even ventured a piastre or so themselves.

In the main, the men listened more attentively to the padre than ever did his pre-war congregations. For was he not one of them, living with them, and nearly always accompanying them on their work? The simple talk on topics nearest their hearts, without too many scriptural allusions, and clipped of the platitudes that may have made him a prosy preacher in the old life, appealed to the listener, whether he was Anglican, Dissenter, or Presbyterian.

This was perhaps the one hour during the whole week when the man thought seriously of the brief span of living and loving that might be left him, and made his weekly amen reverently enough.

When the wind was strong and the dust high, the cinema "palaces"—huge erections of timber covered with native matting or match-boarding, of which there were four or five in the camp—were used for a combined service, and a strange mixture of every creed but Roman Catholics and Jews (who paraded elsewhere) sang lustily such hymns as were familiar to them all.

Christmas came—for the majority, the first they had spent out of Australia—and the authorities did their best to give it a home touch.   A relaxation from the eternal stew was provided in the form of roast meats and tinned plum puddings, the latter a gift from the *Daily Mail* newspaper fund.   Beer was on the tables, and the C.O. and officers made the round of the mess tables, throughout the wooden huts, which had been erected at the rear of each company lines, to the accompaniment of rousing cheers.   New Year's Eve was the occasion of more harmless rejoicing, less exuberant than it surely would have been at home, but the Brigadier (Col. Hon. J. W. McCay) chose to regard it as a widespread debauchery, and next day, ordered a full parade of the Second Brigade.   Accordingly, New Year's morning saw the four battalions drawn up on the sand near B.H.Q., and listening with amazement to the torrent of invective poured over their heads by the irate Brigadier.   It was an unmerited stricture, that rankled deeply in the minds of all, and the crowning insult of "sots, whoremongers and blackguards'' deeply wounded the decent-minded men who were in the majority.   The indigna-tion aroused by this New Year's Day phillipic ex-ceeded the later resentment against Mr. C. E. W. Bean, who had frankly written home of the First Division's questionable methods of enjoying them-selves on leave.

Noteworthy incidents in the desert life were the visit of Sir George Reid, who, top-hatted and eye-glassed, addressed the whole Division in batches, and presented each man with an excellent jackknife; and the inspection by Sir Ian Hamilton.   During this latter function the troops were at some little dis-advantage in that they had to march past in double fours on the narrow *Infantry Road,* one four on the hard paving, the other on the loose sand.   Despite this, the Fifth kept good alignment, but on nearing the saluting base, the Battalion pipers took up the time from the band behind, and threw the whole column into confusion.   That evening, when the pipers began their usual harmony outside the officers' mess, the whole regiment, smarting under the knowledge that their performance of the afternoon was below stan-dard, hooted and catcalled their vigorous disappro-bation.   From these malcontents must be excepted those of Scottish birth or parentage, who strongly up-held the merits of their beloved music.

The training of the last four months had been in-tensely hard.   Bronzed and fit as they became, even on the wretched food and strenuous training, it was indeed a survival of the fittest, and the favorable im-pression that the First Division made on Sir Ian Hamilton is recorded in his diary.   Hard work for six days a week, with a long march after church par-ade on the seventh, gave little time for the debauchery in which their friends in Australia were given to understand they indulged, and the men began to grow restless under this prolonged and seemingly interminable work.   Sneers in the yellow press at "six bob a day tourists" roused their anger at the circumstance—whatever it was—that kept them here, and events in Europe were followed as keenly as the poor cable service of the Egyptian press would allow. Would it be Turk or German?   Bets were freely offered and taken, and canteen talk revolved round this all-important point.   What evacuations from sickness and disease had reduced the Fifth in strength were more than compensated for by the first batch of reinforcements under Captain Permezel, who joined the regiment on January 7th.

The second batch of reinforcements arrived at Mena early in March, having landed from the *Clan McGillivray* under the command of Lt.-Col. R. M. McVea, V.D., a very well known officer of the old Victorian Scottish Regiment.   Colonel McVea had, during training in Broadmeadows, collected as many of Scottish blood or name as possible, and as a consequence brought a strong stiffening of bag-pipes for the Fifth's pipe band.

Despite the fact that none of the bandsmen took their instruments to Gallipoli, one or two of the pipers carried their beloved pipes, and one of them took his last long rest in Turkish soil with the pipes reverently laid beside him.

Wild speculation on the future came to a climax when the battalion were ordered out on the parade ground on a day otherwise remarkable for a passing swarm of locusts that came on the wings of a desert wind, and turned the sunlight a sickly green.   The Colonel, mounted, addressed the battalion.   Something electrical was in the air, and it hardly needed his prefatory remark that he had good news for the regiment, to reveal his secret. Warning them not to cheer, he told them that the period of their training was over, and that they would soon be fighting. To-day he had been informed that they would shortly leave for the front. The warning against cheering was unheeded. The battalion cheered, and cheered again. Hats flew in the air; everyone shook hands a hundred times, and the colonel's horse protested decidedly. There was not one who did not appear glad at the long-delayed news.

Prior to this, there had been the Ismailia affair in February. The Turks had made their foolish thrust at the canal and an engagement had been fought near Toussoum. New Zealand Engineers had gone down the Canal, and the Seventh and Eighth Battalions received orders to move there also. A very real jealousy pervaded the Fifth and Sixth at this undoubted favouritism, and it was with a bad grace that they farewelled the two battalions as they marched out of camp on the third February. In a week they were back again without having had their baptism of fire, and the Fifth were mollified.

Some of the regiment obtained twenty-four hours' leave to visit the battlefield, and going by rail to Ismailia, found the Suez Canal officials only too willing to provide a launch which should take them down to the camp in the neighbourhood of the signal station, Toussoum.

Here on the flat sterility of the desert stretching for miles on the Arabian side of the canal, evidences of the attack and the result were only too clear. To walk into the desert a mile or so was to have reconstructed for you the whole affair. The sand, hard

crusted in places with a salt-like exudation, still held
the footmarks of the tired Turkish soldiery, attempting after a desert march—in itself a wonderful feat
of endurance and bravery—an attack on a strongly
entrenched enemy.

The marching columns here had deployed; there
had scattered out into the long thin firing line as later
they came under long range rifle and machine gun
fire.   Each little mound of scraped-up sand told its
own story.   The depression where the rifleman had
settled his elbow; the deeper holes where his ill-clad
toes had resisted the recoil of his rifle; the little scatter
of used cartridge cases, and lastly perhaps the two
parallel lines his heels had made as he was dragged
off next day to be buried; all these were vivid evidences of the battle.

The pitiful sheet-iron boats they had dragged on
wheels over those hundreds of weary miles to the Suez
lay riddled with shrapnel and bullet holes on the
banks of their achievement, or were settling in the
sand at the canal bottom.

The ill-made graves, wind-blown, disclosed in
ghastly fashion the ragged uniform, the improvised
footwear of socks or rags that had taken the place of
the boots worn out on the flint-hearted desert; or
showed startlingly vivid against the yellow sand, the
swollen, blackened hand flung in a hopeless gesture
to the unpitying sky.

The field was rich in souvenirs—and smells.   The
all-too-plain failure of the attack was emphasised by
the Indian troops of the regiments hereabouts entrenched.   They described, with eloquent gestures
the attack on the forward trenches in the darkness,
the pre-arranged abandonment that lured the Turks

to occupy them, and then the blinding light of the
flares that made them easiest of targets for well-
placed machine guns.

A mad, brave effort, this, that ignominiously melted
at the goal.   The grave of one of the German
leaders, Major von der Hagen, decently surmounted
by a wooden cross, looks from the summit of the high
bank of this great trade artery the misdirected effort
hoped to sever.

Early in March the Third Brigade left camp
for an unnamed destination, a happening which
gave birth to a highly-coloured assortment of
"furphies" about their whereabouts and intended
doings.   Everyone knew later that they had sailed
from Alexandria, presumably for some attack on the
Turks.   Rumour still lied variously as to the course
events were taking with regard to Turkey, though the
naval bombardment had been proceeding since February.

The now historical "Battle of the Wazza" began
on the afternoon of Good Friday, and men of the
Fifth were implicated, in common with men of every
other unit.   Stories of its genesis will always be
many and varied: suffice it to say that a drunken
"rag" in a house in the notorious native quarter
that fronted the Wagh-el-Bukh, and was known as
the "Wazza," developed before nightfall into a seeth-
ing mass of soldiers, mainly New Zealanders and Australians—and mostly sober, be it said—who were
out for fun.   The English military authorities, in
the only way suggesting itself, sent the garrison
mounted police—Westminster Dragoons—to quell the
disturbance.   The sight of the "Red Caps," already
hated for their officious militarism, roused the
chievous mob, hitherto content with wrecking b

furniture and shop windows, to more serious measures, and in the swaying maelstrom of horses and men, a revolver was fired. By whom, Redcap or Colonial, history will probably never agree, but it begat an alarming phase of the disturbance—more shots, and then the Dragoons perforce retreated before superior numbers, using the flat of their sabres.

The next move was to send a battalion of Territorial Infantry, Lancashire Fusiliers, to the scene, meanwhile urgently telephoning A.I.F. headquarters for troops. The Cairo Fire Brigade, a smart, up-to-date corps, with motor engines, had appeared in response to an alarm, though nothing more than a stack of furniture was alight in the street. Their efforts were, to say the least, unappreciated, if one believes the story that the hoses were turned upon the native firemen and then cut up.

The Territorials with fixed bayonets saved the situation by providing the touch of comedy with which tragedy seems always cheek by jowl. Diminutive, fresh-faced Lancashire boys, with a great admiration for their colonial cousins, but also with a stern sense of duty, they marched down the street through the crowd, who obediently let them through, and closed in behind them.

The current catchwords and phrases of the day were bandied about. " 'Aave yer got an 'arf suverin on yer, choom?"—"I'm collectin' coins," "Be 'ee goin' into Cairo?" and the like, were shouted with impish glee. The Tommies went through the crowd, turned, and went through again, but pandemonium still reigned around. Cab horses with fashionable hats and dresses; furniture hurtling from upper windows; a soldier playing ragtime on a much-ʒed piano, are all snapshots of the hectic night.

The arrival of the Australian Light Horse found the trouble over, and only the frightened natives and the rubbish strewn streets as evidence of the outbreak.   A later and more damaging upheaval occurred after the First Division had left for Gallipoli, and resulted in many houses being burnt.

This quarter was a canker in the city life, a festering sink of iniquity that was well purged by fire. The First Division look back on this as the only job they left unfinished.

BOOK II.
GALLIPOLI

Chapter VII.

ADVENTURE BOUND.

THE First and Second Brigades struck camp on Sunday, April 4th, and the Fifth marched into Cairo after tea that evening. Despite—or because of—the desert training, Mena Road seemed long and hard, and the equipment unduly heavy. Tired, and with fine white dust caked over their sweaty faces, the men lay down in the dust under the sputtering arc lights in the military station yard at Kasr-el-Nil, and snatched cat-naps before entraining in the third-class carriages (self-evident "native only" vehicles) which had brought them there four months before.

A tiresome, cramped journey through the night brought them in the pale dawn to Alexandria, where they formed up on the wharf alongside the ship that was to take them on their new voyaging. Whither?

By comparison with the *Orvieto* and with the ships at neighbouring berths, the s.s. *Novian* was, as one man put it, "only a pup." A twin screw iron steamer of 4,200 tons, she had served a long apprenticeship in troop carrying, having completed her twenty-eighth voyage, and had last conveyed the Canadians from Southampton to Brest. Argyle and Sutherland Highlanders, Scots Greys, and other famous regiments had endured the discomforts of this little tramp steamer, and the men had testified accordingly on the paintwork below. The Fifth added to the lengthy list of acid comment, stressing particularly the paucity of the canteen stocks and the charming result of the drainage from the horse decks leaking on to the mess tables below. The thought presents itself that after three weeks' confinement on the *Novian*, the élan of the Fifth's Sunday morning attack was primarily due to a desire to get on terra firma again, whether the enemy was there or not.

On the afternoon of the sixth, the *Novian* moved off, a battalion of the Worcestershire regiment, just arrived from India on an ex-German liner, being interested in the departure, and heartily applauding the post-prandial efforts of the Fifth battalion's pipers. During the night, the wind freshened, and there was a fair sea in the morning, which buffeted the *Novian* uncomfortably. The attendance at mess fell rapidly, and soon the wet decks were strewn with those who did not care whether "Cookhouse" was sounded or not. Twenty-four hours later, the vacant places at mess were being occupied again, and the ship steamed in calm water through the green-crowned rocky islets that so thickly stud the blueness of the Grecian Archipelago.

Four days of sailing through the placid blue of these waters, brought the *Novian* to the harbour entrance of Mudros, the chief town of the island of Lemnos. After some little period of "standing by," a small torpedo boat showed the way through the boom that lay across the harbour mouth, and the ship augmented the fleet that was steadily accumulating here—man-of-war and troopship, submarine and supply ship; accessories in the drama that was soon to break new ground in the world-war.

A natural landlocked anchorage, this Mudros harbor, ringed with hills that were dotted with red-roofed stone houses. A snow-capped mountain rose in the background, and the young crops carpeted the slopes with vivid green, studded with crimson and white poppies.   The Third Brigade were discovered here languishing on transports, and already heartily sick of their floating prison, having endured nearly three weeks of it.

Of the Fifth, a fatigue party from "D" Company were first ashore, towing behind a ship's boat the carcase of one of the transport horses which had died between decks and was to be buried ashore.   The sight of poppies and buttercups set the men gathering these familiar flowers with childish delight, and they returned bedecked in a most unmilitary manner.   In this landlocked harbour, landing practice now took place frequently with full kit, and the long-suffering Navy manfully hid their emotion at the sacrilegious remarks that the Army passed on Jacob's ladders, boats, oars and other seafaring implements.   Once ashore, a short route-march generally took place, and then embarking practice again.   This was the Colonials' real introduction to the Navy, and the beginning of the firm friendship that hereafter existed between the sailor and the Antipodean.   Many famous warships were gathered here, the super-Dreadnought *Queen Elizabeth* out-bulking them all. "Queen Lizzie," as she was playfully termed, was the great attraction for the soldiers, and numerous parties, under command of an officer, rowed over in the ship's boats, to see her at close quarters, some of them being allowed aboard.

The Russian cruiser *Askold*, known as the "Packet of Woodbines," because of her five slim funnels grouped together, was greeted as an old friend, having been met at Colombo on the voyage over.   A persistent "furphy'" had it that her main guns were merely show pieces, owing to the fact that she was cut off from her ammunition supplies.

Too cramped even for "P.T.," the ship offered little facility for inspecting clothing and equipment, a diversion which, with lectures, took up the brief working hours.   Gambling schools—poker, bridge, banker, and "crown and anchor"—flourished, and the arrival of four week's pay (in English money again) gave them a decided fillip.   The canteen stock was now depleted of such trifles as tobacco and cigarettes, biscuits, chocolates and condensed milk, but fortunately remained fully stocked with the things that really mattered—macaroni, mixed spices and bootlaces.

Swimming was a popular pastime, and with the use of horse pontoons alongside, even the inexpert enjoyed themselves.   An incident worthy of mention is that of Second Lieutenant E. T. McVea's swim.   His father, Lieutenant-Colonel R. M. McVea was at that time in charge of Divisional details on board the *Osmanieh*, and while McVea, junior, was enjoying his swim round the *Novian*, Major le Maistre jokingly suggested visiting his father.   Acting instantly on the idea, the swimmer turned round and began the journey of about a mile and a half to the *Osmanieh*. Arrived there, he presented himself to the ship's Adjutant, and learned that his father was absent on the *Queen Elizabeth*. which had left the harbour.   After a brief rest he wished to essay the return trip, but was ordered by the Medical Officer to desist, and rigged out in a blue jacket, Scotch trews and Glengarry of his father's, he returned by boat.

It was at this time that the infantrymen realised for the first time what full marching order meant. Packs filled with overcoat and clothing, forty-eight hours' ration in haversack, two hundred and fifty rounds of ball cartridge, two blankets and ground sheet, with rifle and pick or shovel, made the full load with which each man staggered down the vertical ladder from the ship's side to the boats below. The precaution was taken to have shoulder flaps unbuttoned and belts unbuckled, so that should a man slip into the water, the unlucky one would be able to shed his equipment, and not sink like a plummet.

Captain F. Lind, R.M.O., left the regiment on the 21st of April. It was not his desire; a careless N.C.O. in charge of a fatigue party was really responsible for his transfer to the hospital ashore. A section of the decking had been removed outside the dispensary door on the lower deck, for the purpose of getting horse fodder from the hold, and had been left unguarded. Captain Lind, coming hurriedly out of the dispensary, was unable to avoid it, and fell through the deck to the hold, some twenty feet or so. Striking his head on the steel shaft casing at the bottom of the hold, he sustained a severe compound fracture and concussion. Next day, strapped to a stretcher, he was lowered into a naval picket boat that danced in the choppy sea alongside, and did not rejoin the battalion until some months later, Captain Matheson, A.M.C., meanwhile being allotted to the vacancy.

By this time everyone knew definitely what the objective was, though many shrewd guessers had hit the mark long before, and no one was really surprised to know that we were to land in Turkey. Maps of the Peninsula were issued to officers, and instructions issued to all ranks as to their conduct when in Turkish towns and villages. Turkish phrases and words, such as conceivably would be of use were made known for

the edification of all.   For a few days, "Throw down
your rifle, I will not hurt you," became a common
answer to the query, in execrable Turkish, "Who are
you?"

Even the most careless and unthinking ones could
not fail to realise the seriousness of the task
before them, and a glance at the map indicated a
hilly, almost mountainous country, arbitrarily bisected
by numerous small streams that sprang from the
higher ground and found their way quickly to the
sea through deep ravines.   An air of seriousness pervaded the whole ship.   The officers were closeted
with the C.O. many times.   Equipment was checked,
"Iron rations" were issued, and some of the blood-
thirsty could be observed on deck, sharpening their
bayonets to a more satisfactory point on the ship's
grindstones.

As "iron rations" will probably be mentioned
many times, it will be just as well to describe them
at once.

A white canvas bag, tied by tapes at the top and
about the size—if not of the exact proportions—of
an oatmeal bag, contained two or three handfuls of
small, oval biscuits, considerably thinner and less
adamantine than the ordinary army biscuit, a small
tin of "bully," and an oval tin with removable lid.
This latter contained two paper envelopes with tea
and sugar, and two cubes of beef extract.

Sir Ian Hamilton called a conference of Brigade
and Battalion commanders, and when these had ad-
journed to the *Queen Elizabeth*, that warship moved
out of the harbour and proceeded up the Dardan-
elles for the purpose of showing the officers what sort
of country they and their men were to attack.   The

visitors were much interested in the ship itself, and the ship's officers displayed the famous naval hospitality to the utmost degree. One of the wardrooms bore evidence of a Turkish shell which had pierced the ship's side and exploded in the room, doing only such damage as might supply a small job for the ship's carpenter.

What were the emotions of those officers who stood on the deck and saw the heavily wooded shores of Gallipoli on their left, as the huge man-of-war slowly steamed up towards the Narrows? A good proportion of them had had no more experience of active service than the men under their command, and as they listened to the naval men indicating features of interest, many of them must have been for the moment oppressed with a sense of their responsibility when they thought of the lives that within the next few days would depend in a large measure on their courage, coolness, and good judgment. One of the guns from the Asian side fired at the "Lizzie" as she passed, but the shot fell far short in a geyser of spray, and no reply was made.

The landing places had already been arranged, and the observers gazed intently at the ruined fort of Seddul Bahr on the toe of the Peninsula, standing high on the sandstone cliffs above a maze of old, but strong wire entanglements. They were told that at places near by the English and Indian troops would land. The ground here, though cliffy at the sea, was not very hilly, and undulated gently to the peak of Achi Baba, skirted by the road that led from Cape Helles to Constantinople. As the ship steamed further up towards the Narrows, the ground become more broken, and between the foot of Gaba Tepe and the marshland of Suvla Bay was seamed with innumerable gullies that led from the sea into the foothills that guarded the mountainous country terminating with Chunuk Bahr.

The officers returned from this reconnaissance seriously impressed with the magnitude of the task before them, though just as strongly conscious of the power of the naval backing that would be supporting the landing parties.

The fleet that represented the British and French navies was not now conducting the active bombardment of the Asian and Gallipolean forts which they had commenced as far back as February, but was engaged in minesweeping, patrolling and general reconnaissance so as to retain what slight advantage they might have gained, and to prevent the Turks from engaging in any military movements which would prejudice the chances of the one on which our land forces were about to engage. None estimated more seriously the work in front of the troops than did the Navy. From sea and land and air they had seen the nature of the country to be captured. The determined resistance encountered at almost all points by parties of marines landing from picket boats, and the Naval Air Service's reports of intense military activity on the whole of the Peninsula, indicated the danger and difficulty of the new military thrust. Nothing could now disguise from the Turco-German the fact that the naval attack had been the precursor of a military one, and though the forts may have been more or less damaged, the enemy were profiting by the British habit of wasting time, to defend the peninsula more strongly than ever against the threatened land attack.

It is to be assumed that the naval mind fully understood the dubious wisdom of entrusting a separate landing such as was to be attempted further up the coast from Cape Helles, to inexperienced troops. The physique and general bearing of the Dominion troops had impressed them very favourably, but there was perhaps apparent a slackness of discipline and a carelessness of manner that did not altogether please minds imbued with the high ideals of naval discipline.

The landing parties that were allotted to ''X,'' ''Y,'' and ''Z'' beaches at the southern end were mostly seasoned troops—British and Indian regulars, whose dependability was known and whose fighting ability had been tested. But these untried troops—how would they fare in the struggle against a crafty foe like the Turk, a seasoned veteran who had the enormous advantage of fighting on his own ground?

They were loyal friends, the Navy men, and it is not to be thought that their opinion was uttered outside the confines of the mess, the wardroom, or the lower deck. There already existed between the Colonials and the Navy a mutual attraction, based on admiration for the qualities discovered by each in the other, that was to be transmuted into a very real affection in fires of effort and sacrifice, in the immediate future.

Chapter VIII.

THE LANDING—AND AFTER.

THE morning of the 24th April brought definite orders to move, and the harbour re-echoed to the rattle and clank of the anchor chains as, in turn, each transport moved out to the open sea. The *Novian* left its anchorage at 12.30, and the windows of the little stone houses on the hills of Mudros harbor were winking golden flashes back to the sun, as the ship slowly cleared the booms across the harbor entrance. A rendezvous had been made some distance away from Lemnos, and the *Novian* was due at five p.m.

Unconsciously, men squared their shoulders and took deep breaths as they looked out at the other vessels moving out, for they knew that the curtain was soon to rise on the great adventure that eight months ago had called to them to cross the sea.

Those that dreamed looked out and visioned the battalion landing on some sandy beach, forming up and marching through the Turkish villages (where they were not to molest the women, and were to respect the Muktah, or head man of the village), along the white road that led to the minarets of Constantinople, until the moment arrived when they had to storm the Turkish positions, and forming into skirmishing order as they had done hundreds of times in Egypt, charge with the bayonet. No one, save

perhaps the officers who had seen the country, fore-
saw the boats' parties, shelled and broken, scrambling
up the scrubby cliff, gaining the summit, and then
losing themselves in the scrub and undergrowth until
an unseen enemy's bullet laid them low. The gift of
prescience is fortunately withheld from us by a wise
Providence.

The food on the *Novian* had not been of the best,
and it was here that the Fifth made their first acquaintance with margarine. Although fresh meat
was available, the cooks coped with great difficulties
in cooking for eleven hundred odd men on such a
small ship, and as a consequence, the change from
the camp cooking, which had been interspersed with
numerous restaurant meals, was unwelcome to many.
These remarks are meant to convey to the reader how
the men felt when they were told that they would
land before dawn on the morrow, but that at three
a.m. a good hot meal would be served.

During the night the ship had been steaming
slowly, and the air of mystery and the sense of impending action were strong. Through the darkness
could be seen, now and again, dim hulls of other
vessels, moving slowly and quietly on either flank
with little more than steerage way. Smoking was
forbidden, and necessary noise reduced to a minimum.
The instructions were regarded with a fine carelessness, on the *Novian* at any rate, that might have im-
perilled the whole enterprise. Restless and excited
groups of men stood around the decks, sometimes
under cover, but often not, smoking cigarettes or
pipes, and the flame of a match within cupped hands,
or reflected from the walls of deckhouses, must have
engendered many naval maledictions on the damned
Colonials,

Reveille was set for 2 a.m., and was a needless ceremony. Perhaps some of the men slept. Some of them at least made a pretence of reposing on their kit, but the great majority were quite openly excited over the prospect of fighting soon, and played restlessly with the bolts of their rifles, picked imaginary dirt from their bayonet springs, or wrote in diaries and pocket books last messages for their loved ones.

The ship had been moving more slowly for some time, and now was motionless in the darkness, still surrounded by the vague forms of the remainder of the fleet. The hot meal had been partaken of, but in very few cases was justice done to it. Bully beef stewed with a few potatoes, and a liberal addition of water, was not particularly appetising, but it certainly fulfilled the promise of "a hot meal."

The men were now mustered on the deck, and the position of the shore having been ascertained, all peered anxiously in that direction. The moon, hidden hitherto by dense clouds, was setting behind the high dark mass of land that loomed in front, and as the first finger of dawn made the darkness less intense, a pale streak faintly marked the demarcation of sea and land.

Muffled sounds of oars had been heard by those on the *Novian* for some time before, and it was whispered that the Third Brigade had been allotted the position of honour, and that they were even then on their way to the shore.

Thousands of eyes strained through the impalpable darkness that shrouded the objective, and the watchers listened intently for the first sounds indicating that the landing party had attained their goal.

"Ah! There they go!" A quickly-expelled breath came from all as the darkness at the base of

the cliffs was pricked by tiny spots of flame. A
rattle of rifle fire and a few faint cheers and shouts
were heard, and those on the ships and in boats on
their way ashore knew that the crusaders of a new
nation had leapt to grips with the Infidel.

The knowledge that the fight had begun brought a
sigh of relief from everyone, an involuntary relaxation from the constraint that had been accumulating
for days, and had culminated in the past half-hour or
so.

Dawn had come before "A" Company of the Fifth
had debarked, and now the necessity for caution had
disappeared, all was bustle and noise, attended, however, by a curious lack of excitement.   The forward
slopes of the hills facing the shore were still in dense
purple shadows, and the flashes of rifles, and, higher
up, the larger bursts of flame from a field-piece, still
showed distinctly.

On the right was now discernible the Cape or headland marked on the map as "Gaba Tepe," which was
surmounted by a stone fort.   Firing across the little
bay which stretched between it and the landing place,
the fort opened up with shrapnel on the beach and
the boats, and, at a range which made accurate shooting an easy matter, inflicted a great deal of damage.

The Navy's part had hitherto been a silent one,
confined to the dangerous task of towing the lines of
boats in to the shelving beach as far as the steam
pinnaces could go; but now with the first flush of
light, their guns began.   The *Triumph*, instantly recognisable by the curved cranes that stood out amidships, replied to the fort, and everyone's attention
was turned to the striking illustration of big-gun
fire.   Silhouetted against the pale morning sky, the

black outline of the fort was splashed with orange
bursts of flame, as the naval shells erupted into
showers of earth and stones hurled high into the air,
and falling back into the smother of smoke and dust
almost hid the warship's target. A light cruiser and
a destroyer joined in the attack, and the watchers
cheered each hit.

Gaba Tepe still remained active, however, and the
fire on the boats was still a galling one, the Seventh
Battalion suffering heavily as they went ashore.

The transports were not forgotten, and shrapnel
began to scatter about the ships and rattled against
the *Novian's* sides until the companies who were still
waiting, were ordered below.

The tow of empty boats which were to take ashore
the first lot of men from the Fifth came alongside
with dead and wounded, upon whom the men above
gazed curiously.   They were brought on board, and
the first complement under Major Fethers' command
took their places in the boats, supervised by Lieutenant Caughey, who was disembarkation officer.
Captain Clements was already ashore in charge of a
beach party.

"A" Company left the ship at 5.30 a.m., "B"
at 6.30 a.m., "C" at 7 a.m., and "D" at about 8 a.m.,
although a beach party had left before all of these
to get in touch with the men of the Third Brigade,
and act as guide to the Battalion.

For the reason that they were considered so much
like the new Turkish "Enver" headgear as to be
likely to mislead other of the Allied troops, slouch
hats were prohibited, and orders had been given to
leave them on board.   Many of the men cut the rims
into fantastic shapes, or removed them altogether,

while others threw them to the sailors who were manning the boats. Without exception, the navy on landing duty that day wore the Australian or New Zealand slouch hat, and some jolly tars wore eight or nine perched atop each other. The sea around was strewn with bobbing hats, and very few wore them ashore, notwithstanding the pictures that have been painted of the landing.

Of the calmness and cheerfulness under fire displayed by the Navy too much cannot be said. They struck a keynote that the Dominion troops could not help emulating, and from the chubby-faced midshipmen of fifteen or so, who stood each on the bow of his little pinnace, to the bearded veteran who drank tea whilst steering his boat for the fifth or sixth time ashore, under fire, they set a glorious example of coolness and courage under the most trying conditions.

"A" Company, under Major Fethers, had passed on from the beach up one of the numerous gullies which branched off from the rising ground above the beach, where an old hut stood, and reaching the high ground, advanced towards Olive Grove, where they met with considerable resistance. "B" and "C" Companies followed closely in the rear, while "D" halted under the crest of the hill, where the C.O. had established Battalion Headquarters until the position became clear.

The Third Brigade had cleared the beach and the steep slopes that led up to the high ground where the line was afterwards consolidated, and although there was a heavy rifle and shell fire, no actual opposition beyond the harassing attentions of hidden snipers was experienced until the Battalion reached the ridge, and debouched onto the more level ground that sloped down to the olive grove and the foothills beyond.

The day was a beautiful one, and the sun now shone warmly from a blue sky. So much has been written of the contour and the general appearance of Gallipoli that it is necessary to avoid repetition. The ground was soft and clayey, deeply eroded by the streams and surface water that rushed down to the sea, and still trickled from recent rains. The whole was thickly covered with scrub, bushes and undergrowth, but was without trees of any size, a kind of wild olive being the largest. In such a maze of ravines, the ground pathless, and patterned so that a clear view across more than a few yards was impossible, it was natural that cohesion between Battalions and even companies or platoons, was well-nigh impossible. Struggling and scrambling in single file up a narrow cleft in the ground, that perhaps branched off into many others, and getting out of sight of the sea at an early stage, men soon lost touch with their comrades and wandered over the next saddle of ground into another battalion—or the enemy. So it was that, even thus early in the day, staff arrangements became an utter impossibility, and tragedy must have quickly ensued, had it not been for the initiative of the men.

Except to the early arrivals, the enemy was invisible, though tangible evidence of his resistance was everywhere, and the crack of the sniper's rifle brought unseen death from all sides. Fortunately, the mood of the men was mostly to push on. Inaction led to nothing, and so little groups manned by a surplus of officers, and other groups with no commissioned leadership at all, scrambled and slid and clambered up and down the slopes, not knowing where, but always getting further inland. Already the gullies were being trodden into narrow paths that showed a reddish tinge in the clay, and abandoned equipment and the wounded, showed the tortuous and difficult way to the ragged firing line.

The Fifth's position was to fill in the gap in the line which existed between the Eighth Battalion on the right and the Sixth on the left. Before this could be wholly achieved, one of the Fifth's most gallant and capable officers, Major Fethers, was killed early in the morning, while in charge of "A" Company. A shot through the neck proved fatal, and he died in Major Flockart's arms. As a captain he had taken charge of "A" Company when the Fifth was first formed, and had succeeded to his majority and the command of the new "A" Company in Egypt. It has been rightly said of Major Fethers that duty was his watchword, and in the fearless performance of it he was lost to the Battalion at a time when his guidance and courage were most needed. Steady and capable, he was one of the men who played an all important part in the evolution of the battalion morale.

Many of the Fifth were mingled with others of the Brigade, particularly the Sixth, and some were among the party of two hundred or so who were rallied by Major Bennet, of that Battalion, and steadied by his courageous example, into a resolute body who stood fast to repel the Turks when they broke through.

At about this stage, Private S. Ricketson, of "D" Company, finding himself among a body of men without a leader, took charge, rallied them, and led them forward under heavy fire over the plateau which was afterwards known as Lone Pine. For this and subsequent good work he was awarded the D.C.M., one of the earliest decorations of this campaign.

Isolated groups of men, with and without officers, fought their way through the thick scrub, and in many cases never returned. How far inland the most advanced parties reached will probably never be accurately known, but many of the Fifth were very near the crest of the high ground that overlooked the village of Maidos before they were annihilated or turned back.

The intensity of the shrapnel, rifle and machine gun fire never seemed to vary all day, but curiously enough, very little rifle-firing was done by the attackers. The enemy remained well hidden and was able, by previously marked ground, to determine the range with deadly precision. That they were individually brave fighters was evidenced by the number of snipers who remained hidden in the bushes and wrought havoc until they were cleaned out. The story of the landing day resolves itself chiefly into a sequence of guerilla fights waged between twos and threes and even single combatants, in the midst of the thick scrub, and knowing no boundaries. The experience of many of the Australians was that of advancing under a devastating fire through a bewildering maze of bush, and then being lost, without a visible enemy or objective. It required no little courage under the circumstances, for men receiving no orders, to advance or even hold fast, but it was done, and when dusk gathered in on this Sunday a very large area of ground had been captured by the three Brigades.

When the danger threatening this scattered force was realised, orders were passed through that the men were to retire and form a firing line on the top of the highest ridge behind. The impassable nature of the country, and the consequent difficulty of com-

The Beach at Anzac, some days after the Landing. The 5th landed near here.

[By courtesy Colograph Art Co.]

munication, rendered the transmission of this order and its execution exceedingly difficult.   The order was shouted from one group to another, where possible, but it is highly probable that some of the advanced parties either did not know of the withdrawal or were not in a position to achieve it.   When this new firing-line had been formed, the Fourth Battalion, on its way up from the beach, was diverted to it, and at dusk, as wounded and tired men dribbled back to the crest, organisation had restored order and the line was rapidly being consolidated.

The rattle of musketry and the roar of shell fire never ceased till dusk.   Then the shelling died down, but a more intense rifle and machine gun fire began as the Turks, quick to realise the relinquishment of the ground so hardly gained, cut off the small parties and endeavoured to turn retirement into rout.   They met with unexpected resistance at the new firing line, where desperate labour had won a few feet of cover from the earth, and eager hands had broken down the scrub where it encroached on the line.   The valour of the Turk, now that he had recovered from the surprise of the landing, was immense, and the efforts he made to dislodge the troops from the steep and scrubby hills of the Peninsula was unceasing through the whole of that anxious Sunday night.

Both the darkness and the configuration of the ground favoured him, and creeping up under cover of the scrub he was able to harass the defenders of the shallow trenches with a short range fire and fierce bayonet attacks.

D

Chapter IX.

HOLDING ON AT ANZAC.

THE skill and courage shown by the Indian mountain batteries from the earliest moment of the landing and subsequently, cannot be overpraised. Like the Navy, these seasoned veterans set a fine example of coolness under fire to the raw troops, and their effective shots from most advanced positions saved the situation again and again. Kipling's reference to them—"For we fancied ourselves at two thousand, we guns that are built in two bits," ran through many minds that day, and the cool valour of Major ———, the English officer in charge of the battery near the Fifth, was an inspiration. The mobility of these small weapons, which only throw a three-pound shell, made them of peculiar value in the early hours before the Australian 18-pounder guns were landed. They were capable of being rapidly assembled when taken in convenient sections to a new position, and when it become necessary to move, they were even more quickly dismantled, and would vanish before the Turkish battery had time to reply.

The simple, almost child-like nature of the Indians, the devotion shown to their English officers, and their endless delight in their work, impressed the Australians more than any belief in the accuracy of the weapons they manned. The delighted grin of the gun crew after each shot attracted the grimmer-faced

Colonials, while the stoicism with which the Indians took their wounds won the hearts of men who themselves bore pain silently, or at least only cursed fluently, if impersonally.

Lieutenant Lillie's platoon, No. 15, had covered the retirement of one of the guns whose crew had almost all become casualties, and for a while some of the infantry men helped to serve one of these little guns, that leaped so violently backward after each shot.

Monday morning dawned on a ragged line of roughly dug and disconnected trenches that fringed the hill crest, held by weary men for whom the new day only meant renewed shelling. Throughout the day, the Turks made further desperate efforts to oust the invaders, but with the impartial daylight, a steady and accurate rifle fire foiled their attempts to close on the trenches, and the arrival of reinforcements for the line made the Australians' position less insecure. The attacks during the day were almost as desperate as those of the long night, but it was with cheery confidence that the men holding the hilltops repelled the Turkish attacks, both by sustained rifle-fire, and by the best means of defence—attack with the bayonet. Night came again, and with it the horrible, constant strain of staving off the fierce sallies from the scrub which so closely bordered the now-improved trenches. Momentary enemy successes at one portion of the line were quickly nullified by strong counter attacks, and Tuesday morning must have brought home the bitter truth to the Turco-German leaders that they had lost any opportunity they might have had of pushing off the Australians. Simultaneously the British staff must have realised that the element of surprise had disappeared, and that the struggle must settle down into the trench warfare that follows stalemate. Eight months of fighting was to prove the relative positions of the Allies and the Turks very little altered, whether at Anzac or at the further end of the Peninsula. A little straightening of the line might occur here, a little bending of it there; now the British pushed their holding further forward into the Turkish boundaries; now the enemy reclaimed some of his losses.

No food other than the iron rations issued before landing had reached the Fifth up to the third day, though others were only without it for forty-eight hours, but the haversacks and water-bottles of the dead supplemented to a certain extent this meagre allowance.

Fires of dry wood were now permitted in the gullies, and by means of vigorous fanning it was found possible to boil water with little smoke that would be visible to the enemy and draw his fire on that point. Practically it made no difference, as the smoke of many fires ascended from every part of the occupied ground, so that everyone had a sporting chance of seeing his fire scattered by a shell. Water from the streams that trickled at the bottom of the gullies was odorous from contact with the early dead, and muddy from traffic, but it made passable tea. The first supply of water that reached the line was earmarked for the water-jackets of the machine guns, and the crew thereof guarded the tins with a menacing expression and a loaded rifle.

On the Tuesday, the first supply of rations, including the faithful biscuit, with bacon and cheese, reached the front line, and the savoury smell of cooking drew everyone's thought from the enemy. It is certain that had the Turk descended on the line at this critical period, he would have encountered little or no opposition, unless he had asked for a moderate share of the food that was even then being fried, boiled, roasted, grilled and otherwise treated over little fires everywhere. Bacon, of all things, is calculated to arouse strong gustatory emotion in hungry men, and when the first good meal had been partaken of, most of the troops were in favour of attacking the enemy at once.

On Thursday the twenty-ninth, the defences—for such the front line of the erstwhile attackers had become, were in such condition that the Fifth were withdrawn for reorganisation, the garrison now on this part of the Peninsula being adequate. Accordingly the Battalion mustered on Shell Green, the only flat ground within the sector, a sloping rectangle, cleared of scrub, and evidently once cultivated. The conviction that the Battalion was almost extinct, which nearly everyone seems to have had, was dissipated when the men who had been for the time with other units dribbled in and the roll call showed the strength as being about 390 officers and men. The landing strength had been 32 officers and 1,026 other ranks. Many glad reunions took place among mates who had believed each other killed, but many looked in vain for their pals in each little group that straggled up the gully to augment the ranks.

It was now possible in some measure to ascertain how the Brigade had suffered, and seventeen hundred casualties proved to have been their cost of the fighting. The Brigade staff itself had sustained heavy proportional casualties from a shell which landed near the entrance to the shallow dug-out at the confluence of the Wire and Shrapnel Gullies.

Major Fethers and Major Saker were killed, the latter meeting his death while organising the firing line on the Monday afternoon. Wounded on the previous day, this gallant soldier, with an imperturbility and courage peculiarly his own, carried on with a fine disregard for his own safety, and steadied the reeling, broken line.   Major Saker had seen service with the British regular army in the South African War, and never did this tall, spare man with the grizzled moustache, use his knowledge of men to greater advantage than when he won the hearts of "C" Company. Quiet and serious outwardly, he displayed at the mess-table a side of his nature that proved him the most kindly humourist of all.

The next few days saw little or no change in the position of either side, though no doubt the enemy were as busy 'improving their defences, relieving front-line troops, and amassing stores and ammunition, as were the Australians.   The Navy still bombarded distant unseen objects in a desultory way, and night brought two destroyers close inshore near Gaba Tepe, where their searchlights swept unceasingly from beach to headland throughout the night.   The defences of this part of the shore remained an impenetrable mystery.   The stone fort surmounting the Cape had been so shattered by naval gunfire that barely one stone was left intact.   No reconstruction of the fort had been attempted, nor indeed had a living soul been seen since the Sunday, yet when a party in launches landed on the heavily wired beach at the foot, they were driven off by hidden rifle and machine gun fire with severe casualties. So it remained, except for this, a silent enigma until May 5th, when six shots were fired, evidently from a twelve-pounder, at the Second Brigade, which was being concentrated in readiness to embark for Cape Helles. The flash was distinctly visible, and though the eighteen-pounders on the right, and one of the battleships plastered the face of the cliff where the flash had been seen, the gun was still unsilenced, although none of the shots were effective.

The heroic determination of the stretcher-bearers throughout the whole of the Gallipoli campaign, but markedly in the early days, cannot be over-emphasized. Stretcher-bearing on level ground is trying enough, but when the work had to be carried out on slippery paths that curved and twisted in a tortuous descent, when the unseen sniper waited patiently for you to draw within his focus, where the narrow track struck down so steeply that the helpless wounded slid from the stretcher, and when two journeys to the firing line and back constituted a test of the strongest's endurance, then the stretcher bearers became heroes. Nor did they limit themselves to a given number of journeys, but as long as they had the strength, so long did these gallant men struggle up the rough path with their blood-caked, clay-plastered stretchers, to where the call of ''stretcher bearers wanted'' was never stilled.

It was curious at this stage to see the change that actual warfare had wrought in the personalities of all. Perhaps the most striking result was the recasting of friendships, other than that caused by death and wounds. Men who had been almost unnoticed in the battalion's training days had sprung into prominence by their actions during the fighting, while conversely some N.C.O.'s and even officers found their true level in the eyes of their comrades. Actions spoke louder than words in those stirring days, and the fact of a man having lain beside another in the firing line, facing death in comradely proximity, begat friendships which only death could sever.

All suffered under the common disability of uncleanliness. The man who had been careful of his person, his equipment and his arms, now found himself thinking only of his arms. With unshaven jowl, torn and stained uniform, he thought not of these, but of whether his rifle was clean or not. The man who in camp got up ten minutes before the others to shave himself fastidiously, and clean his teeth, was now to be observed in a deplorable state of dirt and whiskers, scrupulously attending with a sharpened match to his sight and his bayonet springs. True, the first opportunity was taken to clean teeth, shave, wash and brush hair with the help of a single mess tin of clayey water, but until this was possible the Battalion was only comparable to a herd of outlawed criminals. The spectacle of once trim and neat officers, with a week's beard, was gratifying in the extreme to the humorous side of the men's nature, and the sight of a popular officer (who was, to say the least, slim-legged) minus his putties and with a prosperous chin growth stimulated wit to no small degree.

On the first of May the Brigade were withdrawn from the line where they had returned after their first muster, and reassembled on Shell Green, where the Fifth enjoyed two lazy days, and on the third, relieved the Sixth Battalion in the line.

When the Fifth were enjoying this first respite from the line, parties were allowed to visit the beach for bathing, though they were warned that it was under shell fire, and dangerous. The thought of laving their filthy bodies in water was enough to send them down like happy schoolboys, and soon heads were bobbing about, with random showers of shrapnel lashing the water perilously near. Though none of the Fifth were killed, casualties were quite common when the men were bathing.

The Fifth were recognisable by the shoulder color

Using a Periscope Rifle at Anzac.

patch of red and black, which had been issued in Egypt, so it was said, that men on Cairo leave could be readily identified in respect of their unit. Previously, the small metal numerals on the shoulder flap had been the sole means of identification, at least among infantrymen, and these were easily removed when the occasion demanded. On the day of the landing, the Fifth could be distinguished at a much greater distance than heretofore by the watchers on the ships, each man's movement as he clambered up the slopes being heliographed by a flash of light. This strange phenomenon was caused by the presence of the bright tin canister issued to them some little time before, which to outward appearance looked like a long biscuit tin with two handles. The lid resolved itself on examination into another tin with a handle on the bottom. which fitted into the other and longer part. For what use they were intended, no one ever knew clearly, but the majority of the men suspended them to some part or other of their equipment, and did not abandon them until experience taught the danger of the flash of light which accompanied their movements. "The Baking Powder Tins," as they were called, had a brief, inglorious career in the manner originally designed for them, but it is understood that they afterwards made excellent bombs.

Chapter X.

CAPE HELLES. KRITHIA.

ON Wednesday, the 5th of May, the Battalion, in common with the rest of the Brigade, was delighted with the news that ran through their ranks like a bushfire, that they were to be withdrawn from the Peninsula in order to have a rest. No one was heard to demur, for truly the past nine days had been a trying time for new troops. Leaving the trenches, they spread into the dug-outs, some only such by courtesy, that pockmarked the hill near Brigade H.Q., facing the sea, and over their first issue of treacly navy rum, they discussed the doings of the last few days. The sterling qualities of dead comrades were dwelt upon, their shortcomings forgotten; the conduct of this or that man or officer was praised or denounced with the warmth it deserved, and all looked forward to the expected holiday with keen pleasure. But alas! It proved another "furphy!" and the battalion learned with some dismay that they were only to undergo a change of scene, and were to proceed next day to the Southern end of the Peninsula where the English and Indian troops were held up in much the same way as the Australians. The Royal Marine Light Infantry had arrived at Anzac to relieve the Second Brigade in order that the latter might go to this sector. Between midnight and dawn of 5-6 May the Brigade embarked on destroyers and minesweepers for the brief journey, after receiving

two white bags, quite familiar by now, of iron
rations.   Lying huddled closely on the foreshore
until their turn came for the boats, several men were
wounded by dropping bullets, even at this distance
from the firing line.

A different scene met the eye on the sunny morning of the sixth, as the boats came into the piers that
had been thrust out under the cliffs of Seddul Bahr.
The steep walls of limestone upon which perched the
fort, the bustling activity of the cosmopolitan collection of troops and the number of craft, both mercan-
tile and naval, provided much speculation.   Fore-
most in the picture was the stranded bulk of the
steamer *River Clyde,* which had been beached in the
gallant landing by the Fusilier Brigade.   The details of the wonderful story of the Trojan attempt,
in which so many soldiers and sailors perished, were
soon gathered by the Fifth, and glances measured the
steep cliffs as if to compare the difficulties of the
respective landings at Anzac and here.   Landing on
a pontoon wharf alongside the *River Clyde* simultaneously with some Senegalese black troops, the men
were quick to gauge the daring and the perils of this
venture.   Sandbagged and armoured in the bridge
and bows, the ship had been raked with a perfect hellfire at close range, as her honourable scars indicated.
How a single being could disclose himself and live
for a few seconds at that range, was indeed a miracle.
Low doors cut in the sides, whence the troops were to
sally when the landing stages had been thrown out,
bore the legend in chalk: ''Duck your nut,'' a quite
unnecessary admonition when one considers the fire
that was raging outside.

Past old and rusted wire entanglements at the foot
of the cliff, through which the poppies and wildflowers

reared their fantasy of colours, by a steep and winding road, the men gained the summit and looked
curiously on the ruins of the stone forts and the over-
thrown guns, striking evidence of the intensity of the
naval gunfire.

A march of some two miles or so along a well-made
road, winding through farm and orchard land,
brought the Battalion to their allotted position in
"general reserve." They were in high spirits. The
change of scene had wrought sudden effect, and they
found time to admire the contrast between the cultivated fields and the wild scrub country they had
just left. The contours here were flatter, and, rising gradually from the toe of the Peninsula, undulated gently to the foot of the eminence known as
Achi Baba, the strongly fortified position which lay
athwart their road to Constantinople.

In an open field with a clear stream of running
water the Fifth were halted and told to make themselves comfortable. The fresh water suggested a
long deferred pleasure, and very soon a modern ver-
sion of the wolf and the lamb at the stream was being
enacted, save that in this instance the lamb replied
in strongly flavoured language that some blanker further up the stream was dirtying the water for him,
too!

The energetic ones who had been digging ground
shelters to lie in for the night, found that water was
plentiful under the surface, too, and perforce had to
desist, enjoying the fruits of their labour the next
morning in the shape of a bath filled with clear water.

From this position almost the whole panorama of
the battlefield was visible. The main road ran on
the men's right towards the hill Achi Baba, and close
to the foot of this eminence (shaped like an inverted

basin) could be seen the village of Krithia, with some quaint stone windmills on the outskirts. The village had been the scene of the only street fighting that had taken place on Gallipoli, and was even now a bloody stumbling-block to the advance of the Allied troops.

If the Peninsula be regarded as being shaped like a human foot, the fort of Seddul Bahr stood on the toe, and, roughly speaking, the Allied line was flung across the instep above it from sea to sea. On the left were the Indian troops, then the English; on the right the French troops, both white and coloured.

The Turks had strongly-placed trenches with overhead cover, and a good field of fire over the flat fields in front, so that the Allied line could not be further advanced without creating awkward salients. Both the shore batteries and the naval guns were blasting the whole of the enemy's front, but the intense rifle and machine-gun fire of the Turks held up the infantry advance, particularly at the Krithia village point.

A creek (Kirte Dere), with high banks and a slight trickle of water in it, ran from the Turkish lines at right angles to this, and, roughly speaking, parallel to the line of the Allied advance. It provided a slight amount of shelter for our troops up to a point in rear of the support lines, its banks also slightly protecting dressing stations.

Precisely at eleven o'clock on the morning of Saturday, May the eight, after an ominous lull in the fighting, an Allied bombardment began from shore and sea, unprecedented in its fierceness. Between six and seven hundred guns belched forth destruction over the whole of the Turkish lines from the front line trenches to Achi Baba in the background. The

ground trembled and the air quivered.   The enemy's
positions were hidden by smoke and dust, out of which
masses of earth and vegetation were flung to the skies.
The white bursts of eighteen-pounders and French
"seventy-fives," and the yellowish clouds from the
naval shells clothed the fields in a hideous mantle,
and behind the Allied lines fresh troops prepared for
the inevitable attack when the shelling should cease.

The third reinforcements arrived at Anzac the day
before leaving for Cape Helles, and were now appor-
tioned to the companies.   The other men, senior in
service by a few days, already regarded themselves as
veterans, and commented vigorously on the super-
fluous dunnage that the newcomers carried, forgetting
their own heavy burdens of some two weeks before.
Barely was there time for the reinforcements to know
who their leaders were, when the regiment received
orders to move.

The Fifth were ordered forward at a time when
their thoughts were turning toward lunch, and in
"echelon" formation of platoons, they walked easily
and unhurriedly across the fields to where they should
eventually reach the comparative shelter of the creek
bed.

Fruit trees in bearing and crops almost ready for
the sickle spoke of early summer.   Death had already
begun her garnering, and the fields of barley were
scarlet-dotted with poppies waving over the dead,
who had fallen into their cool, green sepulchre.
Purple irises and yellow buttercups turned to the
warm morning sun as the lines of alien troops crushed
the corn underfoot.   A gentle breeze rustled in the
barley heads a soft obligato out of all keeping with
the harsh bellow of the guns.   It all seemed little
touched by the wave of war that had passed through it

and beyond, except for the trodden swathes across the
fields; and here and there the corpse which the green
stalks bent to hide.

Up to this point, shelling had been desultory and
ineffective so far as the Fifth were concerned, and the
cover of the creek bed was reached with slight loss.
A halt was made and lunch prepared. Dessiccated
vegetables had been issued for the first time, and individuals made savoury mixtures of these with bully
beef and beef cubes; but ere they could be enjoyed,
the Battalion moved up the creek in driblets to where
they were to deploy into the open and advance. Until
within about nine hundred yards of the enemy, only
slight losses were sustained, though the open ground
on either side was under rifle and machine-gun fire,
and the regiment sustained casualties while squatting
in the creek bed. A constant stream of walking
wounded, Tommies and a few New Zealanders, passed
along the banks, and news of how the battle went was
gleaned from them. Within a few minutes the
waiting ones learnt that the enemy were driven back;
that they were advancing; and that they could not be
shifted. Then it was they learnt, and remembered
the lesson ever afterwards, not to trust the individual's account of the action he had been concerned in.

The Fifth had been ordered to move to the right
of the line, and their position at this period may be
likened as being at the handle of a spread fan. It
was necessary, in order to proceed to the right corner
of this figure, to move to the right as well as forward,
and it speaks volumes for the discipline of all ranks
that they were able to cross the intervening trenches
and loose wire in the face of such a fire, and gain
their correct place in the line.

Now the word came to advance, and by platoons

as the "hopping off" point was reached, they scrambled out of the shelter of the creek and deployed to the right in open formation.   Several trenches in support of the firing line had to be crossed, most of them manned with Indian troops, who showed no pleasure in being held back while other troops "leap-frogged" over them.   Many of the smaller Fifth men found a lean brown arm hoisting them up from the fire step as they laboriously climbed out of the trench, and heard a voice:—"Tur-kee no good!"

The intensity of the small-arm fire had increased as they moved forward over the flat ground, and heavy shelling was encountered, though the naval gunfire kept the Turks from making as much of the target as they would have wished.

Dead lay thickly impeding the advance at this stage, a large proportion of them being Sixth and Eighth Battalion men, who had preceded the Fifth. At last the panting men, struggling under full marching order with pick and shovel, reached the front-line trench, held by Royal Naval Division Battalions, and, crowded in among the occupants, they took breath for a further advance of some two hundred yards, to where a thin line of the Sixth and Eighth had reached the absolute limit of advance against the terrific fire.

The Brigadier, Colonel McCay, and Captain C. E. W. Bean, the official correspondent, were prominent at this juncture, because they stood up in the open, the former, in his eagerness, too far forward, judged from a military standpoint; the other, in shirt sleeves and spectacles, observing the battle from the most dangerous position that possibly could be found on the whole front, but from which no doubt he obtained an excellent view.

At last the moment came.   The Brigadier's voice
could be heard crying, "Come on, lads! Advance Australia," and with an inspiring yell the remainder of
the Second Brigade moved up to augment the sadly-
thinned line.

The intervening distance was level, thinly covered
with coarse grass that grew here and there in sickly
tufts, and providing no more cover than could be
found on the proverbial billiard table.   The fire
was now so intense that a dust haze lay on the ground
like that which the first drops of a summer storm
produce, and exactly as they would have faced the
elements, the men unconsciously bent their heads and
dashed forward.

Each man had begun the advance with either a pick
or a shovel, but the weight of equipment with full
pack, and the strenuous nature of the rush, had
caused most to part with their burden, so that it was
only here and there that one could be seen with digging tools.   It was now about four o'clock, and the
sun shone warmly.   Onlookers from the slight eminence that constituted at one time British H.Q. could
see among the dust raised by the shelling, the brown
lines of the Allied troops moving steadily forward,
with their bayonets flashing in the afternoon sun.
Here, as at Anzac, the Australians saw little of the
foe, who lay so stoutly entrenched ahead.   On the
right of the Naval Division lay the French troops,
who for some reason did not move forward when
the Australians leapt from the trench.

Gradually the ragged front line of men, for whom further progress was impossible (partly owing to the close
range fire of the Turks, and partly to the barrage of
the French "seventy-fives," which had not been
lifted) was reinforced by rushes of platoons, sections

and twos and threes. The close range fire of the Turks proved deadly, and alternate men began to dig in while the others maintained a steady fire. The naval gunfire was impressively accurate, some of the shells actually bursting above the heads of our men, but the forward burst carrying the pellets on to the Turkish front.

An awkward position on the right, created by the failure of the French to advance, was turned to advantage by the Turks with enfilade machine-gun fire, but the Australian line was amended to overcome this, and the fault made good as far as was possible, until Naval Division troops remedied the defection.

The sun set in a golden splendour, painting the faces of the thickly-strewn dead a roseate hue. Under the cover of the darkness the position was feverishly improved with the picks and shovels which were brought up, and the Turks' counter-attacks being beaten off, the morning found the Australian portion, at any rate, of the line, with trenches about four feet deep. The losses had been necessarily severe, and the strength of the Brigade was again very low, despite the infusion of fresh blood prior to the battle. The death of gallant Dr. Matheson, the R.M.O., who, in the brief time he had been with them, had endeared himself to all, depressed the whole Battalion. While dressing in the shelter of the forward dressing station Captain Matheson heard a wounded man call for assistance, and with a cheery cry went out to fetch him in, but was hit by a bullet in the head, the wound proving a fatal one. Courageous and happy natured, his loss was an irreplaceable one, and the anecdotes of his brave deeds told by his comrades formed a fitting eulogy.

It was unfortunate that none of the officers of the

Fifth knew clearly where the front and support lines were when the advance began, owing to faulty staff work, but common sense and coolness overcame the difficulties, and the success of their part of the job was not delayed.   The knowledge that they had been chosen by Sir Ian Hamilton to act as shock troops in lieu of the regular troops of the Twenty-Ninth Division, who had been so badly smashed in the landing, was indeed gratifying, at least, to those who survived.

The strength of the Fifth on the morning of May 8th was thirty officers and a thousand men, and on withdrawal their numbers had been reduced to seven officers and less than three hundred of other ranks, the great majority of the casualties occurring in the first half-hour of the advance.

Colonel McCay and Major Cass, of the Brigade staff, were both wounded, and for a time during the Saturday afternoon there was no Brigade staff at all.   Major Cass, though lying out wounded, gamely tried to carry on by using passing men as runners, and refused to be carried away until he had done all that was possible.

After two more days in the front line, spent in improving the trenches and repulsing half-hearted attacks by the Turks, the Battalion was relieved on the night of 10-11th May.

A ration of ten cigarettes per man was enjoyed, this being a gift made by the crew of the *Queen Elizabeth,* in appreciation of the work the Australians had done.

Chapter XI.

BACK TO ANZAC—AND STALEMATE.

THE Brigade returned to their former position at Anzac on the 16th May after a rest behind the lines. They bivouacked on Bridge's Road for three days in dug-outs on the side of the hill, two companies being sent into the line, and the remainder resting.

The daylight hours had provided little or no excitement after the first few days, and only the more expert and energetic now devoted their attention to long-range sniping. The others slept. Few had anything to read, cigarettes and tobacco had already become scarce, and the hot, sunny days made sleep the easiest and most natural relaxation from the strain of the night.

The dead of both sides decayed and festered in the scrub, and, where possible, little parties went out to bury them. Death stank continually in the nostrils of the men, and seemed to flavour the food they ate. It certainly flavoured the water that trickled down the ravines, and that the parched men roughly filtered through handkerchiefs and drank. The grumblers complained bitterly of the attentions of the Turkish snipers, who harassed them from long ranges on these burying occasions. "Shootin' at a bloke when 'e's buryin' their own blasted mates. They always smell worse than our blokes, too." Which latter seemed a gruesome fact.

The word ''Anzac'' had not then been coined, and, like ''Digger'' and ''Aussie,'' still lay in the womb of the future.   The slang of the day was limited in range, and ''giving the good oil,'' or ''the dinkum oil'' referred to authentic news or information, while a ''furphy'' was still the current term for rumour or lie.

The primeval instinct of self-preservation led the soldier on the Peninsula to adopt the ways of the cave man, and the nature of the ground, the absence of artificial shelter, and the weather conditions, made the excavation of the hillsides a natural consequence. Within a few days the gullies and hills were honey-combed with roughly made dug-outs, mostly occupied by two, and sheltered from the sun, when necessary, by a ground sheet hung in front.

The ''back walls'' of the front line trenches were excavated with greater art, and supported with pillars of earth.   Small dug-outs were formed into which one man could creep and lie down out of the sun when off duty.   Idle moments when few shots was fired during the hours of daylight enabled the men to improve yet further the trenches (so hurriedly dug in the first forty-eight hours of their occupation).   Niches and recesses furnished neat cupboards for the occupants and their food, and the trenches became models of cleanliness.

Battalion Headquarters were made in dugouts in the side of a gully, and were reached by a path cut into the hillside.   Quite safe from rifle fire, occasional shells made the locality unhealthy, though every part of Anzac suffered this disadvantage.   One of the H.Q. Signallers, while coming round this path, was struck by a shell and was blown so completely to pieces that no suspicion of his death was entertained until blood dripped on someone from the bushes above.   Search disclosed the unfortunate man's blue Morse flag and identity disc, but little else served to reconstruct the tragedy.

Some few days later, a Turkish shell landed in the Headquarters dugout, killing R.S.M. Neilson instantly, and destroying all the Battalion papers and records. Sergeant-Major Neilson was a tried veteran of the South African war, whose age should have shamed many a younger man into the Great Adventure, and whose desire for efficiency in his own and the Regiment's work was almost a fierce one.

An interesting account of the preliminary naval bombardment which preceded the military landing at Gallipoli is that of Mr. G. A. Schreiner, representative of the Associated Press with the armies of the Central Powers. Mr. Schreiner arrived in Constantinople in the middle of February, 1915, and in the course of an article written for *Harper's Magazine* of April, 1918, he gives an account of the engagement viewed from the Turkish side. It may be premised from the tone of the article that the correspondent's sympathies were with the Turco-German forces, so that his details may be pardonably coloured in their favour. Boer as he is by birth, it is a reasonable assumption that Mr. Schriener was not favourably disposed toward the Allied cause.

He advances the theory that the Entente Secret Service agents in Bucharest were primarily responsible for the failure of the Allied fleet to return after their partially successful attack on March 18th. He avers that, in their zeal, they seized upon and disseminated a rumour that big-gun ammunition was traversing Roumania from Germany en route for Turkey and that the Allied fleet commanders, believing that the forts still had armour-piercing shells after

the battle of this date, withdrew.   We have Mr.
Schreiner's word that not a single shell reached Turkey via the Balkans, and that when the action was
terminated by the retirement of the Allied fleet late
that afternoon, the batteries at Kilid-il-Bahr and
Anadolu Hamedieh had between them only twenty-
seven armour-piercing shells!   In his opinion, the
Turks fully expected to see the fleet return next
morning (the nineteenth), and complete what they
had partially achieved, despite the fact that the *Queen
Elizabeth*, the *Irresistible, Ocean, Gaulois, Inflexible,*
and two others, were now the helpless playthings of
the currents, the French ship *Bouvet* being sunk
earlier.   He further adds:—''There is no doubt that
the day had been against the Allied Fleet. . . .''
Referring to the damage done to the Turkish side, he
says: *''The total casualties* in killed and wounded
were less than 100, and only one gun had been put out
of action, while three others were slightly damaged.''

Contrast this with the press despatches of the time,
made available to the British public.

Dealing with the military landing, Mr. Schreiner
states:—''A few weeks later, beginning with April
25th, Constantinople was once more within the reach
of the Allies.   This time their landed forces would
have done it—could have done it—had they cut off
the Peninsula of Gallipoli in the Isthmus of Bulair.''
If we may believe what this correspondent writes in
so positive a manner, Liman von Sanders, the head of
the German military mission in Turkey, had no
greater fear than that the Allies would take the
Isthmus, in which case he and the Turkish Ministry
of War had decided to evacuate the entire Peninsula.
General Sir Ian Hamilton and Admiral de Roebeck
will no doubt have mentally castigated themselves
severely if they have read Mr. Schreiner's article, and

learnt that the landing at Anzac and Seddul Bahr were bad mistakes, and that "another hour's work on March 19th, or within any reasonable time thereafter, would have saved the lives of millions of men, would have preserved the physical fitness of other millions, and made unnecessary the spending of scores of millions."

On May 18th began the fierce Turkish attack which was intended, in the words of Liman von Sanders, the Turkish commander, " to drive the Australians into the sea.'' The Fifth took no active part in the sterling and resolute defence which hurled back the fanatic advance. At no time, in the history of the Peninsular fighting, was the rifle-fire—on either side—so intense or sustained. The Australian front line was packed to the utmost capacity with men who fired into the dense masses of advancing Turks till the rifles scorched their hands, so hot did the weapons become.

Some of the men, in order to obtain a better vantage point, sat on the parapet, and from there—it is to be supposed—shot more comfortably than was possible from the fire-step below. The Australian 18-pounders did terrible execution at this short range, and firing at point blank range, ably supported the riflemen.

The Fifth had none of this excitement, but shared in the dangers. Crouched in the gullies behind the firing line, they heard the crackle of musketry swell into a fierce crescendo, with the louder reports of the artillery overriding the other noises. Most of the Turkish shelling spent itself on the area just back of the line, and the Fifth suffered mentally and bodily during this inaction.

The Turks, under the hail of fire, accurate because the short range made a miss practically impossible,

The Captured Hills of Gallipoli.   [By courtesy Colograph Art Co.]

wavered and melted away, leaving their dead thickly carpeting the ground in front of the Australian line, fearful evidence of their failure.

On the morning of the twentieth, while part of the Fifth were in support to the Fourth Battalion near "The Pimple," numbers of the Turks were seen under the protection of hospital flags and badges, apparently attending to wounded in front of their trenches, but on our fire ceasing, their movements became suspicious, and heavy fire being opened on them they scuttled back to cover, immediately retaliating by half an hour of furious firing.

The twenty-fourth of May saw the armistice properly arranged for, and though the Australians strictly played the game, Johnny Turk did not, and took advantage of the lull to move troops and stores, and otherwise improve the shining hour. The efficacy of our fire was proved by the numbers of Turkish dead which littered No Man's Land, estimated at between two and four thousand.

There were many Australian dead to be buried, and in the brief period allotted there was no time, if there had been any desire, for fraternising. The renewal of hostilities was begun vigorously by both sides, and there is every reason to believe, as stated, that the wily Turk had profited by the foolish British idea of honour.

The record of the succeeding months is largely the monotonous one of a beleagured fort. Digging was the main diversion when men were out of the line, and gun pits, roads, trenches and dug-outs were made and improved. Sickness began to take its toll, and dysentery and kindred ills sapped the vitality of the strongest. During June the number of sick equalled the casualties by deaths and wounds. On the sixth of June Colonel McCay, who had returned after being wounded at Cape Helles, was evacuated sick, and Lt.-Colonel Wanliss commanded the Brigade until the twentieth of July, when Colonel N. Smyth, V.C., relieved until Colonel J. K. Forsyth assumed command. Brigade orders during June mentioned that the M.C. had been granted to Lieutenant A. P. Derham, of the Fifth, an officer who by dint of merit had risen from the ranks, and had done wonderful work during the landing and subsequently. Lieutenant Derham was a medical student, and, in addition to his gallantry, he was conspicuous on the Sunday by reason of carrying a first aid outfit and attending to his own wounded.

About this time, Sgt. Leyland, of "D" Coy., was granted leave to proceed to England. This was unusual, but was explained by the fact that he had some invention relating to warfare, which had been communicated by him to the authorities. So impressed were they by what data he submitted that they considered it desirable he be given opportunities to put the ideas into practical effect, and with that object in view, he said farewell to his comrades, and left for England, via Lemnos.

Here he was stricken with disease before the final stage of his journey could be entered upon, and died. Sgt. Leyland's grave lies in the military cemetery outside Mudros, close to that of Lieut. A. Jackson.

On the twelfth of July, Major Flockhart, a popular and most efficient officer, was killed. Most of the Battalion were occupying trenches at Steel's Point, where the Turks had been shelling during the morning. Major Flockhart was observing the effect of the shell fire, and as he emerged from the traverse, a shell struck the iron loophole plate, and he received a terrible head-wound, from which the died the next day on the beach, without regaining consciousness. He was a very gallant officer, whose untimely death saddened the regiment.

Near the end of July, Colonel Wanliss became ill, and was evacuated.   Fate willed that he should never return to the regiment he had led through the travail of its blooding, but at the time, he and the regiment believed he would be with them again.   His health subsequently forced him to be an unwilling passenger to Australia, but he returned in 1916 to active service, and became C.O. of the 65th Battalion, one of the units of the mysterious 6th Division, concerning whose existence the politicians at home perjured their souls. The first Conscription Campaign was based on the assumption that Australia did not have enough troops in the field, and the Government strenuously denied that a 6th Division had been formed.

The presence of a Japanese trench mortar about this period keenly interested the men of the Fifth. When placed in the line near them, they watched with approval its laying and heard the loud explosion of its projectile in the Turkish trench. To judge by the noise of cries and shouting that followed from the enemy, it was particularly effective.

At the time when the Battalion was in charge of Steele's Post, the presence of rats became an active menace, as well as a nuisance.   Not finding overmuch food in their nocturnal foraging, they turned their attention to the jam tin bomb fuses, and nibbled at these, with the consequence that several casualties were caused from premature explosions of the short-fused bomb before the Engineers were acquitted of the charge of carelessness, and the real cause was discovered.

Reinforcements having joined up at this period, some of the more credulous ones listened with attentive ears to a veteran's tale of Turkish ingenuity, and learned how these rats had been specially trained to the art of fuse-biting. The innocent ones were forthwith instructed to commence a keen search for the rats, but to discriminate between the friendly ones and those of Ottoman sympathies, the latter being easily distinguished by the crescent stamped on the left ear.

In no other campaign of the Great War were the entire units of an army in such danger as at Anzac. Usually there is a safety zone, beyond the edge of which, the Ordnance Corps, the Army Service Corps, and other essential adjuncts to the fighting arms, move in safety. Here, everyone took a common risk. In the front line, in the gullies, or on the beach, Death stalked. It is a moot point whether or not the beach was at times more dangerous than the trenches.

"Beachy Bill" and "Asiatic Annie" were two guns which consistently shelled the beach frontages, and many were the casualties caused by them among the non-combatant workers about the wharves and stores. In addition to this, "spent" bullets finished their flight over the trenches on the ridges in a steep curve that often brought silent death to the beach parties. Then there was the shelling from the front which often favored the beach and the dugouts in the cliffs and hills bordering it.

All of this invested Anzac with dangers that put everyone on an equality, and there was an absence of inter-unit jealousy or contempt which sometimes is manifested by a combatant force towards its non-fighting essentials.

The men who carried water, food and ammunition from the beach to the front line performed a herculean task. In the early days of the investment of the Peninsula, before the roads were perfected, it was a day's work to make one trip to certain parts of the line.

Steep and narrow paths, not always taking the easiest gradients, crossing deep ravines and traversing steeper hills beyond, made the carriage of an ammunition box by two men a feat of endurance. Hauling it up a steep bank, one above pulling and the other helping from below, was a strenuous task. Often the top man slipped and the box and its two bearers rolled into the gully, to laboriously recover the lost ground.

The mules were invaluable in this work, and their sagacity was remarkable. Laden, perhaps, with a box of biscuits on either side, they rarely if ever slipped. They were better able to negotiate the steep pinches than the human bearers. On the top of the descent, mules would halt for a moment, then rush down the steepness with terrific speed, gaining enough momentum to easily carry them up the opposite side. They were also less affected by shell-fire than were the few horses which were on Anzac, and very seldom got "nervy" when a shell burst near them.

Chapter XII.

LONE PINE.

ON the fifth of August orders were received that the Fifth was to move up, and "D" Company to take over from the Fourth Battalion at "The Pimple," "C" Company in No. 2 southern sector, and "B" and "A" on the right stretching up to Wire Gully. This was a Brigade front, the Seventh and Eighth Battalions holding the line from Wire Gully to Quinn's Post, while the Sixth were to make their fateful attack on "German Officers' Trench."

For the attack on Lone Pine, the First Brigade were chosen as the storm troops, probably from the fact that the Third Brigade had borne the brunt of the actual landing, and the Second had distinguished themselves at Cape Helles. The attacking troops were marked by white discs on their backs, and white armlets, an innovation borrowed from the Western Front tactics.

On the early morning of the sixth, the Third Brigade carried out a minor diversion on the right of the Second Brigade near Ryrie's Post, which was quite successful in causing the Turks to open up heavy machine-gun and rifle fire on the front lines at this point.

The method of attack was unique. The usual support and firing-lines, with communication-trench, were already in existence. Weeks of work had resulted in saps being run forward from the firing line, connected with an underground gallery running parallel to it, and of course much nearer to the Turk's position. There were three saps, D 5, D 9, and D 11 respectively. Along the gallery were constructed firing steps approximately five yards apart, and from there working parties were cutting apertures, or "pop holes," in the language of the day. The actual breaking through of the pop holes was timed to take place in the darkness about two or three a.m., and was duly carried out. Everything was now in readiness for the attack at five-thirty p.m. that afternoon.

At half-past four p.m. punctually the artillery bombardment began, amply supported by the men-of-war, and the Turkish trenches were subjected to an intense and accurate fire which should theoretically have damaged and disorganised the enemy lines so as to make the infantry assaults more of a "mopping-up" process than anything else.

"C" Company of the Fifth had been holding the front trenches, but now evacuated in order to allow the First Brigade to form up in the order allotted them. The first wave was to advance from the popholes, and the second, third and fourth were to issue from the trenches behind, and follow up.

When the bombardment was lifted at half-past five, the First Brigade sprang from their pop-holes like a multitude of pantomime demons, rushed forward in the face of a devastating small-arm fire which proceeded from the Turks as soon as they recovered from their surprise (showing how little actual or moral damage had been caused by our artillery), and reached the strongly protected enemy line. It was a deep trench with heavy baulks of timber banked with earth, forming overhead cover, in which the

Turks had been well protected.   The attackers, with
desperate bravery, prised with rifle and bayonet at the
chinks, or dropped bombs through the interstices,
while the terrible fire shattered their line at so close
a range that the uniforms were singed by the flash.

Here and there an opening was forced, and gallant
men dropped into the semi-darkness of the trench
and met their foes with the bayonet.

Gradually percolating through into the dark, noi-
some trench, filled with bomb-fumes, and dead bodies
of both sides, with dim and horrible forms grappling
desperately and giving no quarter, the Australians
fought a bloody way along the trench with bayonet
and bomb.

The three remaining waves passed over the fire-
trench, and captured three lines of trenches which
contained large stores of arms and ammunition.

Barely had the panting men time to recover breath
when the Turks counter-attacked, mainly with bombs
up the communication trenches.   Hastily prepared
barricades or bomb-stops were thrown up to meet
the onslaught, and the trenches were again a veritable
Hades.   The lurid flashes of the bombs, the ear-
splitting concussions, the acrid fumes and smoke, and
the smell of blood and burnt flesh made the conditions
in the semi-darkness terrible.   The attacks, though
desperate, were met with still greater daring and re-
solve; the Turks were beaten back and the captured trenches were safely consolidated and fairly
secure by the end of the day.

During the night of the sixth the Sixth Battalion
made an attack on German Officers' Trench, but it
was foredoomed to failure, and a withering machine-
gun fire crumpled the remaining waves, few, if any

Dugouts and Shelters in a Gully at Anzac.

men reaching the objective, and none returning. When daylight broke the bodies of over three hundred gallant men could be seen lying in the scrub land between the lines.   Lt. R. T. Fairclough, who had been a Corporal in "D" Company of the Fifth, and was transferred to the Sixth on being commissioned, was one of the officers killed. A wonderful conception of the meaning of the word "Duty," and an absolute fearlessness, combined with his cheery nature to make his loss deeply felt by his old comrades of the Fifth, as well as by those of his own men.   Lieut. A. Jackson, formerly of the Fifth, and a noted oarsman, was another sterling officer who was mortally wounded this fateful night, dying some days later at Lemnos.

The Seventh Battalion relieved portion of the First Brigade on the sixth, and it was against their part of the line that the Turks made a determined counter-attack which was responsible for some hard fighting, during which the Seventh gained three V.C.'s, Lieutenants Symons and Tubb, and Corporal Dunstan distinguishing themselves in this supreme manner.

After forty-eight hours "A" and "B" Companies of the Fifth relieved the Seventh, and Major le Maistre and H.Q. moved into Lone Pine trenches.

"C" and "D" Companies were attached to the Sixth Battalion, and, while there, bore the brunt of severe bombing attacks, during which distingished service was done by many men of the Fifth.

Prior to the Lone Pine attack a placard had been hoisted up by the Turks in their front line, which intimated that Warsaw had been taken, a statement received by the Australians with derision as a "furphy," but which was later confirmed.

During the preparation for the attack on Lone Pine, Sergeant Drummond was in charge of a party from

E

the Fifth engaged in bringing up rifle ammunition and stacking it in a hollow in Wire Gully, which was in a convenient position to form a supply dump.   A New South Wales chaplain had also chosen this place as possessing advantages for a position in which he could conveniently hold a Divine service for the First Brigade troops, who were to take part in the impending battle, and Drummond, returning from a laborious trip to the beach, found that the little enclosure lined with ammunition boxes had been taken over by the Padre, and that in this extempore chapel, service was in progress.   The fatigue party had their job to do, however, and the service was accordingly punctuated by the thud and rattle of the boxes being slid down a plank into the hollow.   The interruption proved so disconcerting to the Dean that he informed the Sergeant, with no little asperity, that he had ''desecrated the first church in Gallipoli.''   ''I'm sorry, sir,'' replied Drummond, ''but,'' indicating the ammunition with a wave of his hand, ''all this is just as necessary for to-morrow as your sermon, isn't it?'' The Padre smiled, and supposed that, unfortunately, it was.

Chapter XIII.

SUVLA BAY.

Resting at Lemnos—Back to Anzac.

COINCIDENTLY with the Australian attack at
Lone Pine a diversion was created at Cape
Helles, both of these subordinate to the
landing and advance at Suvla bay, which proved as
abortive and costly an attempt as has ever added a
bloody page to our history, eclipsing even the later
tragedy of Fromelles in 1916.   Supporting this attack, which was thrust inwards from the sea across
the arid, salty plains of Suvla towards the hill of
Chunuk Bair, was the advance of New Zealand and
Indian troops, with whom were a small body of Australians—4th Brigade and 2nd Field Ambulance
stretcher-bearers. A difficult night march by these across
enemy country succeeded through its very daring, and
that part of the scheme, upon which so much of the
success of the whole depended, was achieved.   While
the Colonial troops lay in the darkness among the
scrub on the high hills, awaiting the final phase of the
attack, the British troops were staying their advance
till dawn should break.   The precious minutes fled
by, while the Turks were eliminating the element of
surprise upon which the whole attack hinged.
Dawn's saffron fingers touched the early clouds, and
morning broke rosily over the hill tops and revealed
the whole panorama to the eyes of the watchers of
both sides, up there on the heights.   From their

vantage points above the plain the whole tragic scene lay vividly beneath.

The raw British troops lay there, shaken by the land mines which had disorganised the early advance on the beach lands, tortured by thirst unwisely slaked at the very inception of their arduous task, and badly raked by the Turk's fire, as they advanced across the scrubby plain, through the rolling clouds of smoke from the undergrowth which the wily Turk had fired with a favourable wind.   They had the courage and determination, which, under wiser leadership, would have enabled them to press on to their goal, but the councils of the foolish prevailed, and halting for the night, they gave the feverishly-hastened Turkish reinforcements time which allowed them to anticipate, by ever so small a margin, the delayed advance of the British troops.   A courageous and skilled fighter like the Turk opposing the newly-baptised Territorial troops meant a formidable obstacle, and before it could be overcome, the valorous troops on the heights of Chunuk Bair were dying hard in their vain endeavour.   Below on the plain an impotent army strove to accomplish what now was too late.   The tragedy of Suvla was complete.

After Lone Pine, August was spent in the now monotonous occupation of holding the line, persistently harassing the enemy, digging, and carrying out the fatigues which on the Peninsula became of paramount importance to the defenders.

Dysentery was now a foe as dangerous as the Turk, and the meagre and uneatable selection of food aided the spread of the diseases which sapped the strength of the British troops more surely than did the Turkish attacks.

On the third of September the strength of the front-line garrison which held the Australian front against the vastly superior Turkish force was nine hundred and thirty-five men!   It is not to be supposed that the enemy was ignorant of how affairs stood with us. Very little of the invested ground was concealed from them, and the intimacy of the advanced trenches of both sides was such as to make deception difficult and even impossible.   They were probably fully seized of the fact that despite the lightly-held line, the contour of the ground made a systematic general advance impossible, and that here at Anzac neither side could secure an advantage which would entirely dispossess the other of their hardly-won, and strongly-held positions.

So perhaps Johnny Turk was content to let things be as they were.   Down south or at Bulair perhaps lay the real danger of a successful advance, so that nothing would be gained by a costly attempt to drive the infidel from here.

So the hot weeks dragged on.   The flies were in-numerable and incredibly aggressive.   A newly-opened tin of jam was speedily the rallying-point of legions, and in the processes of transferring jam to biscuit and biscuit to mouth, hundreds of them perished in a tenacious devotion to their objective.

No description of the Gallipoli campaign can lightly pass over the work of the medical services.   The work of the first three weeks was an awful nightmare. Following on miscalculations of the possible casual-ties of the Landing, came the fearful, unending streams of wounded to the temporary dressing stations and beach hospitals.   The stretcher bearers struggled up the arduous heights and slid and scrambled down again with their suffering burdens, till at last, from overwhelming fatigue, they fell on their blood-caked stretchers and lapsed into merciful sleep.

The doctors, piteously few in number, but attempting by superhuman efforts to cope with the rush, worked on and on, till at last they slept while standing, their subconscious selves persisting in their tasks. Twenty hours and more, without sleep, some of these heroic men worked, till nature capitulated and they slept, against their indomitable will.

The casualties sustained in the advance against Krithia (Cape Helles) on the eighth of May intensified the horrible conditions subsequent on the inadequate medical services, and the dressing stations and hospital tents were crammed with stretcher cases. Shipping there was in plenty; but without sufficient medical attention, no wonder that so many hundreds died of wounds who otherwise might have been saved.

One transport that left the Peninsula two or three days after the Battle of Krithia had a freight of some five hundred wounded, with a staff of four doctors and sixteen orderlies. Arriving at Alexandria, they found the hospital accommodation there overtaxed, and perforce had to proceed to Malta. By dint of wonderful and incessant toil, the doctors did attend to everyone, but it was a long time ere they reached the last man, some of whom had been enduring the agony of uncleaned wounds and unset fractures for seven and eight days.

The ship's staff always played a worthy part, and it was a common sight to see grimy stokers when off duty, attending to the wounded in whatever way was possible.

The accommodation of the leviathan *Palace Hotel* in Heliopolis was soon overtaxed, the auxiliary hospital at Luna Park (a pleasure resort similar to the one of the same name in Melbourne), and other auxiliaries in Cairo, were speedily filled to discomfort, and so were the hospitals hastily established in Alexandria. Lemnos was mostly reserved for sick who had a reasonable chance of a speedy recovery, so that it was necessary to look elsewhere. Malta, with its existing military accommodation was not inaccessible, and soon the hospitals there were overflowing, and it was impossible to do other than send the wounded on to England. Obviously this course should have been reserved for the wounded who were permanently incapacitated, or those whose recovery was a lengthy matter, but in practice no classifying was possible, and even the slightly wounded went there, too.

The warm season had begun in Egypt, and only those who endured and survived their stay in hospital there will know what the wounded went through. A hundred and twenty-eight degrees in the shade was reached, flies were an ever present torment and menace, and the danger of blood-poisoning was an acute one.

The Colonial and Imperial nursing sisters were permitted to come only as far as Lemnos, or, at furthest, onto the hospital ships that lay off Gallipoli; but here, and in stationary hospitals, the sick and wounded were tended under these conditions by heroic and devoted women.

Unlucky indeed was the man, suffering from diarrhœa, dysentery, enteric, or septic sores, who was evacuated to Lemnos. The medical arrangements were in charge of the British medical authorities, and, as instances of ineptitude, ignorance, and neglect, they were sufficiently appalling. Over-crowding was unavoidable, and no blame for it could be attached to the subordinate medical officers there, but the filth and vermin which added to the torments of the patients were inexcusable. Beds and bedding were infested with vermin, even the dressings being invaded by the horrible pest, and cleanliness was impossible. At one hospital in particular, no washing accommodation was provided, and each day men could be seen gathering at a nearby semi-stagnant pool, washing, shaving, and cleaning septic sores and wounds in horrible propinquity.

The diet supposed to repair strength in men wasted by disease and exposure was pitifully insufficient in quantity and quality, although Turkish prisoners in the vicinity had bread to waste. The British patients walked to the neighbouring camps to beg food, or traded hospital blankets to the Greek peasants for the sustenance their enfeebled bodies craved.

Made desperate by hunger, the men, improving on the immortal Oliver Twist's example, endeavoured to satisfy their needs by attempting to get two "sittings" at a single meal, but some of those detected in this unpardonable military crime, were punished by the humane medical authorities—incredible as it may seem—by being sent back to their units at Gallipoli!

Following the enervating heat and the ever-present flies, came the early November cold, and the men's sufferings were intensified by insufficient clothing. Even Gallipoli seemed preferable after this life, and Egypt seemed like Paradise lost.

Anzac was peopled by brown savages. Singlet, breeches and boots completed the apparel of most, while the more hardy disdained even the singlet. Breeches were cut down to very abbreviated "shorts," and memories of Bondi and Carrum were revived as the men compared their various degrees of colour.

As the majority of the men were still minus the slouch hats which had been officially discarded prior to the landing, an issue was made of khaki cloth "havelocks," which, in some measure, protected the nape of the neck from the intense heat.

Reinforcements now arrived frequently, as was indeed necessary to restore the depleted garrison to some degree of strength, and so hurriedly had some of these departed from their native shore that they had not had time to familiarise themselves with the service rifle.   Accordingly, the N.C.O.'s (of the Fifth, at any rate), found themselves recalling long-forgotten scraps of detail, as in the gullies back of the front line they patiently lectured the newcomers on the parts of the rifle !   Fortunately the Turk did not disturb this training, and in due course those of the "reinstoushments" who survived sickness and the sudden death that ever winged its way over the area, found themselves peering through loopholes over some yards of scrub at the sandbags of the enemy.

On the ninth of September the whole of the Second Brigade was withdrawn from the Peninsula, their places being taken by the newly arrived Sixth Brigade.   The Fifth and Sixth Battalions and two hundred and eighty-six of the Eighth embarked on the *Newmarket*, and sailed for Lemnos, disembarking at Engineer's Pier on the eleventh, and marching thence to Sarpi Camp.

The Fifth had been reduced by the four and a half months of warfare to a strength of twenty officers and three hundred and eighty-six other ranks, though up to this time they had received six drafts of reinforcements.

Laden with their equipment, so long discarded, and unaccustomed to marching, the men found it impos-

sible to go more than a mile and a half without
resting.

The Australian nursing sisters flocked from the
hospital tents to greet the Battalions as they marched
up the road to the camp.   The nurses had seen the
regiments move out past Mena House five months
before, bronzed and overflowing with gaiety, step-
ping on the hard white road to the band's quickstep,
with the springiness of good health, and with the
light-heartedness of youth—adventure bound.   Bub-
bling with vitality, the men had flung jest and song to
the leafy roof of acacia trees that shadowed the long
road to Cairo.   And now they were returning, recognisable only by the faded colour patches that showed
here and there, browner than before, and leaner and
graver; and the watching women saw the remnant
of the regiments that had gone out in all the pride
of youth and health, drag slowly and painfully past.
Stained and torn uniforms barely covered their brown
nakedness, and their eyes and mouths showed fine
lines that the strain and suffering of the past few
months had graven, making veterans of the youngest.
Still they were not dispirited, only very, very tired;
and as they gave hearty greetings to their sisters,
brave partners in their enterprise, they wondered to
see tears bedewing the nurses' smiles.

These men had indeed seen death, and felt its
breath on their cheeks, but here they were out of it
and free from responsibility and danger for a while,
so that when the company jester called out, "We're
just going home to change for dinner, Sister," there
was a general laugh that showed the cheerful spirit
underlying the weariness.

Two or three days were spent as restfully as the
British Army Regulations will allow, and on the

thirteenth, the Seventh Battalion completed the Brigade.   The old routine of training began anew, and
was carried out in the morning, while sports and
athletics were encouraged in the afternoon.

Cricket matches were played against other units
and the Navy, and the cordial relations between the
sister services were intensified, as was the affection
between the Australians and the sailors which was
before so strongly marked.

The officers of the Fifth bought a small sailing-boat,
and this proved an excellent means of visiting the
battleships in harbour, obtaining stores, and not least
of all, taking the hospital sisters for cruises. Captain
Luxton, and Lieutenants Marshall, Moore and Permezel ventured out one stormy day when the native
fishermen deemed it unsafe, and narrowly escaped
drowning in the fierce squall that almost disabled
their small craft.

The Brigade remained at Sarpi Camp, strengthened
by the seventh reinforcements which had now arrived,
and gradually getting fitter for the intended return to
the Peninsula about the middle of October.   They
did not go there, however, for diphtheria broke out in
the camp, and the Brigade were isolated, much to
their disgust.   On the tenth of October the quaran-
tine was lifted, and the twelfth saw them inspected by
Major-General McGregor.   Captain J. Walstab, the
popular commander of ''C'' Company, was promoted
Major on the third of this month.

It was here the Fifth discovered that they had a
teetotaller among their ranks.   With the idea of
issuing a small bottle of stout daily to each man, as
a strengthening addition to their diet, a return was
called for to show the number of teetotallers and non-
teetotallers in each battalion.   The Fifth's return

showed *one* teetotaller! It will perhaps be as well
to note for the sake of veracity that there were other
abstainers, but they had consented to be branded as
drinkers in order that their mates might receive a
double share of stout.

The eleventh of October was a day of bustle and
preparation, as the whole camp was polished up for
the great Kitchener. With Generals Maxwell and
Birdwood, the famous soldier searchingly looked the
men over, to his expressed satisfaction. He addressed the troops in a clear, though by no means
stentorian voice, and told them that he was proud of
the splendid work they had already done, and that if
they were now doing no more than helping to hold
up such a huge number of men, they were still doing
incalculable good to the Allied cause.

Inspections were rife, for on the sixteenth the re-
novated Brigade was inspected by the Admiral of the
French fleet.

On the 24th of October, considerably refreshed
by the spell, the Brigade, excepting the Seventh Battalion, moved back to the Peninsula. Brigade H.Q.,
with the Fifth and Sixth Battalions, embarked on
the *Abassia,* and the Eight Battalion on the *Princess
Ena.* Rough weather at Anzac made immediate landing impossible, and the ship stood off to Imbros until
the twenty-seventh, when the men set foot again on
"Brighton Beach," if not filled with eagerness, at
least taking up the burden uncomplainingly.

After a little time in dug-outs in the cliff face overlooking Hell Spit, the Second Brigade relieved the
Third Brigade on Silt Spur, the Fifth and Sixth being

[By courtesy Colograph Art Co.]

Chaplain Dexter, D.S.O., D.C.M., holding Communion Service at Anzac for Members of the 2nd Brigade.

in the line, and the Seventh and Eighth in reserve in Clarke's Gully.

This part of the front was a truly wonderful piece of engineering, and by dint of hard and patient work had now been completed. The main communication from Brown's Dip to the front line had been named "Lady Galway's Road," and consisted of a tunnel, in some parts seven feet high.   It broke into the line on the forward slope of Silt Spur, where the trenches were completely underground.   Loopholed at intervals, it provided an excellent vantage-ground for listeners and snipers.   The trenches hereabout were well drained, and even in wet weather, were dry underfoot.

The weather was now rapidly changing, and days as well as nights were cold and wintry. Bitter rain and sleet were at last succeeded by snow, which fell steadily throughout one night in late November. The shivering troops, thin-blooded after a year of almost constant summer, woke to the spectacle of a snow-clad landscape, and the delighted Australians made their first snowballs, and tired not in the promiscuous throwing of them.   Chaplain Dexter, ensconced in the bay of a trench repelled a spirited attack with his stout resistance.

At this time orders were received that a unique operation was to be instituted over the entire Anzac front, officially styled "the silent ruse."   Briefly it was intimated that all firing of artillery and other arms would cease for a period of three days.   The Staff no doubt had in view the imminence of possible evacuation, and intended to prepare the way by treating the enemy to yet another example of our peculiar ways of warfare.

The silence was strictly observed, and the troops kept zealously from the enemy's observation. The long-sustained silence proved irksome to Turkish nerves. Since the landing—nearly seven months before—it had not been possible to count ten seconds between shots, and now the silence of a deserted town hung over the Australian front lines. Observation must have shown the Turks that the area was still occupied, and the everyday business of the beach, so like to a small seaport town, altered not one whit.

The machine-gun duels between opposite posts died into an irritable, stuttering solo from the Turks, who now ran the whole gamut of the machine gun's register. Violent bursts on the loopholes succeeded steady traversing fire that hosed up yellow dust along the line of sandbags, but evoked no more response than before. On the second night of the ruse, a Turkish patrol was observed crossing No Man's Land, and presently crawled through the low scrub to one of our machine gun posts which heretofore had been a persistent annoyance. The listeners heard the rustle of the twigs and the swish of the leaves as the dark forms crawled cautiously forward, and at last our gunner saw a hand protruded through the loophole, and close round the barrel casing. This was too much for the Australian, and orders or no orders, he could hardly resist the target. As chance would have it, the period of inaction and the cold caused his gun to jamb, and the alarmed patrol was away before he could get into action again. A few shots and another jamb, and by that time the wrath of the nearest officer added to the gunner's chagrin.

Another Turkish reconnaissance reached elsewhere in the line that night, and though many rifles were trained on them, and itching fingers fidgetted on triggers, no shot was fired from our side even when the enemy rolled a bomb through the loophole and caused a few casualties.   No finer test of discipline could have been imposed than this Spartan restraint, but the men held fast, and this patrol too reached their own lines safely, no doubt adding further to the Turk's mystification.

Chapter XIV.

THE EVACUATION.

Goodbye, Anzac!

TO those officers who were able to oversee the position not only at Anzac, but at Suvla and Cape Helles, the fact that the Turks were immovable, was by this time patent. Stalemate had set in early at Anzac; little or no progress had been made during the past few months at Helles, and nothing but the danger of a withdrawal from Suvla kept the investing forces on the scene of that direful attempt to break the back of the Turkish defence.

Early in December, orders received by the staff at Anzac authorised the withdrawal of a certain percentage of the troops, and it was in pursuance of this that the Fifth and Sixth Battalions, with Brigade H.Q., embarked on the *Abbassia* in the cold evening of the 12th-13th December. Opinion was divided among all as to whether this meant good-bye or *au revoir,* and many other theories also gained credence. Imbros seemed to be certain as the destination, and even the Brigadier was surprised when the ship's captain informed him that his orders were to take the men to Lemnos.

So they came again to Mudros harbour, which seemed so familiar, on this the third visit. The distant mountain was more heavily snow-capped than before, and the breeze that came down the encircling hills held more than a hint of bitterness in its breath.

But this for the time being was home, and the rascally-looking, piratical, plundering Greek bum-boatmen were hailed effusively, and those of the men who had money basked in the smiles of new-found friends.

None of the glory and excitement that marked the lowering of the curtain on the Gallipoli drama was the portion of the Second Brigade. Thus indeed were so many hundred men, some few of whom had stuck it right through from the landing, cruelly deprived of the right to assert in after years that they were among "the last six to leave the Peninsula."

But while the rearguard fired the dumps, and the last boatload bumped in the surf of "Brighton Beach," the Fifth were already enjoying the rest on their old camping ground in Sarpi Camp, Lemnos, and thinking of their Christmas dinner. Sir Ian Hamilton's report that he considered the evacuation would mean 50 per cent. of casualties was fortunately wide of the mark, though the most sanguine would never have predicted such an easy withdrawal as was achieved.

There was nothing heroic in the actual evacuation. A surreptitious creeping away from the scene of so much desperate fighting, hard work, and mere miserable living, a leaving behind of the many mounds that marked comrades' sleeping places; although each of the living looked back at the ragged skyline of Anzac, the well-worn, dusty paths and familiar gullies, with the thought that perhaps he and his fellows might come again, and with more support win through to absolute victory.

GALLIPOLI.

Night falls dark on the hills where they lie alone,
  The dead who died in vain on a desolate shore,
Far from the land they loved, far, far from their own,
  The ranges and cities and streams that they see no
    more.

Dawn comes over the hills and the graves of the slain,
  And a dew-bright gleam from the least little leaf is
    shed,
And Honour and Youth and Valour shine out again,
  And Love, and the great triumphant souls of the
    dead.

—*Enid Derham.*

Chapter XV.

EGYPT AGAIN.

The Birth of the 5th Division.

AFTER the evacuation the Australian and New Zealand troops were re-assembled in Egypt early in January, 1916, the desert in the vicinity of famous Tel-el-Kebir being selected as the venue for the infantry, while the Light Horse went with unfeigned gladness back to their beloved horses at the camps around Cairo. Various details from the hospitals gathered at Tel-el-Kebir; the ninth, tenth, and eleventh drafts of reinforcements arrived; and the old Battalion detrained and settled down to tent life with the ease of veterans. After their abnormal mode of life on the peninsula, drill came as an unwelcome shock, but the men realised that the Battalion had absorbed so much new blood that it was highly necessary to begin at the beginning and train themselves to the same pitch of physical and military fitness as had been the Fifth's splendid attribute in April, 1915.

Therefore the Battalion split into squads, and for the next three weeks rehearsed again "turning to the right by numbers," "saluting to the left," etc., till, as some one observed, "You wouldn't think there was a war on, would you, Bill?"

On the twenty-fourth of January the Battalion moved up to Serapeum, on the banks of the Suez

Canal, and it was here the Fifth Division was formed. Approximately half of the Second Brigade made the nucleus of the Fifteenth Brigade, these drafts from the Fifth, Sixth, Seventh, and Eighth Battalions forming the basis of the Fifty-seventh, Fifty-eighth, Fifty-ninth and Sixtieth Battalions respectively.

The colour patches of the new regiments were the same as those of the First Division regiments from which they were lineally descended, but were worn vertically instead of horizontally.   Most of the transferees went voluntarily, but the chance to transfer others was naturally welcomed by certain officers.

This radical alteration in the composition of the A.I.F., rendered necessary by the large enlistments in Australia, meant well-earned promotion for the veteran officers and N.C.O.'s of the old Battalions, and also gave opportunity to some of the later arrivals who were aspirants for rank.

Captain J. C. Stewart, who had been Adjutant of the Fifth since its inception, went over as second in command of the Fifty-seventh, while among the officers who transferred to the new regiments were Capt. T. Hastie, Lieuts. B. Jack, Harris, Cameron, Sampson, and N. Marshall, M.C.

On the tenth of February, the Fifth marched across the sand to Serapeum East, a distance of fourteen miles.   With the veterans weakened by their privations, and the new drafts still raw, this march proved an intensely trying one to all.   The sun blazed fiercely down on the column plodding through the clogging sand, and when the destination was reached at dusk that evening, the tired men were allotted outpost groups, and reluctantly dug cover for this purpose.

Front-line Breastworks at Fleurbaix, where 5th were first introduced to Western Front Warfare.

There was still a vague possibility that the Turks might return to the Canal attack, especially now that their occupation at Gallipoli, so to speak, was gone; but it was rather for the purpose of training than as a military precaution that these outpost duties were undertaken while the Battalion was in this zone. The 12th reinforcements arrived just prior to the draft for the new Fifth Division leaving the old regiment.

Here until the end of March the Fifth were continuously training into the physical fitness they needed to face the imminent hard fighting on the Western front, a fitness which the enervating life on the Peninsula had lowered so greatly.

History repeated itself in the matter of desert work, and the "originals" found themselves doing the same desert march as of old, with digging and mock fighting as adjuncts to it. More latitude was allowed in dress, and most of the men wore nothing more than a singlet and "shorts" on the body. Sunday, however, brought the "military maniac" from the lair in which he had perforce lain dormant during the week, and in full dress uniform and with meticulously arranged kit, the men suffered the infliction of inspections, which if productive of profanity among the ranks, also brought the standard of the Battalion to a pitch quite as high as heretofore, judging it from this so important aspect.

Here on the desert, the food was good, though water was precious, for the reason that it had to be transported out to the troops by camel train. An exciting incident occurred one evening when the camel train, with its load of water and rations, arrived. One of the camels was suddenly affected with the peculiar madness with which they are seasonally attacked, and

"savaged" an unfortunate man standing near. He
was in danger of being mauled to death before a
weapon could be secured, but was saved by the
prompt and courageous action of "Tiny" Williams,
of the Fifth. Dashing to the nearest tent, "Tiny"
exerted his strength to uproot the centre pole of the
tent from the ground, and armed with this formidable
weapon, he soon persuaded the beast to quit his
attack, thus saving his comrade from terrible injury.

The action was indicative of the man, for he had won
the D.C.M. at Lone Pine, and later in France gained
the bar to it, a double distinction almost as rare as
the V.C., and often awarded for actions no less meri-
torious than those which won the higher honor.

The desert was left on March twenty-fifth, the
return march to Serapeum being reeled off without
distress, and entraining here in trucks, the Battalion
went on its jerky way to Alexandria, where it embarked the same day. In saying good-bye to Egypt,
which had been their base for some sixteen months,
some may have had regrets, but the majority were
pleased to have left the sandy wastes, heat and flies
of the country behind, and set eager faces towards
the new turn in the road of their adventure.

BOOK III.
FRANCE AND FLANDERS

Chapter XVI.

FRANCE AND FLANDERS.

Steentje—Fleurbaix—The Front Line—Le Nouveau Monde.

TROOPSHIP life commenced anew for the Fifth when they embarked on the third phase of their adventure, the transport being H.M.T. *Briton*, and their destination France. The remainder of the Brigade followed on the Transports *Megantic* and *Ballarat*.

Alexandria was left behind for the second time, and after an uneventful voyage—even the submarine danger proving no more than an invisible and consequently disregarded menace, Marseilles was reached on the night of the thirtieth of March, and at six o'clock in the morning the regiment debarked on the cobbled quayside, and touched France for the first time. Here, but for the turn of Fortune's wheel, they might have landed more than a year before, eager, unblooded troops; but now they looked round with the calm eyes of seasoned veterans, showing something of the Anglo-Saxon aloofness among strangers.

The bustling debarkation officer and his staff, who had safely landed so many thousand troops here and elsewhere, wholly failed to bustle them, and it was in their own good time that they marched without haste trainwards.

What did interest them were working parties of the once proud Prussian Guard, whose regiments they were subsequently to meet and find hard-fighting foes.

The cold and uncomfortable train journey of sixty-three hours was unforgettable, although the old campaigners exerted every art to alleviate the discomforts of the journey.   Paris was passed, or rather its environs, during the night, much to the disappointment of those who strained eager eyes through the darkness for a glimpse of the wonderful city. Wherever the train stopped, the kindness of the inhabitants proved still unimpaired by the strain ever imposed on it by passing troops, and chocolates and flowers gladdened the men's hearts.   The French people thought themselves amply repaid by the tins of bully beef which were thrust at them with easy generosity.

At about noon on the third of April the weary, cramped and dirty men detrained at Godswaertsvelde, a small town, and returned with interest the curious gaze of the villagers, while the C.O. ascertained their next move.

Most of the men knew that they were to follow the prescribed training for new troops on the Western Front, and that in pursuance of this, they had been sent here as to a training-ground—since 1914 the quietest sector on the Western Front, and the one where all the novices were blooded.

Though they may have been considered as having passed the first and other stages of modern warfare with credit, they did not grumble at the implied aspersion on their fighting qualities, and hankered not after immediate strenuous scrapping.

Steentje, a small town some thirteen miles distant, was indicated as the area for the Fifth, but as, naturally, no one knew the road, and no guide was available, the Battalion bivouacked on the side of the road for the night.   Bitterly cold it was, or seemed, that night for the men, thin-blooded from Egypt, and all were glad when the chill dawn broke, with an early breakfast soon following.

Packs were adjusted and the march towards Steentje commenced. The sea and train journeys had not conduced to the retention of their marching powers, and memories of recruit days were unpleasantly aroused by the consequent chafings and blisterings. It was a tired, out-of-sorts, disjointed column that trod the cobbled streets and rough country road through the sweltering air to the little village of Steentje. On reaching here, where the billeting party had preceded them, the men were accommodated in farmhouses and outbuildings. This was their initiation into the billeting system so common in France and Belgium, which the Fifth were to experience in so many degrees of discomfort in surroundings and smell. Every man will remember the filthy farmyard, the unavoidable manure-pit in the centre of the stage; the pigstye and the stagnant, slime-covered pond. Straw for bedding was plentiful, and the men, indeed, had never been so comfortable in France as they were made here.

But the fly in the amber was another insect, so to speak, who with his myriads of brothers came nocturnally. A digger is credited with having said, after some little active service of the kind hinted at, that he now knew why Napoleon always stood with his hand inside the breast of his coat!

The filthy condition of the average French or Belgian village was intensified, let it in justice be said, by the fact that British Cavalry had wintered here, and you may be sure that the Fifth cleaned up after them with a very bad grace, casting pungent criticism the while on all mounted troops.

A fortnight was spent here in getting the rough corners knocked off the battalion, though the men grumbled mightily at the monotony of renewed elementary training.   A course of short route marches rapidly brought back the swing into the step of the men, and the intangible feeling of elasticity and virility that a trained body conveys to the beholder was soon theirs.

While at Steentje the Fifth were marched to a field some miles away, where a Gas School had been formed. Here the use of the gas mask was explained, and after adjusting them, the men were taken through a trench of asphyxiating gas, a process which was accomplished without accident.

Lachrymatory, or "tear" shells were afterwards exploded near enough for the men to feel the effects, and the preventive measures impressed upon them. A strong smell of pineapple characterised this peculiar gas, whose effects were not so dangerous as temporarily inconveniencing to the recipients.

The *estaminets* were patronised freely at night when the training was done, and the euphonious French word quickly superseded "pub" in the men's vocabulary. *Vin rouge, vin blanc,* generally diluted with *grenadine* (which is pomegranate syrup) and the light, innocuous beers of the country, were consumed with avidity, the healthy, vigorous life guaranteeing immunity from after effects.   Those who despised the humble and cheaper beverages paid for "champagne," which more often than not was *Vin Mousseux,* or sparkling wine chemically treated to produce excessive effervescence.

Schoolboy French was revived, and the unoffending peasantry were attacked with a variety of pronunciations that puzzled them greatly.

Bailleul was not far distant.   A town of some few thousand inhabitants, it possessed, in the eyes of the Fifth, a most desirable attribute in the shape of hot baths, a luxury which was freely enjoyed with and without leave.

On the morning of the fifteenth April, the Battalion left Steentje and marched to Fort Rompu. This was not the name of the town, but as Erquinghem-Lys was impossible for Australians, the name of the principal street was chosen to designate the whole place.   Here the Battalion was quartered in wooden army huts, about sixteen men to each.   A sea of mud surrounded the location, and there was again much cleaning up, followed by the "setting-up" training.   Bayonet exercise, the bugbear of the infantryman, was frequently and exhaustingly practised, together with elementary training.

"Anzac Day," the first anniversary of the Landing, was here celebrated as fittingly as the place and conditions would allow, and the toast of "fallen comrades" was drunk in silent remembrance of good pals. Most of the veterans of this day a year ago had clung together in little groups, and the "reinforcement" who was admitted into the comradeship of their circle felt honoured indeed.

Here it was that the Fifth came first into intimate contact with the French people, while, for their part, the French had the new experience of Australian troops being quartered amongst them.   Many and various regiments and nationalities had passed through, or trained in, the town, but it was to the "Rouge et Noir," as the people called them, that they showed the little kindnesses and friendly actions that they had never extended quite so freely to the other soldiers.   The easy-going familiarity that was not impudence, the open-handed generosity and the real homeliness of the Australians won their hearts. That this was not affectation was proved by the reception which the Fifth received from the village when they returned many months later.

On the twenty-seventh the Brigade units were inspected by General Sir Douglas Haig, who expressed himself as being well and favourably impressed by their demeanour, and the next day the A.Q.M.G. of the Second Army, accompanied by the G.O.C. Brigade made an inspection of the billets.

It was now considered that the Battalion was fit to go into the trenches, and accordingly on the twenty-ninth April, fully equipped, and with the newly-issued steel helmet replacing the beloved slouch felt, the Fifth left for Fleurbaix, or Fromelles, as it is rightly called.

Following the usual practice of troops on the Western Front, they were to occupy, as has been shown, a portion of the line on which so little had occurred since the early days of the war, that it was known as ''The School.'' Here raw troops were ''schooled.'' Here they became familiar with loop-hole and parapet, firestep, sap and traverse; were taught not to expose themselves even when all was quiet; learned the arts of keeping the trench clean, of being alert for surprise; of doing sentry and listening-post work; in short, they served the last portion of their apprenticeship to the God of War.

Naturally the Peninsular veterans laughed at the idea of being trained in trench warfare, but they were soon to learn how different fighting on this front was from their experiences with the Turk, and later on they would freely admit the difference.

Poison-gas had not been used at Gallipoli, owing to the unfavourable contour of the ground, but here it was so common a measure of offence as to be no longer remarked upon, and the gas helmet was as necessary an adjunct as the rifle.

Passing through the town of Fleurbaix in the darkness, the battalion stumbled along the road, till turning off into a lane, they came through a hedge into a field, and struck the duckboards, the battened plankwalks that were perforce used in this semi-amphibious trench warfare.

Irregular flares from the distant front showed the apparently endless twisting track but dimly, and in between the fitful gleams the men, burdened with heavy equipment, stumbled and cursed.

Continuing for a considerable distance in this manner, across open fields intersected by small streams, the Battalion at length emerged into dim view of sandbagged parapets, and heard the familiar crack of solitary rifles which recalled strongly the intermittent fire of Peninsular days.

An advance party had reconnoitred the sector allotted to the Fifth, and sentry-posts were quickly formed, the men being told that "Fritz" was three hundred yards away.

When daylight came, it was seen that the trenches were not so much dug in, as built up with sandbags. Looking backwards, one saw a stretch of lightly-timbered meadow land, with here and there a shattered tree, the whole faintly traced with abandoned trench-systems and studded with neglected graves. All seemed so different from the deep, hidden trenches and communications of Anzac, that ran up and down and across the steep, scrubby gullies.   The wiser ones affirmed for the benefit of the reinforcements that there could not be heavy shell fire here, and proved their statement by pointing out the tidy parapets and comparatively shallow trenches.

The enemy drew first blood.   One of the Fifth sharpshooters, who was snugly ensconced in a loop-holed position, was found neatly drilled through the head by a watchful German marksman, who probably knew the range to an inch.

In spite of occurrences as this, the life was one of monotony.   Fatigue parties were employed by day to build up, improve, and clean up the trenches and parapets; and there were ration fatigues by night. The latter job consisted of traversing the communica-cation line to the point where the supply waggons brought their loads to the dump.

From here, a wooden tramline ran over open country back to the trenches.   During almost the whole journey, the parties pushing the laden trucks were exposed to desultory rifle and machine-gun fire, which made the ration party, or "pushing party," as they were more familiarly called, an unhappy band.

Fritz was quite aware that the Australians occupied this portion of the front, and the first of May saw his welcome arrive in the shape of shells.   The rear trenches were more particularly favoured than the front ones, either through bad shooting or design, but considering the number of shells that the Second Division behind received, the Fifth were lucky in having small casualties.

On the third, the enemy shell-fire fell thickly round the neighbouring area of La Boutillerie, and a landmark known as "Tin Barn," continuing steadily at the rate of one a minute.

Apart from this, the battalion was comfortable, and the men were able to send to the canteen in a village close by for luxuries.   Chocolate, tinned fruit, jellies and cake were added to the army fare.

The next day, the gas-alarm was given in the usual manner, by the beating of a suspended brass shell-case, and helmets were donned.   The cause of the alarm proved to be lachrymatory or "tear" shells, however, and apart from slight weeping from those who had been somewhat slow in getting into their helmets, no damage was done.

Nothing more of any moment occurred until the thirteenth, when, their fourteen days duty being over, the Fifth were relieved by the Seventh Battalion. The casualties for their last week in the front line were:— killed, five; wounded, twenty.

Back to "supports" went the Fifth, finding their resting place to be in a ruined farmhouse at the cross roads (Croix Maréchal) and in full observation of the not far-distant enemy.   Working parties were formed, and the usual round of doing fatigues for the Engineers, cleaning trenches, etc., and the ordinary and unending "house maid's work" of the army was entered upon.   The Engineer, being one of a "technical unit," usually extends a semi-contemptuous patronage to the infantryman, and when the latter unfortunate is detailed to Engineers' fatigue, then the technical man reverts to type and becomes a pitiless foreman of galley slaves.   In his opinion, infantrymen are trained to assist Engineers by doing the more laborious work of digging and carrying.

With such diversions as these, varied by frequent dashes for shelter trenches when the spasmodic duel

F

between British and German artillery would begin around them, the Fifth spent another fourteen days, when their turn for the front line came again.

Back to the trenches they went accordingly on the twenty-eighth of May and relieved the Seventh, from whom they learnt, as they handed over, that the enemy was becoming more active and that machine gun fire was very persistent and reasonably accurate. Listening posts had been formed to protect wiring and other parties whose work took them to No Man's Land when darkness fell.

The Fifth experienced the same conditions. Fritz was quiet during the day, and apart from the ordinary sentries, the men did no more than amuse themselves the best way they could. The more energetic sought convenient loopholes, and tried their skill at the opposing trenches in much the same leisurely way in which they may formerly have leant over the counter of an Eastern Market shooting saloon to shatter bottles. There was this difference, though, that here they were not restrained by the cost of the ammunition, nor did they linger overlong watching for the effect of their shot.

The others slept, gambled, wrote, and behaved like other human beings with whom time hangs heavily.

Night brought activity on both sides, and "listening posts" crept out through the rusty wire and shell-holes to the spot where they would lie tensely braced, with their senses alert to distinguish which among the sounds from the Germans near by meant danger to the working-party behind.

Their strained faces showed ghastly for a moment as the light of a flare burst forth, and pressed flat to their little cover, they would wait till the knocking machine gun had spat viciously in the direction of the working party, who had flung themselves unceremoniously on the ground at the first shot.

Perhaps the post on their return would report an enemy working-party in front, and when all had safely returned the Fifth machine gunners would spray a handful of shots at intervals in their sector, in the hope of getting some of Fritz's "night shift."

Prior to the Fifth's arrival, the trenches had been occupied by one of the British "Bantam" regiments, and as a consequence the parapet had to be raised considerably higher so that it might afford the Australians the protection it now denied them.

The centre of the position here was immediately in front of the Chartreuse Monastery. This sector—La Boutillerie—was the right wing of the Ypres front, and here famous regiments of the "Old Contemptibles" had fought in nineteen hundred and fourteen with the wonderful gallantry that brought them immortality.   Behind the line lay Laventie, famous for fierce house-to-house fighting in those early days.

The Fifth were much incensed when they learned of the Hun's challenging placard exhibited soon after the occupation of front-line trenches:—"Advance Australia—if you can."

"A" Company's portion of the trench branched off almost at right angles to the main line, and from its position it might have been supposed to be occupied by the Boche.   To prevent accidents, a notice was prominently displayed on its front, which besought the hot-headed recruit in plain letters:—"Don't fire on this trench—it is ours."

Here the men renewed acquaintance with the rat pest. Quite as impudent and predatory in their habits as their Turkish brothers, they yet afforded amusement to the men during the long hours of duty in the front line. A simple form of destruction to which the rats' raiding proclivities made them easy victims, was to impale a piece of cheese or other food on a bayonet fixed in position on the loaded rifle, which was aimed through the loophole. All that was required was patience, and pressure on the trigger at the right moment. The rat was killed, and there was also a remote chance that, if the rifle was laid in the right direction, the one bullet might rid the earth of two incumbrances.

On the tenth of June the regiment was relieved and was billeted comfortably in farmhouses at Le Nouveau Monde, near Estaires and Sailly. Here the work consisted of four hours training in the morning, the afternoon being free. The men thoroughly enjoyed this respite, and adventured far and near, seeing as much as possible of the country and its people.

This life continued till the nineteenth, and was thoroughly appreciated. One of the incidents here was the memorial service for Lord Kitchener, which General Birdwood attended.

Chapter XVII.

THE FIRST BATTLE OF POZIERES.

Ploegsteert Wood—Albert—Pozieres—Bailiff Wood.

ON the twentieth, orders were received that the Battalion was to proceed to Neuve Eglise, and over the Belgian border they marched to this place, where they were accommodated in small canvas bivouacs. From here they shifted to the famous Ploegsteert Wood, a forest belonging to the King of Belgium, and which became world-famous under the name of "Plugstreet."

Comfortable huts, sheltered by a hill, housed them here, and the inevitable fatigues recommenced. The fatigue parties were introduced to gas cylinders which they carried up into the front line. A heavy and awkward burden for two men, they were laboriously transported and placed under the firing step in readiness for the attack, which took place a few days later, after the usual heavy bombardment.

Only some few of the Fifth, who had been picked for raiding parties, were in the front line during this period.

The twelfth of July saw the Battalion moving towards the Somme, and the people of villages like Flesselles, Cardonette, Rubempré, Warloy, Léalvillers and Senlis, came from their cottages at the steady tramp of armed men, and saw the red and black color-patches of *"ces Australiens."*

Arrived at Albert, the men bivouacked in a field, and on the twentieth moved from their position in reserve to support lines, sleeping in the remains of the old German front line.   Fearful evidence of the struggle that had taken place was visible everywhere.   The ground deeply pitted with shell holes, the abandoned equipment and arms, horribly decomposed corpses partly unburied by the tortured, shifting ground; ruined dugouts, shattered timber—all these marked the path of war.

Between the twelfth and nineteenth of July the First, Second and Fourth Divisions had arrived on the Somme. The Third was still in training in England, and the Fifth was being delayed for the tragedy of Fleurbaix. Here on the nineteenth this newly-formed Division received their awful blooding, which severely tried the courage of even the Gallipoli veterans, who formed its backbone.   It can be but briefly referred to here.   Suffice it to say that the Australians' part in the Battle of Fromelles (as it is properly called), consisted of an advance made by the Fifth Division, in conjunction with the Sixty-First (British) Division, the Fourth and Fifth Australian Div. Artillery, a Brigade of R.A.F., and a large number of heavy guns.   From the military standpoint, the attack achieved the holding up, and possibly the turning back, of forces moving south to Pozieres. Opinion is divided as to whether it was intended to be a ''demonstration'' rather than an actual attack, and a dreadful uncertainty seems yet to linger round the whole story of this action, which cost Australia five thousand five hundred and fifty-three casualties. No one ever received official censure, so none can be allotted here.   Such serious losses by a Division could not easily be replaced, and it was not until the nineteenth of October that they were in readiness again.

Many of the old Fifth were lost in this battle, wearing the colours of the Fifty-seventh Battalion, just a few days before a large number of the original regiment were to go to under at Pozieres.

On the first of July the first battle of the Somme had begun, a struggle that continued with sharply-defined local actions, until the fourteenth of November.

The First Division, under the command of General Walker, received orders on the twenty-second of July to attack and capture Pozieres, a small town on the main road from Albert to Bapaume.   On the evening of this day, the troops lay ready for the advance.   The sky to the north-east was constantly, though fitfully, lit with the flashes of the guns, whose thunder shook the ground underfoot.   The sickly-sweet smell of ''tear'' shells, the fumes of poison-gas and the stink of the dead, tainted the evening air. The Australian Artillery, co-operating with the British, had deluged the town and ridge, and flattened the German wire entanglements.

The First and Third Brigades commenced the attack and achieved their objective.   About 12.30 in the morning of the twenty-third, the attack commenced from the south-west, the Australians steadily waiting behind the curtain of the artillery barrage until it should lift and permit the advance of five hundred yards that lay before them.   When the barrage was raised the men rushed forward over the rough ground in the light of the rockets and star-shells.   They captured the first line without serious opposition, but at the second were checked, and sharp fighting took place before this line was taken.

On the left the First Brigade reached the objective —the Albert-Bapaume road (which ran north-easterly through Pozieres) with comparatively small losses, but the Third only reached their second objective after heavy fighting, which caused severe casualties. The position then gained was one difficult of tenure, as it was exposed to enfilade fire from the right flank. Accordingly the Seventh Battalion moved up in support.

At nine o'clock on the morning of the twenty-third, the Fifth moved into a position of readiness about a hundred yards south of Bailiff Wood, which lay on the banks of a valley bisected by a sunken road leading from La Boiselle to Contalmaison. Battalion H.Q. were established at the south-east corner of the wood, and here the Battalion lay until half-past nine on the evening of the following day. From this position the men could see the battered village of Contalmaison, now a mass of untidy ruins, and on the hillside nearby, swollen and blackened corpses, grim relics of the British charge against the village some weeks before.

A four hours' bombardment of tear-shells in the afternoon, against which the issue goggles proved quite futile, caused much discomfort and profanity, but did not affect the men's morale in the way intended. Streaming eyes, "ticklish" throats, and, in some cases, vomiting, were the physical effects. The moral one was to cause all to hope fervently for an early "hop-over" to be "at the cows." The C.O. Lieutenant-Colonel F. W. le Maistre, with the Intelligence Officer, the Brigadier, and others, reconnoitred during the day, and after their return the Battalion moved forward, at about nine in the evening. Each man carried two hundred rounds of ammunition, two empty sandbags and two Mills bombs, in addition to web equipment in "fighting order," *i.e.*, minus pack and spare clothing.

[Copyright by Australian War Museum.]

When the Wild Flowers had grown over the Battleground of Pozieres.

The operation order directed that they were to move from the wood in single file *via* Black Watch Alley, Walker Avenue and Pozieres trench, then left wheel into No Man's Land, turn to the right, and form four lines. This would be a simple manœuvre on a drill ground, but under the conditions obtaining was a most difficult one to achieve. Only one officer had seen the objective, there were no landmarks or a "hopping out" trench, though the Intelligence Officer had laid a white tape to mark the line.

In the darkness, under these difficulties, accentuated by numerous and unaccountable halts, the men filed into position. None too soon were they there. The artillery barrage which had been hammering the objectives since midnight, was timed to be lifted at fifty-eight minutes past one. The last man got into place at fifty-five minutes past, though, according to calculations, the troops should have been in place by midnight.

On the right of the Fifth was a Welsh regiment, and on the left were their old comrades of the Seventh. The rough and shell-torn nature of the ground, the thick darkness and the absence of any points to guide the men, militated against the success of the movement. At fifty-nine minutes past one they began the advance. but soon lost sense of direction. Rallying round their officers, as much lost as they, the men sought the enemy in all directions, much to the danger of their comrades. A liberal issue of rum had infused some of the officers and men with more than their habitual recklessness.

Whenever a German machine gun spluttered, there was no hesitation about direction, and these positions were rushed with grim determination.

Soon, however, by great luck, small groups did find their objective (a trench called O.G.1), mainly by means of the enemy's fire, although Fritz was now only holding it lightly, and gradually the remainder of the battalion filtered in and the position was held. At twenty minutes past two the barrage was timed to lift on the second objective, a line between Munster Alley on the right and the railway on the left. Some more constant land-mark might have been chosen than this latter, for when the spot was reached the railway had disappeared under the rain of shells. Faced with the same difficulties as the Fifth, the Seventh Battalion had been late in getting into position. No sign could be descried on either flank of the units supposed to link up, and with this in mind, as well as the necessity of restoring order in the confused ranks, the officer in charge of operations (Captain Lillie) issued orders that the second objectives were not to be attempted. Evidently the order did not reach the left flank, for, some five minutes after the barrage had been lifted from the second objective, the troops on this side commenced moving forward.

In order not to leave them unsupported, the right flank moved forward too, leaving only "moppers-up" behind. These were men who had been detailed to clean up dug-outs, machine gun posts, etc., after the main advance had passed over. It was a favourite and effective German trick to conceal machine gunners so that the advance would pass over them, thus giving the opportunity for deadly work from the rear, than which nothing tends more to harass and disorganise. Accordingly, experts with bomb and bayonet raked the fastnesses for the lurking Hun, and where doubt existed as to whether there might be some one in this dugout, or behind that parapet, they threw a bomb first and investigated later.

The second objective (called O.G.2) had been evacuated by the enemy, and was taken without resistance. The Fifth were not to hold it so easily, for a fierce counter-attack soon developed.   In the light of the German flares, the peculiarly isolated position of the regiment was only too clearly revealed, and for their part the men could see a strong post on the right front some fifty yards ahead, and another behind them and to the left, which had been missed in the advance. The enemy quickly grasped their opportunity, and came from the flank down the trench first taken (O.G.1), now behind the main body of the Fifth, and thinly held by the moppers-up.

Bombing their way down the trench the Germans drove along the few men there, still determinedly bombing back.   Lieutenant Fitzgerald, who commanded a bombing party on the right of the advanced line, brought his men to their aid, and a fierce bombing fight ensued in the darkness, lit only by the pallid light of flares or the fearful red flashes of the bombs. The German bombs, with their longer range, compelled our men to retreat slowly, inch by inch, along the narrow trench.   For an hour and a half, with fresh men replacing the heavy casualties, the brave officer commanding our bombers of the Fifth encouraged his men to sustained effort until he was killed just before dawn, a very gallant soldier.

Daylight came and showed the Battalion's dangerous position.   The bombers still fought desperately down the O.G.1 trench, half of which now belonged to the enemy, who had also attacked the left flank of O.G.2, where the majority of the men were still isolated.   It was obviously necessary that the trench behind should be re-occupied, and accordingly the men retired from O.G.2.   Throwing themselves

with desperate courage into the bombing fight in
O.G.1 they succeeded in driving back the enemy and
regaining the greater portion of it, and also a portion
of a trench which led to a German strong post. About
fifty yards along the trench, the enemy offered strong
resistance, and here again close bombing began with
furious intensity and grim determination on both
sides, and lasted till nine o'clock.   In the fight the
Battalion bombing team of thirty-six men, who had
taken part in the O.G.1 struggle, were all killed or
wounded, with but one exception.

The position was now desperate, and uncertain, but
it was essential that it should be held at all costs.
Its seriousness may be gauged from the fact that could
the Germans advance down the treach for a hundred
and fifty yards they would capture the communication
trench, thus cutting off the troops on the right flank.
To add to their perils, the supply of bombs—depending, as it did, on the reckless bravery of those men who
survived the journey across the intervening fire-
swept ground—became seriously depleted; indeed, between daylight and seven o'clock the number dwindled
till a very small reserve was reached.   Accordingly
the Third Brigade bombers, a company of the Seventh
Battalion, and a platoon of the Sixth, augmented
the defenders of the trench.

At this critical stage, the heroism of Private Skilbeck made the holding-on possible. With his Lewis
machine-gun he dashed across to the German trench
under a heavy fire, mounted his gun on the enemy
parapet, and swept his fire down the trench till the
drum was exhausted of ammunition.   Again, and yet
again, as the failing bomb-supply rendered some desperate diversion necessary, did Private Skilbeck
repeat this daring feat—and yet lives to tell of it.

For this bravery, he received a Military Medal, though acts in no degree more brave or more opportune won the greatest reward of merit.

Back and forth the fortune of the bombing fight swayed, the Fifth now losing fifty yards of their ground, and now, by grim effort, regaining it.   After seven o'clock the supply of bombs, thanks to the Battalion pioneers, became more plentiful.   Encouraged by the fact, our men even left the shelter of the trench and from the vantage-point of the open ground above, threw with terrible effect.   Till nine o'clock the fight raged furiously, and then slackened, as the Fifth gained the ascendancy. Six hours of nerve-straining give-and-take fighting had won the position for them.

At this time, a Stokes trench-mortar came into action from the direction of Battalion Head Quarters, and quickly obtaining the range, dropped shells at the rate of fifteen a minute, some thirty or forty yards in rear of the German bombers.   A quarter of an hour later, the enemy retired from this phase of the fight.   It was estimated that in this small sector ten thousand British bombs were thrown.   The casualties on our side were between four and five hundred, of which the Fifth lost about two hundred.

Majors Walstab and Luxton were able now to come forward and take charge of the front line, the former relieving Lieutenant-Colonel Le Maistre at Head Quarters, and the latter reorganising the front line. A company of the Sixth Battalion reinforced the exhausted Fifth, who had just repelled a counter-attack which melted away into shell holes under artillery fire and their own rifle fire.

During the next two days, a welcome lull in the fighting gave every chance of consolidating the position, and at the expiration of this time, the Fifth were

relieved by the Eighteenth Battalion.   The exchange was not accomplished without casualties.   The
trenches, crowded with relievers and relieved, proved
an excellent target for the 5.9 shells, which the Boche
sent over, and the "coal-boxes," so called from the
heavy black smoke of the explosion, made havoc in the
brief time of the taking-over.   The Fifth's strength
was not then much more than three hundred.

The weary Battalion marched back two miles or so
to trenches at La Boiselle, and had their well-earned
rest interrupted by an intermittent "tear shell" bombardment.   From here to Albert they marched again,
now so far recovered from the fearful experiences of
Pozieres as to be able to raise their voices in singing
as they went.

Pozieres had been taken and the key to the success
of the Somme battle turned by the bravery of the
three Australian Divisions.   The German artillery
fire, with its fearful magnitude and accuracy, should
have been sufficient to have smashed the British infantry—and it did.   But persisting through the battering—this grim orgy of blood—the spirit of the
Australians overrode the weariness and weakness of
their bodies, and through the seemingly impenetrable
barriers they burst with the *élan* which had made the
Landing, Cape Helles, and Lone Pine bright honours
on their standards.

From Albert, through the blackness of the night,
only accentuated by the fitful glare of the guns still
at work behind them, marched the depleted ranks of
the Fifth.   Steady rain wet them to the skin, the
memory of those who now lay on the blood-sodden
field of horror so lately left, was still in their minds,
yet the French peasant raised himself in bed to listen
to these men singing "Three Blind Mice," in chorus
parts.

Chapter XVIII.

SECOND POZIERES STUNT.

Bonneville—Vadencourt Wood—Belgium—Ypres—
Ottawa Camp—Pommières Redoubt.

THROUGH Lavicogne and to Bonneville the men marched next day. Here they spent the night in the open fields, the town being crowded with troops moving forward. From the thirtieth of July to the seventh of August was spent here in resting, re-organising and training for wood fighting. This latter was needed in view of the forests that studded the line of the Allied advance; Delville Wood, High Wood and others being considered as offering opportunities for strenuous German resistance.

This training, largely based on the ideas given in the technical manuals, proved to be mostly a waste of time. When the places mentioned were reached, they were such ghastly scenes (with battered stumps and confused litter of corpses and equipment), that the name of "wood" seemed a misnomer indeed.

Eight o'clock on the morning of the seventh of August saw the Battalion moving toward Albert again, and after bivouacking at Lavicogne, they proceeded to Vadencourt Wood. It was here that most of the men caught their first glimpse of King George, who passed through in a car, saluting in answer to their cheer.

Vadencourt Wood was a restful scene. The tall trees were yet unharmed, the grass was long and fresh, and wild flowers spangled its inviting greenness. In these rustic surroundings the men regained much of their old spirit, and cheerfully received their seventeenth batch of reinforcements.

Camp fire concerts were held under the elms and beeches, with song and jest—and now and then, let it be written, the strains of such hymns as "Lead, Kindly Light," rose to the leafy canopy in full-throated resonance.   A spectator of these scenes came away with an indelible memory of the lean faces lit ruddily by the fire, the moon fretted by the branches overhead, and the grand hymn that these lads of all sects sang with such unity and fervor.

While the Battalion was in this area, the stretcher-bearers were issued with "anti-gas capsules," an easily-administered alleviative in cases of gas-poisoning.

A church parade here was notable for the fact that Lieutenant-General Birdwood attended, and afterwards presented decorations to the Fifth.   The D.S.O. was conferred on Captain A. E. Lillie; three Military Crosses, three D.C.M.'s, and a large number of M.M.'s, distinguished some of the men in a Battalion where all had distinguished themselves.

After about six days in this delectable spot, the Battalion moved towards the line again on the fourteenth of August, with all the encumbrances of "marching order."   Rain fell heavily, and discomfort of body accentuated the not-too-cheerful frame of mind attendant on the fact that the fateful "storm-troop" patch had been issued for the mens' backs. All knew that another "stunt" was imminent. Three o'clock, and the column had reached La Boiselle, and had halted in the vicinity of the immense mine crater that marked the starting point of the Somme offensive.

The C.O., followed later by the Company Commanders, went forward to reconnoitre the Pozieres trenches they were to take over, and after several experiences consequent on losing their way, found the battalion they were to relieve, and made the necessary arrangements. Next day the Fifth moved into reserve, and on the same evening took over the trenches on the right of Pozieres at the head of Death Valley, with two companies "B" and "C," in the front line, and the others behind in support.

These Companies made themselves fairly comfortable in ruined dugouts in the rear slope of Death Valley. Shell-fire was intense and continuous, and the men performed front-line fatigues under the most unhappy and dangerous conditions.

Now in their constant journeyings on fatigue work for the front line, these men were able to observe more closely the conditions of the ground on which they had fought those few fearful weeks agone. The front line was a hardly-existing German trench, reached by battered communication trenches and saps. The whole of the shell-rent surface was torn into the ghastliest commixture of decaying dead, tattered clothing and broken equipment that the mind could conceive. Stinking corpses, or portions of them, everywhere exuded their foul gases, which sometimes ironically moved the lips of these long-dead men as if they would still speak of their shame at lying unburied. Protruding from the sides of saps and trenches, forming a dreadful paving on which perforce the men walked, German and Australian dead indiscriminately offended the eye and nose.

The "Second Pozieres Stunt," so called, proved a time of nerve-racking passivity for the Fifth. How uncertain was the Australian hold on this hardly-won portion of the line can hardly have been gauged by the Boche, though he constantly drenched the front with shells of all calibre, and caused severe casualties. Daytime was occupied in digging improvements and new saps, and the approach of night brought the danger of an attack on the insecure line.

The Seventh and Eighth Battalions were timed to go forward from their positions in reserve to attack an objective overlooking Martinpuich, a village northeast of Pozieres, and to assist this advance, the Fifth commenced the digging of a hopping-off trench, known officially as ''Secret'' trench. It was so in name only, and the working parties were harassed and cut up by the persistent shelling of the line. The attack was not successful.

Here Lieut. Hooper was killed in the early morning of the eighteenth while supervising this dangerous work. The enemy's rifle and machine-gun fire was also sustained and effective, and the Fifth sustained many casualties. Lieut. W. B. Grantham and Sgt. Looker were constantly exposed while superintending ''D'' Company's work of linking up the disconnected shell-holes, and were marvellously lucky in escaping death. Grantham had bullets pass through his gas-helmet, his tunic and his puttees, but was not hurt. This luck attended him throughout the whole of his service, 1914-1919, and though wounded on six occasions, his native cheerfulness and amiability were unimpaired. Sgt. Harrison, one of the ''original'' men, was mortally wounded during the night.

On the afternoon of the eighteenth, a portion of the line held by the Fifth had to be abandoned on account of the damaging shell fire which blew up three out of the four machine gun teams there. Here Sergeant L. Pearce won the D.C.M. for gallant conduct with

his gun.   Rain fell heavily, and had the possibilities
of the night been fully exploited by the enemy, "B"
Company's position would have been untenable. Daylight brought the strain to an end, and a little later
the Eighth Battalion took over this part.

On the night of the twenty-first, relief came in the
midst of a nerve-racking bombardment, and the exhausted men gladly vacated Pozieres for the second
time.   For some it had been as trying as the first
battle, this patient waiting under heavy fire.   No
chance here to go forward in hot blood with the
bayonet—just a weary crouching under battered parapets, with the men nervously chewing or smoking,
waiting for the next deafening concussion that might
only splash them with dirt and mud, or perhaps anni-
hilate them.

The Fifth had been in touch with the Black Watch
Regiment, who occupied Black Watch Trench adjoining, and with these Scottish troops they formed a
strong and indissoluble attachment.

Under heavy shrapnel fire the Fifth moved towards
Albert, past the ruined church and towards the outskirts of the town.   At about two o'clock in the morning they were halted in an open field, and despite the
steady rain, soon slept in the stupor of exhaustion on
the wet ground.   Next day they moved westward
some few miles to Warloy, to billets; the following day
to Rubempré, and on the evening of the twenty-
fourth of August, the Battalion reached Orvillers.

The First Division were now bound for Belgium
again, and on the twenty-fifth, the Battalion were at
the railhead at Authieule, a small town on the Authie
river, and just east of the large town of Doullens.
Here they loaded transport, guns and the impedimenta
of a Division into huge trains, and on the twenty-

seventh they themselves followed suit, and commenced the weary journey in the now-familiar, dirty trucks, labelled "40 hommes 8 chevaux," bound for Belgium.

Detraining at Godswaertsvelde, they came, after a four-mile march, to Poperinghe.

Poperinghe was a large and once-prosperous town, but now deserted by the population. The Fifth were billeted in the vacant houses, still intact, but bare of furnishings. The outskirts of the town were still being shelled by the Germans. Some of the 29th British Division were here, and the Fifth renewed acquaintance with their comrades of Gallipoli, a mutual admiration making this an easy matter.

After a brief spell here, the men moved into Ottawa Camp, a Divisional Rest Camp. It belied its name, as far as the Fifth were concerned, for the first of September saw them, like the Wandering Jew, on the march again to billets near the ruins of the Chateau Belge, where through the service of the Y.M.C.A., they fed themselves like schoolboys in a tuck shop.

Working parties to the trenches, beginning at about four o'clock on these cold autumn mornings; occasional shellings, fairly frequent gas alarms, mud, and good beds back in billets at night, comprised their life for the next few days. The quietness on this sector after the strain of Pozieres was very grateful to the men, and one of them observed, after a quiet day up in the front line repairing the trenches, "they are almost neutral up here."

It is not to be thought that the "quietness" connoted restfulness. Fatigue parties endured reveille at 3 a.m., breakfast at 3.30, and fall in at 4 a.m. Two hours' journey over duckboards laid through beautiful meadows, including the collection of tools at

"Bedford Farm," a chateau on the route, brought the workers to the trenches, where they remained till 3 p.m., when the return journey was commenced.

The landscape showed but little signs of war, and the front line came quite unexpectedly into view. The trench system was the most complete and elaborate one that the men of the Fifth had seen, the absence of heavy shell-fire enabling their construction and maintenance to fulfil all the theorems of military engineering.

The working parties unwittingly exhumed, in their digging operations, the bodies of many French troops, casualties in the earlier battles of Ypres.

On the thirteenth of September the Battalion relieved the Eighth in the firing line, and took over the sector, extending from Lovers' Lane (where it was comparatively unsafe for lovers to walk) to the Ypres-Menin railway (where the trains for the present were not running). The first two days passed quietly enough, but the early hours of the third brought heavy shelling, which was continued during the day. Snipers were active also, and generally the position became more lively.

"D" Coy.'s position in the line here was a peculiar one. On both sides was an unoccupied area, which was believed to be mined. Sentries patrolled these portions and linked up with the next line of trenches, firing occasional shots to delude the enemy into the belief that troops were holding it in the ordinary way.

So close were the opposing trenches at this point that the Fifth could hear the German transport arriving with rations, and could have joined in the conversation, had they known German. The Fifth transport also brought their loads to the supports line, a very rare occurrence indeed.

Rain fell heavily, and so did portions of the trenches, the loose nature of the ground making it difficult to retain the earth in position.

Rifle grenades and minenwerfers (or "Minnies," more popularly called) arrived frequently from the enemy, doing great damage, while the Fifth experimented with parachute flares quite successfully.

The Second Battalion relieved on the twenty-sixth of September, and through a heavy bombardment on the left flank, the Fifth moved out along a tram track through Ypres to the railway siding, where in the darkness they entrained again for the short journey to Ottawa Rest Camp.   At this stage, Lieutenant-Colonel le Maistre left the Battalion, and Major Walstab succeeded to the temporary command.   Soon after came Major Walstab's promotion to Lieutenant-Colonel, and the permanent command of the Fifth.

Major-General Walker and Brigadier-General "Bull" Antill inspected the Battalion on the morning of the twenty-ninth, and two days later Lieutenant-General Birdwood inspected the Brigade and presented decorations.

For ten or twelve days the Fifth remained at Ottawa Camp.   Training days, interspersed with football matches, and nights enlivened with concerts, helped the time to pass quickly.   On the ninth of October a move was made to Halifax Camp, and on the fourteenth Ottawa Camp housed them again.   Preparations for a long march were made, and on the next day the ten miles march to Steenvoorde was completed by four o'clock in the afternoon, and the men were billeted in farm buildings.   Next morning orders were received to march *via* Cassel to Bussy Chere, and in full marching order, with the men in high spirits and fitness, the regiment moved off singing and whistling.   The rough cobbled streets and roads meant footsoreness, and the distance to the village chosen as a billeting place for the night, was fifteen miles.   The men were tired, but cheerful, when this was reached.   Kits were dumped, and the prospect of a comfortable rest was an alluring one.   It therefore required no little courage on somebody's part to break the news that an infectious disease was present in the village, and the Battalion must move further on.   Accordingly the column moved off again, grumbling vigorously, but soon regaining their spirits. Another five miles was covered ere darkness fell, the twenty mile pad still leaving the men with enough energy for a song during the last mile.   Night, however, brought steady rain, and no accommodation being available, the Battalion turned into a meadow to sleep perforce in the open, the officers electing to spend the night under the same circumstances as the men.   The profound depths of misery in which the tired troops were steeped were magically dissipated by the news that the store carts were being brought into position.   The word ran round that a rum issue was imminent, and the companies were lined up in the wet darkness, and duly received their issue—of—acid drops!   Where they came from is a mystery, but the inventor of acid drops had fearful aspersions cast on his parentage and upbringing by the Fifth.   As they made themselves uncomfortable for the night, the profanity was slowly being exhausted, when a plaintive voice from the darkness came :—''Father! Have you given Willie his acid drop ?''

More cobble stones and rough roads, ten miles of them, were encountered next day, on the way to Houlle, passing near St. Omer.   Blankets and clothing wet with the overnight rain, and a six-in-the-morning start, made the men slightly uncheerful, but their spirits rose with the warm sun, and ere long they sang again.   Houlle and comfortable billets were reached at half-past three in the afternoon, and the tired men sought beds early in the Brewery, where they had been allotted billets.

On the nineteenth the Fifth recorded their vote on the first conscription issue in Australia.   Many, with the horrors of Pozieres fresh in their minds, argued that others should not be compelled against their will to participate in such a fearful struggle as they had just survived.   Others argued that it was no business of the soldier, or of the people at home to decide such a momentous question, and if conscription was so urgently needed, why did not the Government introduce it without reference to the people?   Generally, the opinions expressed seemed to indicate a preponderance of ''Noes.''

Next day, Houlle was left behind and a march of eight miles through the outskirts of St. Omer brought them to the railway station at Arques, and they entrained in trucks en route for the Somme again.

Through Watteu, Calais, Boulogne, Étaples, Abbéville, to St. Riquer they went, detraining at the latter place at four in the morning, and marching four miles to billets at Gorenflos.   Heavy frost covered the village with a mantle of white, and, tired after their cramped train journey, the men slept most of the morning, devoting the afternoon to an exploration of the few shops and estaminets.

On the march again next day to Argnies, some five miles away, where the regiment boarded French motor transports for a long ride.   Though bitterly cold, the change from ''footslogging'' was most welcome. and the men settled down to enjoy the sights.

Switch Trench, near Guedecourt.

Through Flixecourt, Bellot-sur-Somme, La Chaussée
Tirt; Pirancourt, St. Sauveur, Argœuves, Longpre,
Amiens, and at last to Dernancourt, where billets were
arranged for the night.

After dinner the following day the marching began
again, through Mametz and Fricourt Woods to Pommières Redoubt. The scene was unforgettable. Prolonged rain and heavy continuous traffic had made a
quagmire of the road, and progress was cruelly hampered. Men and horses splashed painfully through
the mud, and constantly fell into fathomless pits of
it. The struggling, sweating, trembling animals and
dirty, cursing men, plunged miserably through, the
sorry condition underfoot obliterating for the time
the menace of the shells which burst in a far-flung
deluge of mud.

A few small shelters, roughly constituted of boxes
and tarpaulins, was the Fifth's resting place for the
night, and into these the mud-caked men squeezed,
and slept, standing up for the most part, despite the
depressing conditions, and a heavy bombardment.

Here, in a trench near the road, the Fifth saw their
first "tank." It was derelict since a previous engagement, and now lay in the mud.

Throughout the day of the twenty-sixth, rain fell
heavily, and everyone reached the nadir of discomfort, misery and bad temper. Fatigue parties were
employed in futile attempts to make roads in the
mud, and though shells fell closely, no one, by good
fortune, was hit. Labour battalions from the West
Indies were working in the vicinity, and our men
were much impressed by the coloured men's industry
and cheerfulness. Good humor in these surroundings was worthy of remark. Nearly all spoke good
English intelligently, and quickly fraternised with

the Fifth, who derived much pleasure, tinged with amusement, from their naive simplicity.   The company wit, who asked in the words of a popular song, "Are you from Dixie?" was quickly answered, "No, me from Jamaica, Boss."

Chapter XIX.

THE SOMME MISERY.

High Wood—Bull Trench—Flers—Grease Trench.

THREE days later, the weather still providing the same miserable conditions of cold and wetness, preparations were made for moving into the line.   At one o'clock in the morning the Battalion moved forward with great difficulty, through the sea of mud, knee deep in wretchedness.   Progress was exasperatingly slow, and was delayed by men becoming bogged helplessly, till dragged by their comrades from the mud's tenacious hold.   A halt was made at the side of the "road," among some timber close to High Wood.   No spot in France saw more furious fighting between British and German troops than did this once lovely wood.   Dominating the surrounding country for some considerable distance; overlooking Bapaume, Guedecourt, and further towards Bullecourt, the tide of war had ebbed and flowed ceaselessly around it.   It was now a collection of shattered stumps, lifeless for the most part, but with here and there a shoot of green defying man's destruction, and waving gently over the unburied dead that lay so thickly and ingloriously among the ruin.   The place had been won and lost; attacked and counter-attacked.   Twenty thousand corpses of Briton and German eventually lay there in a chaotic welter of fallen trees, shattered transport and equipment, when at length the Boche had been driven far back beyond it.   It is a high place of

honor in English hearts, for here lie men from the
the farthest flung outposts of the Empire.

From their position the Fifth could see Flers,
Bazentin, Montauban, unknown even by name to the
majority, but soon to be ineffaceably marked in their
memory.   An issue of ''iron rations'' was made here,
and toward evening the men started for the line.
Wading, crawling, wallowing in mud for hours
through the darkness, more than once lost by their
leaders, they at length stumbled and splashed into
the support trenches which they were to occupy.   On
the way they had passed the Essex Regiment and
the Enniskillen Fusiliers, of the 29th Division whom
the Fifth were relieving.

It would defy imagination to picture the difficulties
of the men's struggle through this veritable Slough of
Despond.   Weighted down as they were with web
equipment in fighting order, they had to carry, in
addition, two hundred and twenty-five rounds of ammunition, two bombs, two sandbags, two gas helmets,
provisions for two days, blanket, waterproof sheet,
and rifle.   They fell, and could not rise without
assistance, so great was their fatigue under the weight
of equipment.   Still they found it possible to joke,
and made the most incongruous remarks about roller
skating, promenading ''The Block,'' and summer
evenings; thus they kept their spirits up.

At half-past twelve in the morning then, utterly
fatigued and wet and mud-plastered, they reached
''Bull Trench,'' where they relieved the Second Battalion of the Worcester Regiment.   The Fifth were
ironically told to make themselves comfortable, which
they did.   In wet dugouts, knee-deep in mud and
water, or leaning against the sodden wall of the open
trench, the night air freezing them to the bones, the

men slept fitfully, or not at all, till daylight tardily came.

The cold light of morning showed them the trench, or drain, as it resembled, a huge trough in a sea of mud. Looking back towards the support lines, like a derelict steamer on a reef, could be seen a ruined tank round which the Hun artillery still spitefully dropped shells that flung geysers of mud heavenwards.

The exposed position of Bull Trench made it the recipient of unwelcome shelling. The rain came down again, and the cold persisted. Nowhere, even in the half-ruined dugouts, could a dry spot be found, though in the best ways possible the men endeavoured to lessen the fearful discomfort of their surroundings.

Difficulties of transport caused the rations to miscarry or delay, and the men subsisted on what little was left of the iron ones.

Fortunately the shelling appeared to be indiscriminate, and only one man was wounded. The next day the shelling increased, and the casualties numbered four. On this night, the last of the month, "C" Company went forward to relieve a company of the Sixth in "Grease Trench," while "D" relieved another in "Biscuit Trench." This half of the Battalion experienced fearful difficulties in reaching their objective. Lost in the darkness, falling into shell holes, being hauled out to perform a similar kindness the next minute for their whilom rescuers; floundering on hands and knees in the tenacious mud, lying there exhausted till impelled to rise from fear of being left behind; with no light, save the brief flare of a shell near them, they did, after some hours of this fearful plight, reach the trench which was to be their post for the next few days.

The ground was so rain-soaked that it was impossible to form dugouts, and the most that could be done with the treacherous soil was to scrape a shallow ledge to sit on.   The water was knee-deep, and here they had to stand watching towards the enemy, leaning against the mud, drenched with cold rain, only moving when they felt that the oozing filth was ominously closing round their feet.

With all their misery came the pain of "trench feet."   Some of the men became delirious.   Weak with fatigue and tortured with rheumatic pains, their feet and limbs aching and swollen, the only bright spot was the fact that the enemy did not shell them.

Subsisting on cold rations, they gazed at the enemy trenches across the quagmire of No Man's Land, where the slain lay half entombed in the mud, and they gained a negative satisfaction from the thought that the Boche was suffering just as badly as they were.

The carrying parties achieved wonderful feats of perseverance and endurance daily, in bringing forward the rations through the muddy, water-filled trenches, where they waded to their hips.   At length they would scramble out of the trench and take the risk that the open offered, if in this way they could move quicker.   Two of the Battalion's heroic Lewis gunners who had brought up ammunition, arrived at the front line in a condition that made even the miserable occupants laugh.   Hampered by their clothes, they had stripped to the shirt, and with only this garment on, they arrived mud-plastered to the armpits, but with their nether garments in a comparatively dry bundle.   How they got them on again, under the prevailing conditions, history does not tell.

Orders to make an attack were daily expected, and dreaded by the half-battalion in the line, and the

other half who were back in Pilgrim's Way, Bull
Trench and Pioneer Trench.   For four days the opportunity was waited, but the thigh-deep mud con·
noted failure.   A stunt was actually attempted by
the First Brigade, some three hundred yards away,
and was defeated, not by the enemy, but by the all-
enveloping mud.

It was at this place that the Battalion experienced
the danger of the artillery fire of their own forces,
which for some three hours was directed on them by
error.   Fortunately no great harm was done, the
mud proving an effective if unpleasant "cushion,"
which decreased the danger of flying fragments.
While here, too, the men witnessed what must have
been one of the biggest air-fights of the war.   As far
as could be seen, about eighty machines were engaged,
and it had to be reluctantly admitted by the Fifth that
our airmen appeared to have the worst of it for the
once.

Mention has been made of the difficulties attendant
on carrying rations and ammunition to the front line.
This was only the last stage of a Herculean task.   The
transport lines were back at Pommières Redoubt,
where the wretched pack-horses stood belly-deep in
the mud sea.   From here the animals took them to
within six hundred yards of the front line, to Battalion Head Quarters.   The mile journey usually
took an hour and three-quarters !   It was not un-
common for the beasts, struggling to free their legs
for the next step, to leave their shoes in the
agglutinous mixture, which had been churned to a
fine degree of stickiness by the never-ending traffic
and shelling.   Here would be seen the transport man
riding one horse and leading the other laden one,
bending over his mud-caked mount and vainly endeavouring to urge haste where none was possible, to

escape the shells which burst round.   During the
first period the Fifth spent in the line at Guedecourt,
twelve horses were lost, and on the second, seventeen;
some through shell-fire, but the majority drowned in
mud.

It was now found possible to get hot food to the
line in the "hot boxes" which retained the heat by
non-conducting material packed round the food recep-
tacle.   The claim of one of the battalion officers to
have suggested their use, if not actually to have discovered the idea, caused the nickname of "Hot Box"
to be irrevocably attached to him.

The Eighth Battalion relieved on the Fifth of
November and as if to celebrate the day by fireworks,
the German artillery fire became intense, the Fifth
having five men killed, besides those wounded. Leaving the slimy trench behind with thankful hearts, the
relieved men slid and floundered in the darkness towards the rear, and reached "Gap" and "Switch"
trenches, on the eastern side of Flers, at 20 minutes
to five in the morning, having picked up the half
Battalion from supports en route.   Conditions here
were better than those they had left, and the over-
wrought men slept heavily, though wet to the skin
and plastered thickly with foul mud.   In the afternoon, the Fifth were in reserve at Bernafay Camp,
where they were housed in large underground dugouts.   Dry clothing for the first time in so many
days, a welcome rum issue, and dry quarters, all made
for happiness.   Down below in the warm air, tainted
with the wood smoke of the braziers, rum and tobacco,
the men grouped round the warmth, talking and singing, looking, with their unkempt beards and long
woollen jackets, like Polar explorers.

Factory Corner, near Flers. [Copyright by Australian War Museum.]

The care of the men's feet was one of the most important duties of the officers during the winter in France. So many of the British soldiers were suffering from the dampness under foot, as indeed the men of all the armies were, that every care was taken, when the men came out of the line, to combat the crippling conditions that long soaking in cold water generated. Whale-oil was extensively used as a liniment, and was undoubtedly effective if applied in time. The only other practical safeguard was a change into dry footwear as often as possible, which, while the sufferer's duty lay in the front line, was practically never.

Apart from "carrying" fatigues, which were enlivened with a little bombing and shelling, time passed pleasantly enough till the twelfth of November brought orders for a move further back from the line. Marching through Dernancourt and Ribemont, the men left the latter place on the eighteenth for Vignacourt in motor 'busses.

On the road they had passed the Guards Brigade. No greater contrast could be imagined than that which the two bodies of men presented. The Australian regiment was weary, untidy, and muddy to the last degree. Some of the men were minus rifles and equipment, and many hobbled painfully with "trench feet." The English regiments were spick and span and fresh, and marched smartly to the music of their band. At Dernancourt, the Companies of the Fifth were addressed by their commanders, who urged the men to "buck up" a little. This referred to their spirits, as their despondency was noticeable, though not to be wondered at, when one remembers the misery of the preceding days in the mud.

Vignacourt was the third largest French town the

G

Fifth had yet been in, but it was still mediæval in its street construction. Winding, cobbled streets were irregularly bordered with narrow footpaths arbitrarily blocked at intervals by the stone steps that sprawled from the house doors.

The Fifth underwent a rigid course of training in Vignacourt. New clothes were issued, and the men were refitted generally. Five hours daily of hard work soon had its effect, and the Regiment rapidly regained its physical and mental fitness.

On November 30th, refreshed and reorganised, they entrained and left for Buire, *via* Amiens.

Detraining here they marched to billets, and remained until the fourth of December, when the march was commenced to Sydney Camp, near Becordel, a village of which only ruined traces remained. The well-constructed, comfortable huts of the camp were left behind the next day, however, and New Carlton Camp was reached; a miserable collection of tents and dug-outs, but one which served the purpose of preparing the men for the miseries of the front line, so soon to be endured once more.

Reveillé was set for half-past three, and the men plunged dismally into the mud and rain, bound for the front line. Progress was slightly less difficult this time, owing to the work that had been done in road-making since the Fifth's last visit. Arrived there, "C" and "D" Companies relieved two companies of the Thirteenth Battalion in Grease Trench and Goodwin's Post, while "A" and "B" did a similar service with the other half of the Thirteenth in Pilgrim's and Pioneer support trenches.

An enemy bombardment at half-past four in the afternoon resulted in fourteen casualties, with addi-

tional ones during the three days that the shelling
continued. The rain continued, and trenches and dugouts began to crumble away under its insidious per-
colation, and the old, intense misery of the men's first
sojourn here re-commenced, frost bite and trench feet
claiming more victims than the Boche.   Corporal D.
Johnston, one of the original Battalion, was killed
and buried at Goodwin's Post that night.

"C" and "D" Companies were relieved in the
front line four days later by the other half, this
operation, always a critical time on the Somme, being
attended by some casualties.   During their period
in the line, the weather grew colder and the shelling
heavier.   "B" Company reached Switch Trench
with only eight men fit for duty!   During the bombardment of the next few days, Sergeant Wood,
D.C.M., and some of his men, were wounded. Woods
was sitting on the parapet swinging his legs when the
shell arrived.   Portion of his leg was blown away,
but he insisted on the other wounded men, none so
seriously hurt as he, being attended to first, and
before being taken away, had made arrangements for
the burial of one of his mates, Private Legge, and the
identification of his grave by a cross.   A wonderful
example of grit and cheerfulness that rose triumphant
over suffering.

The Fifth were relieved of front line duty by the
Seventh on the fourteenth of December, returned to
Gap and Switch Trenches, and for the next six days
did yeoman service in working and carrying parties
to support and front lines.   On the twentieth they
were relieved by the Fourth Battalion, and left the
waterfilled trenches and damp dugouts to their unfortunate successors.   The entrances to these dismal
shelters were covered with blankets and waterproof

sheets frozen as hard and stiff as boards by heavy
frost and icy winds.

Bernafay "B" Camp was reached and the men
slept the night in huts there.   A shell from a naval
gun fell short, and one of the huts in which a platoon
had just settled down was blown to pieces, four men
of "B" Company being killed and eleven wounded.
Corporal Williams, though wounded, performed with
admirable coolness the task of extricating and re-
organising, and richly earned the Military Medal,
which he afterwards received.

Chapter XX.

FLERS—BULLECOURT.

Mametz—Meaulte—Suicide Camp—High Wood—
Factory Corner—The First Raid Fails—Thilloy—
Haplincourt—Lagnicourt—Bullecourt—Beifvillers
—Hénencourt Wood.

ON December fifteenth the Battalion moved to
Melbourne Camp, Mametz, and for the re-
mainder of December stayed here in Divisional
Reserve.   All manner of fatigues were their portion.
Unloading trains, salvaging and sorting of defective
ammunition, occupied their time.

Christmas dinner, the third that the Fifth had
seen on service, was spent as joyously as possible, the
army issue comprising a small box of comforts, bully-
beef stew, plum pudding and beer.   New Year's Eve
was only marked by a strenuous endeavour on the
part of all ranks to drown the sorrows of the past
and the dread anticipations of the future in a not
ungenerous issue of army rum.

So in the mud of Meaulte, not far from Albert, the
first two weeks of the new year nineteen hundred and
seventeen were spent.   Two companies had been
quartered at Buire for some days, and then moved on
to billets at Warloy-Baillon, where they trained on a
bleak common just outside the town.   The training of
the batch of reinforcements who had joined them
here, and N.C.O.'s classes, exercised them till the
whole Battalion marched to Albert on the twenty-
third of January, and billeted in ruined buildings
there.

Two days later, they were on the march again. Past
La Boiselle, Contalmaison and other places of famous
memory, now snow-mantled, bleak and inhospitable,

they went, past Bazentin, till they halted at a camp at High Wood West, a collection of huts with the pleasant appellation of ''Suicide Camp.''   During the Battalion's stay here the cold increased in severity, and, with it, the suffering of these men from warmer climes.   Water froze in the water bottles, and mess tins of snow were heated on the braziers for washing and shaving.   Moustaches and hair froze spikily, fingers and toes were chilled to insensibility, and eyes suffered from the blinding snow-refraction. The men were heavily clothed in vest, shirt, cardigan, tunic and woollen jacket, and with such excellent harborage the lice pest became intensely and painfully aggravating.

Short route marches were undergone, despite the slippery roads, and other training was carried out. A working party from the Battalion, mostly ''old hands,'' were billeted at Bazentin le Petit and formed a ''pushing party'' on the High Wood-Factory Corner light railway.   Beginning when darkness had set in, their task was to load trucks with engineer's supplies, and with three men to a truck to push across the open, snow-covered ground to Factory Corner, under shell and machine-gun fire.   If rations constituted the load, they had to be man-handled some quarter of a mile to Head Quarters, which was in the cellar of a ruined building.

The return load was a grimmer one, consisting of corpses which had to be taken from Headquarters to Suicide Camp.

The Fifth carried out its first raid on the tenth of February, a position opposite Bayonet Trench being chosen, Lieutenant H. M. Griffiths, with Second-Lieutenants F. Langford, H. C. Morrison, W. M. Taylor, and a hundred and three N.C.O.'s and men com-

prised the party. The raiders surmounted the first
row of enemy wire with duckboards, and crawled
under the next row, but were held up at the third
obstacle and severely bombed. One section, under
Second Lieutenant Langford, succeeded in entering,
cleaned up the part of the trench they had gained,
and accounted for those Huns who were ensconced in
the deep dugouts, by the simple process of throwing
bombs down the entrances.

On the whole, the raid failed, mainly through in-
accurate Intelligence information, and lack of Artillery support to destroy the enemy wire, despite the
keenness and gameness of the personnel. The return with the wounded was achieved under a heavy
fire, and the roll call revealed that eight men were
killed, three missing, and forty wounded.

Captain H. I. Carlile, the regimental medical
officer, very gallantly accompanied the raiders, and
was himself severely wounded. A few days later,
Captain J. C. Mayo was attached in his stead.

A sermon, given by Chaplain Miles to the Fifth
whilst in Egypt, dealt with the doings of a tribe
mentioned in Deuteronomy, and called the Zam Zum-
mim, noted for their huge proportions and strength.
It was an interesting discourse, but, as is often the
case, the peculiar name was remembered by the men
long after the moral effect of the sermon had been
dissipated.

When the first raiding party was chosen at Ploegsteert Wood, the men were segregated for the special
training necessary, and on the door of the hut they
occupied was chalked in bold letters—"The Zam
Zummers," a half-serious allusion to the sermon
heard many months before. Ever afterwards raiders
in the Fifth were known as "The Zam Zummers."

Less one company, the Battalion relieved the Sixth on the following day, "A" and "B" Companies occupying in the front line. After five days, during which the enemy shelled freely and slight casualties were sustained, the Seventh relieved and the Fifth moved back to supports in the Flers line, "A" and "D" Companies going into camp at High Wood East, where the remainder of the Battalion joined them on the twenty-second. "A" and "C" Companies relieved the two companies of the Seventh in "Yarra Bank Trenches" a few days later, with "B" and "D" in support in the Flers line. "A" Company took over advanced posts in "Rye" and "Barley" Trenches, while "C" moved forward and occupied "Bayonet Trench."

Captain A. H. O'Loughlin, who had been Adjutant for over two and a half years, was killed by a stray bullet on the twenty-eighth of February. This popular and efficient officer had just been chosen for training as Staff Captain on Brigade Head Quarters. Leaving Australia with the Fifth as R.Q.M.S., he had seen constant service with the regiment, with the exception of two months absence through sickness, and had been through every engagement with them. His gift of organisation, aided by a keen memory, had contributed in a very great degree to the men's well-being, and in his untimely death the regiment suffered an irreparable loss.

Lieutenant E. Williams was appointed acting Adjutant, and afterwards was confirmed in his appointment.

On the first of March the Fifth took over additional frontage from the Fourth Battalion on the left, "B" and "D" Companies occupying a line of strong posts

Life on the Somme, 1916. [Copyright by Australian War Museum.]

in front of Thilloy. Battalion Head Quarters were
now at Luisen Hoe Farm. Strong enemy patrols
attacked the next day from the direction of Till
Trench, but were beaten off, and thirty prisoners
were taken. The Fifth casualties were eight killed,
two wounded, nine missing. Later the same day the
Battalion was relieved, and was distributed as supports at Factory Corner, Flers line and Yarra Bank
Trench, during which time they sustained slight
casualties. The fifth of March saw a move being
made towards Melbourne Camp at Mametz again,
where Lieutenant-Colonel Walstab left to take charge
of the Second Training Battalion, and Major D. A.
Luxton succeeded to the command of the Fifth.

Moving to Dernancourt on the seventh, the Battalion underwent easy training till the thirteenth, living in billets. Then they moved back to Mametz
"A" Camp. After a week here, they marched to
billets at Buire-sur-Ancre, where drill, route marches
and other training were done. Major Luxton was
promoted Lieutenant-Colonel here.

The Battalion took the road again on the fifth of
April, and marched some eight miles to "Carlton
Camp." Two days later another march of nine miles
brought them to Haplincourt. Their way led them
past the old front line, skirting the Guedecourt Wood,
on through the shell-scarred ground into the more
open country through which the Huns had retired in
February. Haplincourt was situated on a wooded
rise in gently undulating grassy country. There was
no need to be told that the unspeakable Boche had
passed here. The houses were levelled to a shapeless mass of debris, or burned to a charred heap;
fruit trees had been wantonly destroyed, the village
church mined and reduced to a desolate heap of

masonry, a white flag fluttering dismally from the apex of this mournful pile.

The Fifth accommodated themselves as well as possible in the cellars and ruined houses, and lived peacefully enough until the sixteenth.   The untold luxury of a bed was the portion of some few of the lucky ones, prepared by Huns who had perforce left hurriedly. The fifteenth was notable for the counter attack by four picked divisions of the enemy on the line on the front of the First and Second Divisions.   Despite heroic resistance, during which little bands resisted till ammunition ran out, and hordes of Germans decimated them, the line was pressed back in places, and Lagnicourt was temporarily lost.   A splendid rush by the Australians recaptured Lagnicourt, and some guns which had been lost, and with grim determination the men took three hundred and fifty prisoners, and killed hundreds. The Fifth were in reserve only, within sound of this furious fighting, but were not called upon.

In torrential rain the Fifth moved out from the quarters they had made so comfortable in Haplincourt, on the night of the sixteenth, and marched unhappily about six miles to Lagnicourt, where they halted in a sunken road, which had shallow dugouts scratched in the side, affording fair cover from shell fire, but not from the rain, which still poured down, causing most of the men to walk the road till dawn came.

Here some reinforcements came under shell fire for the first time. From the seventeenth to the nineteenth the Battalion did duty in this vicinity in support, and furnished patrols, during which slight casualties were suffered.   On the twentieth the Battalion moved back to the village of Lagnicourt to the sunken road. The village contained elaborate and safe dugouts constructed of tir ıber from the houses which lay in absolute ruin and desolation.   The dugouts contained easy chairs and beds; a chaos of German bombs, equipment and arms hastily abandoned; and the heap of "dead marines" which one inevitably looked for. Dead Huns in more or less offensive stages of decay, and hideously rat-eaten, lay around.

Enemy shells drenched the valley with gas during the night, and sleep was impossible.   Next night the same bombardment, and a heavy shelling during the following day, caused serious casualties among the Fifth.

The Battalion moved forward and occupied the front line on the twenty-third, manning secret outposts in the trenches, from which the men were not allowed to move in daylight.   The enemy retained the village of Quéant in front of the formidable Hindenburg line, and from here a few hundred yards to the front, they could observe plainly the Fifth's position.   Ration parties came up after dark, when movement was possible. Shelling was heavy, and the Battalion suffered losses.   Night patrols did fine work, and it was an unfortunate incident which caused an outpost that had not been warned to machine-gun one of our patrols on its return.   The Corporal in charge escaped a bullet by a graze, only to be killed by a shell a few days later.

The second anniversary of Anzac Day was celebrated here more gloomily than the last, and little more than reminiscences of the comrades who had been with the regiment then, and now had gone, were exchanged.

On the evening of the second of May the Seventh relieved, and the Fifth took up positions at the cross roads in the village till relieved on the fourth by London Territorials.   At midnight a move was made to billets in Vaulx Vraucourt, a ruined village out of range of shell fire excepting for a few long range shots.

In this village an incident occurred which is worthy of mention as showing what one man called "the luck of the game."   In a barn the Y.M.C.A. had their canteen and in the evening many of the officers of the Second Brigade were gathered, making as merry as possible over coffee.

A terrific crash, and a long range shell came through the wall and landed in the floor.   For the fractional part of a second everyone held their breath waiting for the burst of flame that would send them to eternity.   The long second passed—and nothing happened. It was a "dud."   The pent-up breaths were released in a combined sigh of relief, and when someone shouted facetiously, "Time, Gentlemen, please!" the tension was broken, and they repaired with alacrity to safer shelter in which to spend the rest of the evening.

The evening of the seventh saw the Battalion again in the front line, this time on the right of Bullecourt, which had been captured the same morning by the Ninth Battalion. For the next forty-eight hours the Fifth endured a shelling more furious than anything they had ever experienced, together with the furious counter-attacks of the enemy, who came forward, unsuccessfully, for the thirteenth time.

During this critical period the Fifth fought splendidly until relieved on the night of the ninth of May. This period in the line corresponded with the Battle of Cape Helles, on the eighth of May, nineteen hundred and fifteen, where the Brigade had won imperishable honours. Now, as then, they came from the fight with renown, but with sad gaps in their ranks. Captain H. M. Griffiths, M.C., was killed by a shell on the ninth, and the death of this beloved officer roused his men to such a pitch of cold fury that they took unusual risks in getting at the enemy during the counter attack. When the Company left the trenches, tired and spent though they were, they insisted that they should carry their commander's body away for decent burial, so through the night from Bullecourt to Vaulx, they formed a reverent cortege for this brave man's remains.

Arrived at Vaulx at five o'clock in the morning, only four hours rest was had before they moved again to Beifvillers, where Lieutenant-General Birdwood stood beside the road and inspected them as they marched in. Here they enjoyed the well-earned rest that was theirs. The severe winter conditions had penetrated the armour joints of all but the most hardy, and evacuations for trench feet, and sickness arising from exposure, were alarmingly on the increase. But considering all, the general health was wonderful, and the men's spirit something to be marvelled at.

Ovillers, the scene of hard fighting before Pozieres, saw the red and black colours on the twenty-first of May and some of the old officers and some new ones came to the Battalion. Next day they marched again to Hénencourt via Albert and Mélincourt. Ten months before they had moved through Albert by night, with their faces grimly set towards Pozieres. Now they sang through the cobbled streets, a thinner, older regiment, with all the memory of that fierce fight and the unutterable misery of the Somme winter behind them. In the sunshine of late spring, the countryside seemed to be recovering from the tides of war that had so lately flowed over it, and branch and blossom and bird seemed to tell them that all was well.

Hénencourt Camp was a clearing in Hénencourt Wood, which surrounded it on three sides.   The wood was intersected by numerous well-made roads, which all converged on the chateau some half-mile distant from the camp.   To the west the ground dipped steeply down to a plain which formed an ideal terrain for parades and sports, with a series of long-ago constructed terraces making the descent an easy one. The men were housed in huts of wood and canvas in these delightful surroundings, and were destined to remain here till mid-June.

Chapter XXI.

HÉNENCOURT WOOD.

*Resting at Hénencourt Wood—Engelbelmer—Hénen-
court Again—Bray—Hondegehm.*

D URING June, July and August, nineteen hundred and seventeen, the First, Second and
Fifth Divisions were all resting after the heavy
and continuous fighting that had been directed against
the Hindenburg Line from January to May.

Lieutenant-Colonel Luxton now enjoyed well-
earned leave to London, where his recently awarded
D.S.O. was presented to him by the King, Major
Harry Carter, formerly O.C. "D" Company, taking
over. Major Carter had organised the Public Schools
Company, which in the old Broadmeadows days
had enlisted as "F" Company, and since had provided so many excellent officers for the Fifth and
other regiments.

On the fourth of June the first concert was held,
the newly-constructed boxing stadium at the foot of
the hill forming the stage, and the terraced hill ac-
commodating the spectators as well as any Greek
amphitheatre might have done. The enthusiasm
of the audience was remarkable, and the cautionary
hand of the chairman, newly-arrived Chaplain Captain C. Neville, was often necessary to restrain the
applause which threatened to prolong the programme
indefinitely. Altogether it was a huge success.

Next evening the Battalion received "surprise
orders" for a route march, and they proved that they
had not lost their old dash. From the time of receiving the order until they moved off in marching

order only twenty minutes elapsed, and the satisfaction of Brigadier-General Heane was duly communicated to all ranks

Lieutenant-General Birdwood visited the Fifth on the sixth of June, and decorated eight officers and men of the Battalion.   He was accompanied by the Hon. A. Fisher, who, politician-like, seized the opportunity to address the helpless troops.

Football now held sway, and the gossip and the wagers that ensued upon the game made France seem like home again on a Saturday afternoon. Challenges were flung broadcast, and inter-company and inter-battalion matches were arranged.   The Fifth team, under the captaincy of Sergeant-Major Collins, and with several players of no little fame in its ranks, succeeded, after strenuous if somewhat unscientific contests, in gaining the Brigade Championship. Going further afield, they defeated teams from the Twenty-first and Twenty-third Battalions. The officers became infected with the football virus, and the Fifth and Seventh Battalion officers met in an historic contest.   The Fifth rallied to a man to the support of their commanders, and wagered magnificently , if recklessly, with their old rivals. In this game, as in others that had been played on the same ground, strength overshadowed science, and giants clashed in combat.   The game was almost ended, and the redoubtable red and black were eclipsed by the red and brown, when ''Rooster'' Morrison, with fragments of what might once have been football togs streaming from him, came to the rescue with three wonderful goals, and the Fifth were victors by four points.

Cricket, too, had its votaries, but the lack of material and the limited number of enthusiasts caused

this sport to languish.   Soccer and Rugby football
matches were played, but only faint interest was displayed in the English rules, and the Australian game
was always paramount.

In the boxing-stadium, which stood at the foot of
the hill were staged many fine bouts, and here the
sporting spirit was given full vent.   The vast audience ranged on the terraces above gasped with enjoyment as the uppercut got home, or howled with
approval when the clever sidestep foiled the straight
left's knockout intention.   Shining skin and rip-
pling muscle marked the perfect health of the combatants, and the utmost good humour distinguished
both the efforts of the boxers and the rich vein of
comment that flowed from the highly appreciative
audience above.   Such hefty fighters as Sergeants
Barker and Bowman, men who stood firm-footed in
the ring centre and swapped Homeric blows with un-
flinching earnestness, will ever be remembered.
Others, who had enthusiasm but lacked science, de-
livered mighty swings that whistled through the air,
but landed on nothing, and it was a moot point which
type of contest pleased the crowd more.

Some of the figures in these contests fought after-
ward more gloriously on sterner fields, and fell at
the portals of Valhalla with the smile on their lips that
had carried them honorably through the mimic battles
of the squared circle.

On the ninth of June, the Battalion sports were
held, and a programme of over thirty events brought
to light the champions who, two days later, so worthily represented the Fifth in the First Divisional
Sports, held by permission of Major-General H. B.
Walker, C.B., D.S.O., Commanding the Division. The
Anzac Press produced an excellently printed pro-

gramme for the gathering of twenty thousand khaki men which assembled on the hills above the amphitheatre.

Other inter-battalion contests in rifle shooting, bayonet fighting, and road racing were held, the Eighth winning the first-named, but the Fifth being victorious in the others.

Orders appearing on the tenth quoted the names of several officers and men of the Fifth who had been mentioned in despatches, and various promotions were also made.

Church Parade on the seventeenth was attended by the officers commanding the First Division, and Colonel-Chaplain Crookston and Captain-Chaplain Walker conducted the service.   At its conclusion, Major-General Walker distributed the prizes gained by the Fifth at the Divisional Sports Meeting.

Next day the Battalion left this haven of peace in Hénencourt Wood at half-past six in the morning, marching *via* Senlis and Engelbelmer to Mailly Maillet, and went into camp in cupola huts near Baussart. Field manœuvres were conducted en route in sweltering heat, and the apocryphal patrols operating in the vicinity of Engelbelmer were driven off in the most approved manner by the sweating Fifth.

The huts at Mailly Maillet were old, filthy and leaky.   Much cleaning was necessary before they were comfortable, but the next few days brought heavy thunderstorms and rains, which penetrated the roofs in a hundred places.   The news that the Battalion was to remain here for another ten days was received with unrestrained disapproval, but on Sunday, the twenty-fourth, camp was broken unexpectedly at eight o'clock in the morning, and the

Battalion marched to Engelbelmer, where they went into billets in the village.

Like so many other French villages the Fifth had seen, this one was in a lamentable state of ruin and dilapidation, and the dirty sheds, stables and ramshackle houses made unlovely sleeping places.

Here the men were exercised in attacks on systems of defence and in the relief of advancing troops by night.   Unusually interesting manœuvres were these, from the fact that the operations were carried out over country from which the Huns had recently been driven.   Such places as Anchonvillers, Beaumont Hamel, Beaucourt-sur-Ancre, Thiepval, all of which the Fifth traversed in this training, were names that had been written large in history by the heroism of British troops.   The apparently impregnable ground before Beaumont Hamel, from which the enemy had so lately been driven, was a source of wondering admiration to the officers and men.   Here so many thousands of Britons had fearlessly laid down their lives in the bloody assault on the German stronghold, and, by awful sacrifice, had succeeded.

Promotions and transfers were effected at this time; three officers were seconded for duty with the Second Training Battalion, and four returned from this Battalion to their own regiment.

On the twenty-eighth of June, the Battalion moved *via* Warloy to Hénencourt Camp again; usual parades were resumed, with the afternoons and evenings free for recreation.   All ranks marched on the third of July to the Divisional Gas School, *via* Lavarvilland and Ribemont.   The Divisional Gas Officer lectured on the nature and effects of gas, and the men being supplied with the necessary anti-gas apparatus, tests of "smoke" and "cloud" gas were applied without

mishap.   On the third of July, after another march
via Bresle, the Gas School was again visited, and
the use of "flammenwerfers" with which the Germans projected the fearful liquid fire, and which the
British adopted in self-defence, was satisfactorily
demonstrated.

A Divisional memorial to the memory of the men
of the First Division, who had given their lives at
Pozières, was erected in a little military cemetery
on Sunday, the eight of July.   Pozières once stood
here, and the men who had made the taking of the
position possible, now lay round in the sacred dust
of the ruined town.   The memorial had been designed and erected by the Divisional Engineers, and
it was now unveiled by General Birdwood, after a
service conducted by Major-Chaplain McKenzie,
D.S.O., First Brigade, and Major-Chaplain Dexter,
D.S.O., D.C.M., a popular padre who had left Australia with the Fifth.

So many of the Fifth now lay in their last resting
place round the shattered town, where they had given
their lives during July and August of the preceding
year, that a movement was initiated to erect a Battalion memorial.   The Battalion pioneers completed
a sturdy oaken cross, on which the following inscrip-
tion was placed:—"In memory of the officers,
N.C.O.'s, and men of the Fifth Battalion who fell
at Pozières, July-August, 1916.   'Greater love hath
no man than this, that a man lay down his life for
his friend.' "

This simple shrine was erected at the head of
Death Valley, where the Fifth had fought through
such tremendous odds to victory.

During their stay at Hénencourt, the men became very fit and cheerful, the only shadow on their happiness being the news that mails, both outward and inward, had been lost at sea by enemy action, which happened now and again. The Australian soldier was an inveterate letter-writer, and no keener pleasure came into his life on service than the bugle call for mail, "There's a letter from Home, Sweet Home, boys; There's a letter from Home, Sweet Home." Unlucky the man who did not get a letter at this time, and many the commiserating glances cast at him before someone could pass him over an Aussie paper, to cheer him in his loneliness.

General Birdwood endeared himself still more to the Fifth when he moved freely and naturally among them, asking questions about their homes and loved ones, which every man felt proud to answer. His free and easy manner gained their hearts, and the expression of opinion, "He should have been an Aussie," was more than once voiced by his Australian admirers.

Leave was given to Warloy and other places near by, and to places still further afield, such as Amiens "Orderly Room" produced usually no more heinous charge that "A.W.L.," although the canteen was a "wet" one. In this connection the opinion of Chaplain-Captain C. Neville, then attached to the regiment, is quoted. He says:—"The canteen was not a 'dry' one, and under wise supervision it proved more successful than if it had been. Most men liked their beer, and there could be no fault found with the moderate way in which the great majority of the men used it."

The opportunity such as now lay at hand to tune the Battalion to a high pitch of efficiency and harmony was not lost by the C.O. and the other officers. They tried in every way to inculcate ambition for higher rank in everyone, and in the allotment of duties, special effort was made to utilise a man's pre-war occupation. "It's this way," said the platoon commander, explaining the system to a little group: "If a man is a plumber by occupation we would perhaps made him a pioneer; and if he is a mechanic, we would make him a Lewis gunner; if he is an accountant we would make him a company clerk,"—"and if he is particularly dirty we would make him a cook," came a voice from the rear. This allusion to the black-faced figures who presided over the dixies met with unanimous approval.

Though the camp was ideal in most respects, the men were never free from the vermin which they now fatalistically regarded as one of their trials on active service. To be free of "chats" was impossible; to be less lousy than adjoining regiments was a laudable ambition which no C.O. ever seemed to achieve. Fond relatives at home sent insect powder; woollen cords were wound round the midriff; tussore silk underwear was tried by some lucky ones, but all proved ineffective. As one private was heard to say regarding a celebrated brand of insecticide, "Why, I believe that's what the little beggars were brought up on!" Memories of Gallipoli were recalled when one saw the half naked men searching the seams of their underwear, candle in hand, ready to administer "ordeal by fire" to their unwelcome parasites.

At this camp, Captain Carlile, A.M.C., who had been wounded in a raid, returned to the battalion and was promoted Major; while Captain Willis, who had so ably filled his place, returned to the Second Field

Ambulance.   During one of the route marches on the Albert-Amiens road, the King passed slowly in his car through the cheering ranks.

Signs that a move was contemplated were plentiful. Orders contained warnings anent the weight of officers' valises.   Men were ordered to rid themselves of "private" kit.   The practice of carrying letters, papers or sketches, which in the event of capture would prove of value to the enemy, was strictly forbidden, and a special order threatened trial for espionage to anyone detected with photographic apparatus, which latter made the men much more careful with their Kodaks.

The necessity of each man making a will was regarded seriously by the army authorities, and forms were issued to everyone on which they were required to (a) make a will forthwith; (b) give particulars of will already made, or (c) state that they did not desire to make a will.

Badges for long service, combined with good conduct were issued and worn after the fashion of the British Regular Army; an inverted chevron on the lower part of the right sleeve being worn for each year of good conduct completed on service.

On the thirteenth of July Hénencourt Camp was left behind for ever, and the Battalion moved *via* Lavieville, Buire, Dernancourt and Meaulte to Bray-sur-Somme.   All ranks left this camp with happy memories of the sunny days spent here, far from the menace of "Minnies" and "9.2's."

The huts in the camp at Bray were different from any the Fifth had experienced.   Originally constructed by the French, they had afterwards been occupied by various regiments of the British Army, as the walls testified.   Large and roomy, they were excellent, except for the earthen floor, but as the weather remained warm and dry, that disadvantage did not strike the new occupants.

Here for the first time for many months, the whole of the Second Brigade were together, and both officers and men exchanged visits and renewed old acquaintanceship.

The Somme river at this part widens out into deep lagoons, which afford excellent swimming facilities, and soon the banks echoed the joyous shouts of the swimmers, or the resounding smack as some aspiring diver "came a thud."

Brigade concerts, more Battalion concerts, and Y.M.C.A. activities contributed to the social life of the camp.   The Fifth formed the nucleus of a library, and good literature charmed away the hours for those inclined.

The dispiriting news that all letters to Australia between the twentieth and the thirty-first of May had been lost through enemy action, made the Battalion gloomy for a while, but a gift from the Australian Comforts Fund, through the efforts of Major-Chaplain Dexter, of a complete cinema outfit, together with a piano, did much to disperse the "grousing" mood that was upon the men.

In warm, sultry weather the Fifth marched from Bray to Meaulte and billeted here for two days and three nights.   The village offered little opportunity for Battalion manœuvring, and the troops enjoyed a rest for the main part of the time.   Hot baths, arranged in a building attached to the local flour mill, were priceless luxuries, and the sunny banks of the river Ancre nearby were dotted with figures in "the altogether."

On the twenty-sixth of July the Second Brigade was transferred from the Third Army area to the Second, and accordingly the Fifth moved *via* Albert to Avelvy at five in the afternoon, and entrained late the same evening.

Travelling north all night, at seven in the morning they stretched their cramped limbs at Caestre in the Ste Marie Cappel area, where Brigade H.Q. was established.   Y.M.C.A. cocoa warmed the inner man, and the march to Hondegehm billets was accomplished in comfort.

The change from the scenery of the Somme was remarked upon, and the attitude of the population here soon brought about a lively friendship between them and the Fifth men.   Prosperous, cheerful and kindly, the inhabitants received both officers and men gladly, and the best of feeling was exhibited.

Billeting arrangements necessitated the dispersal of the Battalion, and companies found themselves isolated.   Enemy aircraft was active, and all billet areas in this district were defended against their attacks.   Lewis guns were arranged for defensive measures, and a sentry equipped with binoculars kept watch day and night, the gun crew being within easy call.   The battalion parades were guarded with four Lewis guns as anti-aircraft weapons, and all windows and doors of huts and billets were screened at night.

"Mustard" or "Yellow Cross" gas was being freely used by the enemy on this front, and lectures were given which warned the men of the insidiousness of this gas, which could be retained by the clothing and cause disablement some considerable time subsequent

to its arrival in the form of gas shells.   The issue
of "gas rattles" to the extent of two hundred per
mile front, and the constant wearing of the "box"
respirator ready for use, were the official precautions
against the menace.

Regimental discipline reached a very high standard
at this time, and cases of slackness or slovenliness were
summarily punished.   Men grumbled under the
restraint, as was only natural, but the effect of the
firm administration was evident in the bearing of the
regiment on parade and in other more subtle ways.
A tangible result was shown in the Divisional Lewis
Gun School held at this time, when the Fifth gained
the highest percentage of passes, with no failures,
and was adjudged to have acquitted itself better than
any other Battalion in a route march of fifteen miles
with full pack and equipment.   Their reward was a
special march past General Sir William Birdwood,
when they proved worthy representatives of a fine
brigade.

During the stay in Hondegehm, leave to Hazebrouck, a flourishing and important town of Northern France, was allowed, but Cassel, the headquarters
of General Sir Herbert Plumer, G.O.C. Second Army,
was taboo.   The Hun turned his attention to Hazebrouck at this time, and refugees began to arrive at
Hondegehm who had been driven from home by the
shelling.

The third battle of Ypres had commenced on the
thirty-first of July, and English, French, Australian
and New Zealand troops all participated in the advance.   The Second Army advance was not pushed
far, as their operations were considered to be more
in the nature of a demonstration.

On the morning of the eighth of August the Fifth
moved out from this friendly village, set in a chequered pattern of green fields and ripening corn, and
left with the more regret when they understood that
they were due for the front line again.   For some
reason, plans were changed, and a long and severe
march of fourteen or fifteen miles brought them to
billets in a locality between Doulieu and Estaires.
They were nearer the line than they had been, but
were still evidently a reserve force.

Again the companies were scattered in various
billets as in the last area.   Aircraft activity
was immense here, and bombing from the air was experienced day and night.   Occasional shelling occurred too, but most of the big shells passed over high
up, en route for the unfortunate Hazebrouck.   At
night the trembling fingers of searchlights ceaselessly combed the sky, and the unfortunate 'plane
caught in the vivid beams became the target for the
ever-alert anti-aircraft artillery.   British 'planes
scouted tirelessly, and aerial contests thrilled the
watchers below.   Most of the battalion developed
"aeroplane neck," consequent on these exciting
scenes.

Though the men were so near the scene of the
battle that had raged almost constantly for so many
weeks, it was a curious anomaly that they had to
wait two days for news of happenings only a few
miles away, and had then to receive it through the
medium of the London dailies.

Since Gallipoli the band of the Fifth had been quies-
cent, but now the instruments were obtained from Kit
Stores in London, supplemented by new ones, and
soon the other Battalions of the Brigade, as well as

the Fifth, were in a fair way to restore the brassy harmony of other days.

In the surrounding district, harvesting operations were being carried on by the little labour that was there available. No able-bodied Frenchman, except rarely a soldier on leave, might be seen; but in the fields the extremes of age and youth lent feeble aid to the brave and industrious women folk. Here the Australians did a useful and timely work, which must have been of incalculable assistance to the peasantry. Harvesting, to so many of the men, was familiar toil, and with the aid of the sturdy Australian transport horses, details from each Battalion took tyrannical, though good-natured command of the cornfields, and soon housed the harvest in the approved "Aussie" way.

More promotions, transfers, etc., took place at this time, and at a church parade on the twenty-sixth of August, at which there was an imposing array of "brass hats," General Birdwood presented decorations to members of the Brigade.

Chapter XXII.

THE FIGHTING ROUND GLENCORSE WOOD.

*Doulieu-Estaires—Dickebusch—Zillebeke Lake—
Glencorse Wood—Black Watch Corner.*

SEPTEMBER opened with delightful weather.
Bright and cloudless days, and clear moonlight
nights made one feel that it was good to be
alive. Aircraft and artillery took advantage of these
conditions, and the crash of the big gun duels dominated all other sounds by day, swelled into thunderous
climax at dusk and dawn, and through the night made
sleep almost impossible, even far behind the lines.

In the clear blue above, the sun glinted on the
wheeling, diving 'planes, and woolly balls of smoke,
like cotton wool tufts, dotted their paths with the
danger of bursting shrapnel. The Battalion machine-
gunners now and then had the opportunity of firing
a few bursts at Fritz's machines as they swooped low
to bomb.

Propaganda by means of pamphlets, which came
fluttering down, shining in the sun, from the German
'planes, told the French inhabitants how well the
people of Lille were being treated by the Hun, and
further assured them of the success of German arms
on all sides. French aviators, in a similar manner,
told the truth to those imprisoned in Lille, and no
doubt heartened them greatly. Indications that
the Fifth's time for front line duty was imminent
became unmistakable. A picked company of
raiders went through an exhaustive course of training under Lieutenant Anderson; a strict censorship
on all correspondence was inflicted; deficiencies in
clothing and equipment were made good; revolver

practice, gas helmet drill, and special lectures were carried out.   All these were unmistakable signs of impending trouble.   An inspection of two companies from each Battalion made by the G.O.C. Second Army, silenced even the confirmed doubters.

All unserviceable clothing, and other articles of woollen manufacture were at this period carefully salvaged and returned to Ordnance in view of the decreasing amount of shipping available for the import of wool into England.   As even before the general incidence of this order, fifty per cent. of the woollen garments issued in the field were returned to England to be remade into cloth, it is to be assumed that the effects of this saving throughout the huge army then in France was to make available a very valuable addition to the country's needs.

The work that lay in front of the First Division was now made known to all ranks.   Nearby, at Reninghelst, a scale model of the country to be attacked had been prepared by the Engineers of the First Division, and was laid out on about three acres of land.   This the officers first visited, and later the men of each Battalion.   Nothing more unique or typical of the democratic army now striving against the menace of world militarism could be imagined.   To show all the dangers and difficulties of the impending battle to the men in the ranks, who would lose so many of their number in the attempt, was an innovation that, to say the least of it, would not be successful in the German army.

The intelligent interest taken by the men was remarkable.   Not only did they discuss the various points during their inspection, but they talked over and argued the pros and cons of the scheme at greater length, when they returned to billets, than even the most ambitious commander could have expected.

At the beginning of the second week in September the officers visited the front line, and returned after exciting adventures, fully seized with the seriousness and difficulties of the hard fighting that lay ahead of the Division.

On the twelfth the Battalion was given a dress rehearsal near Merville, on the plan of the attack to be launched, and the next day, with their steel helmets, newly painted with the red and black badge, they moved off from the Estaires-Doulieu area at six o'clock in the morning, through Doulieu, Bailleul, Ste Jan's Cappel, marching about thirteen miles to Berthen, and billeting here for the night.   They were minus five officers, and about a hundred and forty other ranks, who had gone into camp at Caestre, where it was intended they should be available to reinforce the Battalion after its first engagement.   Five weeks had been spent in the area they had just left, a considerably longer time than would have been possible had the programme of the Allied attack moved without a hitch.

Approaching Caestre, signs that "things were doing" were plentiful, and the roads were thick with the passage of men, transport and guns, all moving up.   The Battalion went forward again on the fourteenth *via* Boescheppe, across the Franco-Belgian frontier, and camped in a small field near Reninghelst, a place that had known them before.   Here it was that the men inspected the model of the terrain to be attacked, which has been referred to.

The agglomeration of guns and ammunition in this area was stupendous.   Fields were literally packed with artillery of all calibre, and everywhere were the

shells which would feed them.   To a depth of six
miles behind the front lines the British artillery
belched destruction on the German positions.

Moving again through Dickebusch, the men
bivouacked for lunch, and a few hours rest, at Chateau
Segard, where they could see our guns at work behind a newly-captured ridge.

Later that afternoon, the transport and quarter-
master's stores moved back to lines near Dickebusch,
while the regiment, with a strength of twenty-five
officers and six hundred and seventy-seven other
ranks, occupied dugouts in the vicinity of Zillebeke
Lake, prior to moving forward to the assembly position.   The ''hop-over'' had been fixed for the early
morning of the twentieth.   Then ensued a monotonous wait, men lying perdu under the danger of enemy
aerial observation, and whiling away the time by
sleeping and reading in their shelters.

At nine o'clock on the evening of the nineteenth,
rain began falling steadily and increased to a downpour.   The anxiety of the men was intense, and the
fear that the elaborate preparations which had been
made for the morrow would be rendered impotent by
the bad weather was generally felt and expressed.
Was the tragic failure of the August advance to be
repeated?   Undoubtedly the weather had ''showed
itself Boche,'' and too much depended on Providence
treating them kindly in this regard for the men not
to rail bitterly, even against Providence itself.

About midnight, the rain ceased, and depression
was quickly succeeded by restrained excitement.   At
half-past two in the morning the Battalion went forward, silent companies going out into the thick darkness.   They moved confidently over this strange
ground which study of model and map, and good

The Church and Lake at Zonnebeke after the 3rd Battle of Ypres. [Copyright by Australian War Museum.]

Intelligence work, had robbed of its strangeness. The assembly position lay in front of what had been the old front line. The "hopping-off" point had been "taped" on a line extending from Jap Avenue, near Inverness Copse, on the right, to the centre of Glencorse Wood on the left, a distance of about six hundred yards. The line extended into the wood itself about a hundred and fifty yards. It will be seen that the Battalion had approximately one man to a yard, a very thin attacking formation. The objective lay about a thousands yards ahead on a line running past Lone House and Black Watch Corner.

The inky black night and the ground made slippery and muddy by the rain, rendered progress slower and more difficult than had been anticipated, and there was difficulty, too, in preserving communication between platoons which marched at an interval of a hundred yards.

Headquarters, Signallers and Intelligence Sections led the way, followed by "D," "B," "C," and "A" Companies in that order, who preceded the Second A.L.T.M. Battery, the Second Machine Gun Company, and the Hotchkiss Gunners. Delay was caused through the wrong tapes being followed by Headquarters and "D" Company. It was necessary to lay these aids along the track to be followed, and the fact of the tanks, which were co-operating, having laid one to their rendezvous, easily caused an error in the darkness. The other companies kept on the right track, and after some detours the erring ones reached the assembly line in safety.

Enemy shelling during this dangerous and difficult night march was fortunately intermittent, and few casualties were sustained.

H

At three o'clock on this morning, the twentieth, all Companies reported themselves in position. The obstacles of darkness, wet ground, length of approach, and the multiplicity of tape lines had been surmounted in a way reflecting credit on all, and the first act of the drama had been successful. A moment of apprehension was felt when Verey lights were fired somewhere on the right flank, but the enemy evidently suspected nothing, the burst of fire which the men feared was not heard, and everyone released the breath they had been holding in painful anticipation.

Anxiety was felt, too, for part of the M.G. Company and the Hotchkiss gunners, who were missing, but eventually found their right position in the line.

Companies were now formed into two lines, with sections hidden in convenient shell holes. From this moment the regiment was subjected to one of the severest tests of courage and discipline—waiting calmly for an attack.

Sitting there in the cold, dark hours of the damp, misty morning; waiting through an eternity for the dawn, was a fearful test from which they emerged with honour. Desultory shelling from the enemy began about four o'clock, and some few shells burst around the Fifth's position, but from then until the zero hour —twenty minutes to six—casualties were small, and the Boche still was unaware of those crouching lines of tensely waiting men out there in No Man's Land.

The plan of advance was for two companies to form the front line and the two others to follow in support. The men advanced in ''artillery formation,'' that is to say, in sections, with a regular interval sideways, but ranged at varying distances ahead and behind each other, with the idea that a shell bursting among the Company would thus do the least damage—its effects most probably being confined to one section.

Punctually on time—twenty minutes to six in the morning—the overture to the second act began.   If the fearful artillery bombardment which commenced at this time surprised the expectant British troops, then the effect on the unprepared Germans must have been tremendous.

It seemed as though hell's gates had opened, with the frightful thunder and the glare of the bursting shells.   From the eighteen pounders to the "heavies" five miles in the rear, every gun avaliable added its quota to the rain of shells that descended on the first objective.   The front and both flanks joined in this awful devastating fire, which blasted the whole line of the German front.   Shell holes appeared and disappeared in the mud as bubbles in a pot of boiling porridge.   The air quivered and roared as with the rush of a hundred express trains; the earth shook as with the advance of a thousand infuriated steam rollers, and through the murk of this September morning, the flash of the bursting shells made hideous illumination against the wan background of the dawn.

As soon as the barrage commenced, the men lit cigarettes, and springing from their shell holes, mustered in their sections with the coolness and jauntiness they evinced on an ordinary parade.   Keen and fit, they went forward, confident that such a mighty sweeping curtain of shell fire must unquestionably demoralise any Fritzes still alive in that inferno. Their keenness to get to close quarters led some of them to press too quickly forward, with the result that a few casualties were suffered from our own barrage.

The enemy system of defence along this ridge was a series of reinforced concrete blockhouses, known from their circular form as "pill-boxes." They were of varied sizes, some of them capable of housing thirty defenders.   At the S.E. corner of Glencorse Wood, these pillboxes were thickly scattered and presented formidable and almost impregnable shelters for the vicious machine guns, structures which the British artillery fire had not wholly destroyed.   Although some of these monolithic pill-boxes had withstood the fearful battering of high explosive shells, the unfortunate occupants were dazed and bewildered by the awful concussions, and haggard, shaken men emerged in ready surrender to the Australians, waving bandages and handkerchiefs in token of their submission.

The plan of attack provided for the Sixth Battalion taking the first objective, the Fifth capturing the second, and the Seventh and Eighth passing through and assaulting the third and final line. So eager were the leading waves that they would not suffer the rear waves to go forward alone, and a motley tide of all four regiments swept forward.

It needed tremendous courage on the part of the enemy after the furious bombardment, to give opposition to these impetuous Colonials, but in places the German morale was not altogether gone, and on the right particularly the Fifth encountered strenuous resistance from the occupants of the pill-boxes further on and round Lone House.   The right support Company, under Captain H. Burke, however, were able to beat down the enemy's resistance here, and Major Caughey's Company pushed on.

Individual "scraps" were plentiful, and it was near Lone house that Sergeant C. J. Farnington, single-handed, captured a machine-gun and nine Boches, though seriously wounded himself in the exploit.   For his bravery he received the D.C.M.

Meanwhile on the left, "D" Company, under Captain Moore, moved steadily forward toward Black Watch Corner, meeting with slight opposition till the objective was reached.   It had been expected that stern resistance would come from the direction of Verbeck Farm, but the fierceness of the artillery preparation had pounded the enemy here only too thoroughly for this, though this Company experienced harassing machine-gun fire from the extreme left.

As soon as the British barrage lifted from Black Watch corner, the enemy machine-gun fire recommenced with such intensity that the Seventh Battalion were held up, and it was imperative that the stumbling block should be removed, whatever the cost. Immediately, the pillbox from which the fire came was determinedly rushed by a platoon of the Fifth under command of Captain Moore and Sgt.-Major H. Collins.   The position was outflanked, charged with the bayonet, and the pillbox taken, together with two machine-guns, an officer and fifteen men, survivors of the garrison.   As the victors commenced to consolidate the position, the British barrage fell on it again and they were compelled to withdraw some hundred and fifty yards.   The rifle grenadiers were hurried forward to cover the approaches to this stronghold, and by firing on enemy positions to the rear, prevented the enemy from regaining the newly-taken strong post.   In this connection, as in others on the following evening, Second-Lieutenant Hansen was conspicuously gallant, and was awarded the M.C.

Later, the opposition was broken down and the Seventh went forward. Black Watch Corner had been taken, but at a cost. Part of the heavy price the Fifth had to pay was the loss of a brave and brilliant soldier, Captain F. L. Moore. One of the original officers of the Battalion, his youthful enthusiasm and fearless behaviour earned him the admiration and confidence of his men. Ever first in danger, he had led a charmed life through all his years of service, and his coolness again and again brought him and his command out of particularly tight corners. He was killed by a treacherous Hun officer who had surrendered and was standing with his hands up when Captain Moore approached. When the Hun saw that Captain Moore was an officer, he quickly reached for his revolver and shot him, putting his hands up again. The horror and anger of the men at this cowardly act was indescribable, and retribution came so swiftly that no one ever knew who of the many who sprang to avenge their beloved officer, killed the unspeakable Boche.

Captain Moore was still alive and was carried with all possible haste back to the First Aid Post, but expired soon after his wound was dressed. His grave in the military cemetery at Menin Road Advanced Dressing Station was marked by the Fifth with an oaken cross to the memory of a most efficient and fearless officer.

Two other gallant young officers gave their lives this morning, Lieutenant J. R. Stock being killed by a shell while advancing towards Black Watch Corner, and Second-Lieutenant E. Kernan dying of his wound at the C.C.S. at Remy Siding. Before Kernan died, he murmured, "The luck of the game!" and "went West" with a smile on his lips, dying as he had lived—a cheerful and gallant soul.

The enemy by now were re-organising their shattered ranks, and the Australian front line companies were suffering more heavily as the German defence strengthened.

The casualties among the Fifth officers were heavy. Major Caughey, and Lieutenants Burleigh, Anderson, Maunsel, Maloney, Madox and Grantham had all been wounded, and the loss of so many leaders momentarily disorganised the men.   The left flank Company Commander, Lieutenant H. F. Morrison, learning of the situation, sent two of his officers, Lieutenants Bechervaise and Cameron, to the rescue. "B" Company had only one officer and twenty-five men left, so that their hope of digging a trench to connect with the consolidation proceeding on both flanks was small.

Captain Burke now took charge of the right flank companies, and very capably reorganised.   His instructions to establish a strong post on the right flank of the line could not be carried out owing to the heavy shelling on this spot, and he accordingly shifted operations further towards the centre.

The whole line was now busy digging in and consolidating against the inevitable counter-attack, but on the right it was found impossible to dig a trench deeper than two feet, at which depth the water soaked in.

Communications between Battalion Head Quarters and the front line during the action had been early established by telephone through the splendid services of the Signal Section, but their work was soon scattered by shell fire.   The weather conditions made

visual signalling impossible, so that the whole of the
messages were carried by the heroic Battalion runners,
who repeatedly ran the gauntlet of the shelling and
sniping that made their track a very perilous one.
The first message from the advancing companies was
brought by Major Caughey, who was retiring with a
head wound.   He reported that they had got into
touch with the Twelfth Battalion at half-past eight
in the morning.

The Fifth took about two hundred prisoners on this
day.   Generally, they were not the be-spectacled,
puny, spiritless Germans who so often gave feeble and
short resistance.   Hefty, hardbitten, and well fed,
these men gave little support by their fighting to the
theory that the man-power of the German army was
deteriorating in quality.   For the most part they
were willing to pay tribute to the deadly accuracy
and intensity of the British artillery barrage.   A
good proportion of the men, and nearly all the officers,
spoke English tolerably well.

The captured pillboxes contained an abundance of
good food, and in some cases, luxuries that were
rarely seen by our men in the fighting zone.
Liquors, wines and cigars were part of the booty,
and the fragrance of good tobacco arose from the
little groups of the Fifth who discussed the events of
the day over choice liquors.

The prisoners carried our wounded from the front
line, and greatly lightened the burden of the over-
worked stretcher-bearers. One of the Fifth, unarmed
in the excitement of the moment, took charge of a
stretcher for his wounded mate, and requisitioned five
Huns as bearers. One proved recalcitrant, and the
Australian, after searching in vain for a weapon, at
length clenched his fists and threatened to punch the

After Menin Road.

German's jaw if he didn't get on with the job.   On
the way back, a halt was ordered by the defenceless
guard, the Huns were ordered to turn out their
pockets, and then—smoking a cigar—he ordered the
procession on its way again.   The prisoners provided
the humor that lightened the ghastly scenes of battle,
and the spectacle of one Fifth man wounded in the
foot, riding "pick-a-back" on a particularly fat Hun
to the dressing station, was a joyous one.

Some of the captives freely offered their belongings,
and the Australians made their choice from the contents of parcels which had evidently just been received
from home by the Germans.   One man collected
eighteen watches and two purses from prisoners, and
strongly resented the implication that any duress had
been used in obtaining them.   "They must have liked
the look of my face," he explained to his scoffing
comrades.

The enemy shelling and machine-gun fire still continued from hidden positions, but the men lay low in
the trenches, and reading papers which had been sent
up, smoking German cigars and preparing a meal
for themselves, made the best of their respite.   One
man actually lit a fire in the open, boiled his dixie of
water, and nonchalantly strolled back with his tea
under fire.

The advanced position of the front line made the
evacuation of the wounded and the carriage of rations
to the men in the trenches dangerous and arduous
tasks.   The distance that rations and ammunition
had to be transported was eight thousand yards, most
of it under heavy shelling. The work of the stretcher-
bearers was thus rendered unusually difficult, and
they performed prodigious feats of courage and endurance.

Night came, and with it the expected counter-attack of the enemy. The whole of the Australian front line shot flaring S.O.S. signals that were instantly answered by our artillery with a rapidly increased rate of fire, thus discouraging the advance of the enemy soon after it commenced.

On two subsequent occasions the enemy were seen massing on the left front, but each time the co-operation of the artillery was so promptly and effectively given that the threatened attack crumbled impotently away.

The Second Division had fulfilled their part of the attack in a manner equally determined and courageous to that distinguishing the First Division's effort, and word was soon received that they had captured "Anzac House," a landmark on the ridge through Glencorse Wood on the left of the Fifth.

The dominating ground that lay between Glencorse Wood and Inverness Copse was the ridge that the Second Brigade had captured, and it proved, as had been expected, to be the key to the whole position. The unexpected suddenness of the Australian dash, following on the destroying and demoralising effect of the heavy artillery barrage, had thoroughly routed the enemy, and the expectations of the British leaders were more than realized in the brilliant results of the day's fighting.

What impressed observers of the battle was the extreme cheerfulness of all the men. A good-natured optimism as to the result of the day persisted even in the seriously wounded. A padre on duty at the C.C.S., relates that he could not help observing this attribute among all the wounded men. An American doctor on duty at this particular station, mentioned, in the hearing of wounded waiting their turn outside the tent, that the man whom he was then attending must have some blood if his life was to be saved. There was an instant response from two wounded men. The padre, complimenting them on their action in offering blood when they had lost so much themselves, was surprised at the attitude adopted by both—one, a lad of nineteen, and the other a man of about thirty. That they were doing anything more than they might have done, say, in sharing their last cigarette or dividing the contents of their mess tin with their comrade, had not struck either of them.

He also mentions the case of a man who had had one leg blown off and the other badly mutilated, whom he was steadying while the wounds were dressed.   Talking to him to take his mind off himself, he found this man wondrously cheerful.   ''Well, padre, I'm glad I've got at least one leg; I can still do something if they'll let me back to have another go. . . .   Write to my Battalion and tell them they must have me back. . . .   And write to my girl, will you, padre? . . . I don't suppose she'll have me now, but tell her if she doesn't, I'll have no one else . . . and tell mother that I have a bit of a scratch, but can't come home till this show is finished.''

The majority of the wounded, when asked how they were feeling, said—''If I had a cigarette I'd be righto!''

The fighting had covered two days and nights, and when success was assured, congratulatory messages from other Divisions and Army Corps quickly followed.   A special Divisional order, published on the twenty-third of September contained messages from the Army Head Quarters, Corps Head Quarters, Fifth

Australian Division, and their old comrades of Gallipoli, the gallant Twenty-Ninth British Division.   In
the Brigade order, issued by Brigadier-General
Heane, he referred to the capable leadership and the
dash of the men in carrying out one of the most successful operations in which the Division and Brigade
had taken part, and remarked on the gratifyingly
small number of casualties.

The Fifth's roll of honour in this action included
the names of ninety-four killed or died of wounds,
two missing, and a hundred and eighty-three wounded,
a total of two hundred and seventy-nine casualties.
The Regiment moved from the line, worn out with
the fearful nervous strain of the past few days, with
stubbled cheeks, torn and muddy uniforms and
springless step.

There is always the same definite contrast between
the feelings and the appearance of fighting men before and after action.   Their case is very similar to
that of trained athletes.   There is the same alert-
ness, elasticity of movement and sense of excitement
and expectation before the effort.   If there is any
foreboding of defeat it is quickly lost as they crouch
ready on the mark.   Then the same tense striving
for the goal, the same complete physical and nervous
strain, and after victory, the feeling of used energy
and lack of elation that every athlete knows who has
"run himself to a standstill."

To these tired fighting men, weighed down with the
depressing after-effects of that drug—excitement;
silent with memories of comrades who had been with
them so long and now lay "out there," the blessed
anodyne of sleep was all they desired.   This period
of extreme mental depression, following the nervous
strain of fighting or front-line duty, rarely lasted

The Memorable Road to Ypres, September, 1917.

[Copyright by Australian War Museum.]

more than two days, and by that time, the old gaiety seemed to have returned.   Only another tired line at the corners of the eyes and a slightly graver set to the face in repose, told of the effect on mind and body.

The Y.M.C.A. did striking work in providing comforts for the troops during this action, and it is mentioned that the supply of chocolate alone cost nearly a thousand pounds.   Stalls were established in dug-outs-in Warrington Road, Zillebeke Road, Halfway House, and Hooge Crater, all of these being places not far from the firing line, and under shell fire.   From these depots hot cocoa, biscuits and cigarettes were dispensed to the troops going forward, and subsequently, depots at all the dressing stations, including the advanced one in Menin Road, did incalculably good service.

Under Mr. Charlesworth, the Y.M.C.A. representative, the whole organisation performed its immense task in a way that left no man unprovided for.   In the forward area depots alone were distributed thirteen thousand cups of cocoa, ten thousand five hundred and eighty packets of biscuits, and twelve thousand two hundred packets of the cigarettes that everyone smoked while in action. The special thanks of the Divisional Commander which Mr. Charlesworth received could not have been higher praise than the "Good Old Y. Emma!" of the grateful Digger.

Many decorations for bravery were gained by officers and men of the Fifth during this battle, Captain H. Burke, Lieutenant H. F. Morrison and Second Lieutenants C. C. Hansen and R. H. Barber gaining the M.C.; four Sergeants the D.C.M., and a long list of others the M.M.; forty-six decorations in all.

Chapter XXIII.

YPRES.

*Steenwoorde—Yser Canal—Ypres—Broodseinde—
Passchendale Ridge—Vancouver Camp.*

ON Sunday, the twenty-third of September, the Fifth withdrew to Palace Camp, a place west of Dickebusch. Spending a night here, the Battalion marched about ten miles on the next day to billets and tents near Steenwoorde, where the next few days were to be spent. Reorganisation had to take place quickly, as further attacks were imminent and the period of unfavourable weather would soon be upon them. Parades and training in the morning left the afternoons free for sport, cricket and football proving the main diversions.

Camp was broken again on the twenty-eighth, and the Battalion moved from the Steenwoorde area in motor 'buses to Hallebast Corner, *via* Abeele, Boescheppe, Reninghelst and Westoutre, familiar names and scenes to those who had been with the Fifth for any time. Taking to "footslogging" again, they marched through Dickebusch, along the Ypres Road, past the Café Belge and Swan Chateau, to dugouts along the Yser Canal.

The Battalion was now close to the ruined and desolate city of Ypres. Some of the men were accommodated in a deep tunnel some hundred yards long, dark and dank with moisture, while the remainder occupied dugouts in the canal bank, whose yellowish waters were redolent of the gas shells which had so thickly fallen in this vicinity. Though the town

was now some distance behind the line since the
British push of the twentieth, shells still fell on it,
and aerial raids were frequent at night.   Several
batteries of artillery and some observation balloons
in close proximity to the Fifth's position were unwelcome neighbours, but the Battalion escaped the
casualties which other units suffered from the Huns'
attentions.

Ypres was a grim example of the horrors of modern
war.   Formerly a prosperous city, whose architec-
tural beauties alone were enough to make it noted, it
was now nothing but a devil's dustheap.   There was
not a building, public or private, that had not been
hammered and blasted to a shattered ruin of tottering
walls, or lay so much more cruelly smashed that
nothing but a heap of stones and splintered timbers
littered the spot where once it stood.

In this city of crumbling stone, the German shells
still whined and crashed, grinding to finer pieces the
ruin they had already achieved.   Ypres was very
unsafe, even in the crypts and cellars that sheltered
most of the troops, and the vicinity of the railway
station and Lillegate was always most unhealthy by
reason of the shelling that these places constantly
received.

Around and in the city were other signs of the
bloody and desperate fighting of which it had been
the centre.   The graves of Hun and Briton were so
many thousand separate proofs, if such had been
needed, that War had passed through the place.

Till the evening of the thirtieth of September the
Fifth kept the shelter of their dugouts, and then
moved to the front line once more.   It was Sunday,
a day momentous to the army.   History provides
many precedents for Sunday warfare, and in every
age, after some curious manner, the Sabbath has been

found a convenient time for going forth to slay. The present Sunday had begun bright and almost cloudless, but the atmosphere had thickened with the smoke and dust of the intense artillery duel that had been in constant progress for twenty-four hours.   At half-past seven in the evening the Battalion moved forward by platoons under the light of a golden moon that shone from a clear sky.   The night was glorious, but the humans who moved on their sinister purpose that night gazed at the harvest moon with unfriendly eyes.

The journey towards the front line was tedious and intermittent, with the enormous congestion of traffic on the road.   The stream of horses, men and guns was frequently held up while the débris and casualties of the shell-bursts that made the roads paths of danger were removed, and the shell-craters were filled in.   Terrified, plunging animals, swearing men, choking dust, and the glare and crash of the shell-bursts, all made the march of the Fifth along Menin Road, as far as Birr cross roads, a memorable one on that moonlit night.

At this point, each Company picked up their guide, who was to direct them to their positions in the line, as arrangements could not be made for an assembly-point.   Some of the guides proved very poor ones, and, as a consequence, the anxiety of the commanders was acute until all Companies were reported in position at four o'clock on the morning of the first of October.   Shelling had been continuous, and it was feared that the men had at times been seen by the enemy.   Apparently it was not so, and although "B" Company came under machine-gun fire as well as shell-fire at one period, this was evidently only the usual haphazard "strafe."

This first stage of the action, a very critical one, considering the brightness of the night, was achieved with slight casualties.

"C" and "D" Companies relieved companies of the Forty-Sixth Battalion, while "A" and "B" Companies remained in close support.   The front line which the Regiment had now taken over extended from Carlisle Farm, south-east of the now familiar Black Watch Corner, to Broodseinde, a point east of Zonnebeke Cemetery, the First Division holding two thousand yards of the front line in all.   The Fifth held the whole of the Brigade front at this time. Behind this line and parallel to it, ran a sunken road on which very heavy enemy shell fire was concentrated, and all Battalions of the Brigade suffered heavy casualties while traversing it.

The first objective lay about fifteen hundred yards in front and beyond the further boundaries of two woods known as Romulus and Remus.   To the Eighth Battalion had been allotted the taking of the first objective, and the second, lying about a thousand yards further on, was to be taken by the Sixth and Seventh.   On the left of the Fifth's position was the Second Division, and on the right the First Brigade in turn joined up with a Scottish Regiment.

Soon after the Battalion's occupation of the line, the enemy shelling became intense, more especially on the right flank of the sector, where "A" Company were.   Their S.O.S. signal to the artillery was promptly responded to, and the reply quickly had its effect on the German fire, though not before portions of the Fifth's trench were blown in and several men killed and wounded.

Throughout the day the British artillery, especially the eighteen-pounders, became very active. Several casualties were unfortunately sustained by the Fifth through our own shells falling short.

At seven o'clock on the evening of the first, the artillery-duel on the right became intense, the enemy putting down a barrage that called for S.O.S. signals, again quickly responded to by our guns. About half-past nine, trial barrages put forward by the British artillery proved an unfriendly protection for the poor infantry, "A" Company being the chief sufferers in the Fifth from the violent retaliation of the Boche guns. The trenches were blown in all directions, and at one period at least a dozen men were being hurriedly dug out by their mates.

From the Sunday night till Wednesday night, the third of October, "A" Company, although not in the front line, suffered badly from the shelling, without hope of doing aught in revenge. Lieutenant W. Gash deservedly gained the Military Cross for his courage, which, masked in imperturbable cheerfulness, was displayed during this trying time. Parties, frenziedly digging out their buried comrades, were in turn buried by another explosion, but the conduct of all ranks in this danger was admirable.

The night of the second-third of October found two officers' patrols reconnoitring in No Man's Land. They reported that certain positions in front were unoccupied by the enemy.

The Companies not in the front line or support were engaged during this time in carrying ammunitions and stores to the Brigade dump. Though nerve-shaken and fatigued, these men refused to take the opportunity of carrying half the ordinary load when it was suggested to them, and struggled forward with the stuff they knew would be so urgently needed.

Lieutenant C. C. Teesdale, a young and popular officer, was killed on the morning of the third, when holding his portion of the front line, in face of the intense shelling directed on it.

In the early morning of the fourth, the remainder of the Second Brigade—the Sixth, Seventh and Eighth Battalions—moved up in readiness for the hop-over.   Mustering on the tape line in the sunken road at the rear of the front trenches, they were evidently observed by the enemy, for a heavy bombardment descended on this spot at half-past five in the morning, causing many casualties among the waiting men.   The numerous dead who lay at the starting point of the attack inspired the survivors with a fearful determination as they went forward.

At half-past six the British artillery fire began with a terrible precision.   For half-an-hour the thunder of the guns that stretched for miles behind the British line stifled all other sound.   Under cover of this curtain of fire the three Battalions moved forward, the Fifth's stentorian cheers drowned in the ocean of clamor that enveloped them.   Some of the Fifth men could not be restrained, and leaping out of the trenches, went forward with these sister Battalions, glad to leave the trying inactivity of the front line for the excitement of the advance, however dangerous it might prove.

Amid a storm of wind and rain that seemed provoked by the impious thunder of man's artillery, the Australian waves swept forward, and took the first and second objectives without serious opposition.   The artillery fire had been as effective as ever, and the enemy who had still held to their positions were

almost entirely wiped out, the survivors having little
fight left, and surrendering as freely as in the battle
of the twentieth of September.   It was evident that
a German attack coincident with the Australian one
had been planned, as the barrage had accounted for
numerous Germans in fighting order with trench mortars and flammenwerfers.   Some of these men were
of the famous Prussian Guard, who had been freshly
brought into the line to face the Australians.

Papers discovered on prisoners indicated that our
offensive had just anticipated the German one.   The
enemy barrage which opened so disastrously for the
Second Brigade in the sunken road was preceding
the German advance timed for six o'clock.   The
fact that their time being ten minutes slower than
ours, made it ten minutes past six by the British
watches, gave just enough margin in those few
minutes to enable the fierce British barrage to smash
the waiting Huns completely.   Along a front of something like eight miles, at least five German divisions
had been prepared for a violent attack, which should
regain the ground lost between the twentieth and
twenty-sixth of September, crack divisions which included the Fourth Guards Division, the flower of the
German infantry.

The objective gained, the work of consolidation, of
turning attackers into defenders, began, considerably
hampered and damaged by a heavy German barrage
on the front line just left.   Six officers and fifty
other ranks were quickly added to the casualty list of
the Fifth by this intense and accurate shelling.

From the second objective, which formed a spur of
the Passchendale Ridge, the Australians had, for the
first time, a panoramic view that spread over the German positions.   The Hun forward artillery positions

[Copyright by Australian War Museum.]

The Ramparts of Ypres, where some of the Troops Sheltered when not in the Line.

were speedily under our fire, and amid a welter of confused men, horses and wreckage, they hurriedly moved back.

The ground was ours, and despite the fierce retaliatory shelling, the Hun knew that he would never regain the country from which these British had driven him. The Second Brigade had upheld all their glorious traditions by the manner in which they advanced through the dense barrage of high explosive shell-fire, or, like the Fifth, performed the more nerve-racking work of holding the front line under heavy and effective shelling. None of the fighting that appeals to the imagination was the portion of the Fifth, but how readily would all of them have followed the few disobedients and hopped over into the attack, rather than stand and endure?

The result of the battle was to make the Hun grasp on West Flanders less secure. The atrocious weather which followed the advance was more to the enemy's disadvantage than to ours, and the motto of the First Australian Division—''What we gain we hold,'' was likely to prove unshaken. The greater part of Passchendale Ridge still lay in German hands, but the dominating portion was ours.

On the afternoon of the fifth, the Second Brigade were relieved by the Third Brigade, except as regards the Fifth Battalion, who continued to hold their position of the line during the sixth and seventh, losing many men from the enemy's persistent shelling during this time. During the seven days in the trenches, the regiment's casualties were little short of two hundred.

The evening of the seventh of October saw the relief of the Battalion from the front line, and the night was spent in the damp dugouts along the canal

at Ypres. Next morning, in cold, wet weather, they
moved, with mud over their boot tops, *via* Café Belge,
to huts at Dickebusch. Rain still fell heavily, and
the protection of the huts was enjoyed by the tired
men till the afternoon of the ninth, when a short
march brought them to tents in a field near Reninghelst. The place was the one they had camped in
when approaching for the first battle, and the men's
worst fears of its condition after the rain were more
than realised. Previous occupants of the tents, in
endeavouring to obtain some little protection from
the frequent bombing attacks with which the place
was favoured, had dug sleeping places somewhat in
the fashion of shallow graves, which were now mostly
filled with water. The cursing Fifth, smothered in
mud, and weary of everything in general, exploded in
a last damp splutter of profanity at their predecessors,
and settled down to make the best of things.

A week was spent in this quagmire—one of the most
dismal weeks that the regiment had ever spent. Soul-
torturing idleness bred ill temper, and the leaden
days dragged by in all discomfort.

Lieutenant-Colonel Luxton, the C.O., accompanied
by Major Carlile, R.M.O., left for London leave, followed by envious glances. Captain E. Permezel, returning after a lengthy absence at the Second Training Battalion, took temporary command, Captain P.
Young, of the Second Field Ambulance, taking Major
Carlile's place.

Monday, the fifteenth of October, found the Battalion turning their backs on this desolate scene
thankfully enough, even though they were again moving towards the front line. Marching *via* Reninghelst
and Ouderdom, they went into huts at Vancouver
Camp, near Vlamertinghe.

They were soon welcomed by a Hun bombing squadron dropping missiles on the camp, a sleep-disturbing visit which was repeated later in the same night.

Nearly a week was spent here, during which time two football matches were played under strange conditions. No doubt some of the players had played on fairly rough country grounds in that wonderful period—"before the war," but here the obstacles to the game were more obvious. Shell-holes were sprinkled plentifully on the ground, all full of water or mud, or both, and the rest of the ground was ankle-deep in slush. The spectacle of the mud-covered "ruck" waiting round the rim of a shell-hole while a semi-amphibious "rover" rescued the ball, was a delightful one—for the onlookers.

Reconnoitring parties made trips to the line, and the expression, "We're in for it again," became the most frequently used phrase in the regiment's vocabulary, closely followed by the remark, "Well, we've got nice weather for it!"

This latter comment persisted from the old days in Egypt, where at one time it became an obsession with everyone. It embodied a common philosophy that covered every incident or remark with the fatalism of the soldier.

The irritation that the frequent bombing attacks engendered was partly allayed one morning by the destruction of a new pattern German 'plane, which was brought down behind the lines. One of the occupants jumped from the machine when it was hundreds of feet from the earth and reached there some second or so before the machine crashed. It seemed as if the whole British army stampeded, and within a few minutes, late-comers could not approach within

a hundred yards of the scene because of the dense
crowd, while souvenir-hunters gleaned tribute from
all removable parts of the wrecked 'plane.   It is
told that the thoughtlessness of the Hun who had
jumped out was bitterly complained of by one of the
men, arriving early on the scene of the crash.   "'E
might have turned over on his back when 'e fell.   'E's
broke 'is watch somethink awful."   Which might not
be true, if it were not so like an incident of real life.

Canadian troops passed through the camp in great
numbers on their way to attack Passchendale Ridge.
Though they captured this, they were, at the outset,
driven back from it: advancing again, they took and
held it.   The Fifth stood beside the road and exchanged cheery greetings with the Canadians, as regiment on regiment went up to the ordeal that our men
knew from recent experience awaited them.

During the occupation of Vancouver Camp, General
Birdwood attended and invested officers and men of
the Second Brigade with the ribbons of their well-
earned honours.

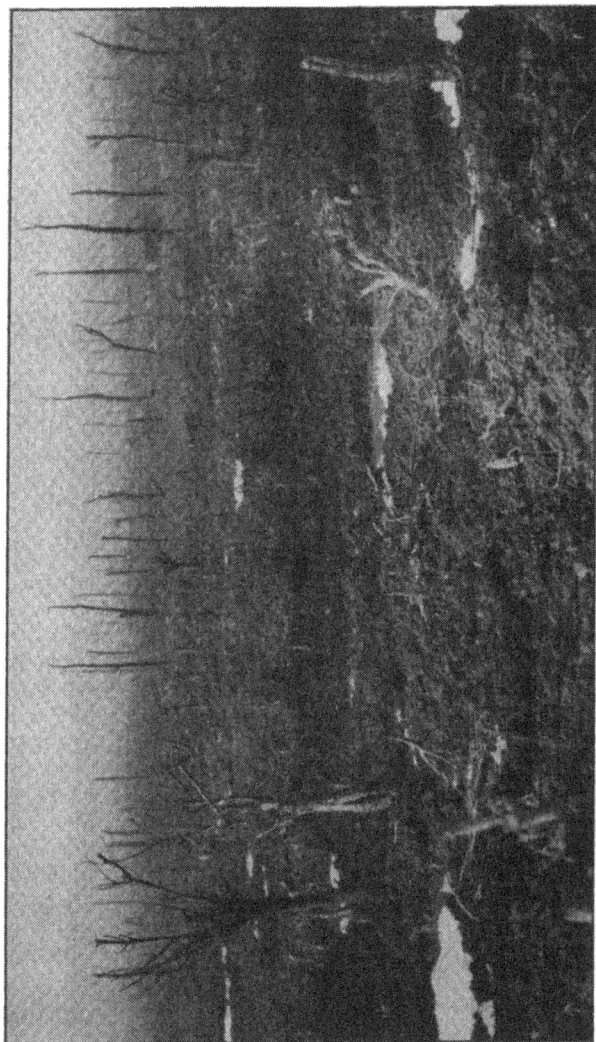

Looking across Remus Wood to Zonnebeke from Broodseinde Ridge.

[Copyright by Australian War Museum.]

Chapter XXIV.

THE BROODSEINDE AND WESTHOEK RIDGES.

*Westhoek Ridge—Zonnebeke—Belgian Chateau—
Desvres—Comines Canal—Locre—Curragh Camp.*

RECONNOITRING parties now visited the front line, and the waiting regiment knew from these ominous signs that further trial was soon to be theirs. Monday, the twenty-second, saw their departure from the camp, and through driving rain the Fifth marched ankle-deep in slush *via* Belgian Chateau and ruined Ypres to dugouts beyond the ramparts of the flattened city, where they spent the night.

Next day, moving forward by platoons to minimise the effect of shell-fire, the Battalion marched along the Menin Road and the Ypres-Roulers railway to Westhoek Ridge, where they relieved the Eighth Battalion in the reserve line. The men were in "fighting order," with greatcoat, waterproof sheet and sandbags. Four of these latter requisites of modern warfare were carried, one under each shoulder flap, and one tied round the putties. With this grotesqueness added to the mud which splashed them everywhere, they went grimly to their job.

The sector taken over by the Brigade was known as a "two-battalion" front. The front line was held by the Sixth and Seventh, with the Eighth in support and the Fifth in reserve. From the fact that the enemy were showing signs of retirement towards the East, it was possible to extend the men to a greater interval than would have been justifiable had an enemy attack been probable. The risk of casualty from shell fire was considerably lessened by this thinly-held line.

The Brigade lines at this time stretched from a position on Broodseinde Ridge, north of the Zonnebeke road, to a point near the junction of the Beclaere Road, with the Ypres-Roulers railway. Despite the imminent enemy retirement, military preparations to defend the front now held were deemed necessary, and the work of the front-line troops consisted mainly of the improvement of existing strong points and trenches, and in defensive wiring.

Rain and cold made the conditions wholly wretched, and the desolate surroundings added to the misery. Dreary expanses of mud, pitted with flooded shell-holes, formed an interminable vista, broken here and there by the mournful uplifted nose of a derelict tank. The shell-holes, trenches, and even dugouts needed constant bailing. The danger of trench feet, in these circumstances, was one that exercised the minds of the commanders, and every effort was made to combat this very serious form of casualty. When practicable, daily inspection of the men's feet was carried out, and with the aid of powder, soap, and the three pairs of socks that each man carried, cleanliness was sometimes, if not always, possible. The result of these precautions was evident when, at the end of the ten days' duty in the line, only six men in the Battalion were evacuated with trench feet, a remarkably small percentage under the conditions.

On the twenty-seventh of October the Fifth relieved the Seventh Battalion in the front line. This section of the front contained eight strong points, "A" Company holding two, and "B" Company manning the remainder. "D" Company were in close support, while "C" were situated at Zonnebeke and became the "pack horses" who carried supplies to the trenches.   Battalion Head Quarters were at the Gasometer, on the north side of Zonnebeke Road, near Desmond Trench.

The move forward from Westhoek Ridge to relieve the Seventh was only achieved after a critical and dangerous march.   The narrow track along the duck-boards was sprayed with shells by an enemy who knew the range to a nicety, and sections of the track were scattered broadcast.   Through this danger area, the men moved steadily, every minute bringing the nearby crash of a shell that scattered whining metal and mud around and about them.   Full of hairbreadth escapes, the journey was completed and the men marvelled to find that there had been no casualties.

In their new position the Fifth were heavily shelled at intervals, and little rest was possible either by day or by night.   Gas shells caused many casualties at this time, though the Second Brigade suffered less than the others.   Though prepared for gas attacks, the men did not anticipate the ingenuity of the Hun in this regard.   The gas-shells were not sent over con-tinuously, but interspersed with high explosive and other ''stuff'' with which he plentifully besprinkled the area at night, so that many were caught unpre-pared.   The gas was insidious in its effect, for men who had inhaled the fumes often did not go under till two days later.   Stinging blindness was the main symptom, and down at the dressing station were to be seen pitiful queues of gas-blinded men in single file, each clutching the tunic of the man in front, and so being led.   Bereft of their voices by the gas, the men profaned in sickly whispers, while their eyes streamed moisture.

Deaths from this form of attack were not frequent, but the pain and discomfort, not only of the kind mentioned, but that arising from the painful blisters that the gas-impregnated clothing made wherever it touched the skin, caused many evacuations from the line.

While the regiment was in reserve at Zonnebeke, the first Canadian attack on Passchendale took place. At twenty minutes to six, after a night of unusual calm that boded ill, the still morning air was rent with the furious thunder of the British barrage. Intense and continuous, the drumfire of the multitudinous guns beat down on the enemy positions on the ridge and round the village. The Fifth, on the right of the Canadians, rejoiced soon to see the German S.O.S. signals. Green flames, quickly followed by red ones, pierced the dark morning in jewelled brilliance along the whole German front line. This, their signal of distress flung out to their artillery, was hailed with delight by the watchers.

The Canadians' impetuous attack carried them four hundred yards forward, in the face of desperate resistance, but here they stayed till the fury of a determined German counter-attack pushed them back to the original line. The German success was short-lived, and two gallant Canadian attacks in quick succession regained the lost ground, as has been said, and pushed further on, capturing the whole of the ridge and the village beyond.

How much of this brilliant success was due to the efforts of the Australians, only they and the General Staff knew. The hard, bitter work that preceded the push had been theirs; the spectacular part of the attack had fallen to the Canadians. Whatever the envious thoughts that filled Australian hearts, they were unspoken, and every man was only too ready to concede to his Dominion comrades the fullest praise for their undoubtedly fine work.

No further counter-attacks were attempted by the enemy from their now distinctly unfavourable position, and until the thirtieth the Fifth experienced a quieter, if still an uncomfortable, period in the front line. Marching out without casualties, on that night they passed, *via* Hellfire Corner, along the Menin Road through Ypres, and camped once again in dugouts along the canal near the railway.   Enemy bombing and shelling were still persistent, and aerial torpedoes added to the din of the night.   Next day the regiment moved to a camp opposite the Belgian Chateau, where they were destined to remain in huts for the next ten days or so.   .

This time was not spent in idleness. Each day four officers and a hundred and fifty men were detailed as a working party, and every morning went to the work in the forward area, near Westhoek Ridge. Royal Engineers were constructing a light railway forward through the newly-won territory, and the infantry's work with them was always arduous and exciting. No sooner was a sector of track laid than enemy shells might, and it often did, scatter it far and wide. On some days, practically nothing was accomplished, the shelling being so intense that the workers lay under cover all day. When this seemingly futile work was over for the Fifth, they were heartily glad, though fortune had favoured them in that only one man was killed, though several were wounded.

During the days spent in the Belgian Chateau Camp, the percentage of sick increased tremendously. Delayed effects of the gas, severe colds and chills, all began to take their toll now that the reaction of front-line excitement set in.

The weather was wet, and mud was attendant on every phase of the monotonous life here; life none the less monotonous, because salted with danger.   The boredom of return to infantry drill was accentuated by the memory of recent stirring events, while the tremendous aerial activity contributed risks that everyone wished to avoid. The humiliation of being wounded while going to dinner, or coming from a concert, was a very real one, and added to the many incongruities of the men's strange existence.

The presence of the First Divisional Concert Party, under the name of "The Kookaburras," provided the one bright spot in the men's dreary, muddy existence. Every afternoon, in a hall opposite the camp, this talented combination played to crowded houses, whose applause evidenced their deep appreciation.

On Saturday, the tenth of November, amid rain and mud, and the never-ending crash and rumble of shells which burst round shattered Ypres, the Fifth moved out of the camp and turned their backs on the front line. Along the traffic-congested roads, the regiment threaded their way as best they could, the men soon losing all sense of direction through the frequent turnings. At length, the Vlamertinghe-Reninghelst Road was reached. Here the traffic was as thick as before, and the mud thicker, and the men plodded through on the side of the road as best they could.

Canadian troops were going forward, and in passing the Fifth, banter and the rough humor of the day were flung across and back between them. "A fine body of soldiers, I guess," said one Canadian loudly. "They're not *soldiers*, they're Australians," replied a nasal voice. "Where are you going, digger?" asked one of the Fifth. "Up to finish your ———— job, while you have a ———— holiday!" was the ready answer. "Oh, are you? Well, we're going down to finish your job and take Lens," was the reply of a Fifth man. This reference to the Canadians' last affair was highly satisfactory to the Australians, and they pushed on through the slush greatly heartened by the exchange of badinage.

Passing by their former quarters at Vancouver Camp, the regiment came through the village of Ouderdom to Cornwall Camp just beyond. Wet, cold, and miserable, all ranks were depressed and ill-tempered, and grumbling and quarrelling were very natural results of these circumstances. With the adaptability that ever characterised them, the Fifth "discovered" a coal dump nearby. The regulation issue of braziers was quickly supplemented in some mysterious manner, and impromptu ones made from petrol tins. Within half an hour, the whole aspect of the cold, wet surroundings was changed. Little groups gathered around the glowing fires, the consciousness of the front line misery was left behind, and comfort and good fellowship succeeded the dismal spirits in which all had been enveloped.

In this camp, a day and a half and two nights were spent, during which time a not unwelcome nor premature change of underwear further helped the men to endure the depressing weather and surroundings. One of the incidents that lightened the monotony of these dull days was the pleasure the men experienced from watching the rat-hunts conducted by a fox-terrier named "Somme," which derived its name from that part of the country whence it had been brought by the cooks of "D" Company.

On Monday, the twelfth of November, the Fifth boarded motor 'buses and char-a-bancs to go further back. The morning was clear and sunny. Autumn's chilliness was nicely tempered, and everyone was in high spirits when the convoy of some

twenty vehicles moved off. Through Reninghelst, and
skirting Poperinghe, they passed through Steenwoorde, and thence to Abeele.

After Abeele had been left behind, the flat and
uninteresting nature of the country began to change.
The evidence of war was not so plentiful now. Camps
were more infrequent, and only the countless mounds
surmounted by white crosses told that the struggle
had passed over here. Undulating green pastures,
dotted with sheep and cattle, alternated with fields
where women and old men were gathering the root-
crops into the quaint three-wheeled carts, or covering
the heaps with straw and earth against the coming
winter.

Through such peaceful scenes as these the vehicles
rolled along the road to Cassel. Familiar to most of
them, the sight of the town was doubly pleasant now.
Autumn had tinged the hedges and trees with rich
browns and yellows, and the sun bathed the whole
countryside in mellow tints.

The highest point for many miles around, Cassel
was reached by a road which wound through avenues
of tall trees and hedges. The multitude of staff-cars
and staff-officers was an unfailing indication of Headquarters, and here General Sir Herbert Plumer had
his staff.

Over the crest of the hill, on to Arques in the direction of Wandrecques went the Fifth, and, alighting
near the little old village of Hendringhem, they came,
after a short march across the fields, to billets in comfortable farmhouses. The stillness of the surroundings was only broken by the now-distant thunder of
the guns, and here, in cosy billets, the regiment rested

A Typical View of the Ypres Sector, during the latter part of 1917.

till the Wednesday.   Another move then, this time on foot, and the Fifth reached Elnes, near Lumbres (ten and a half miles away) by a quarter-past one.

Excepting a few men who still felt the effects of the gas, the regiment stood the march well, and the music of the band made the journey a pleasant one, though the route was hilly.

Only a night was spent in billets at Elnes, but the people made it a pleasant one, and the various little kindnesses rendered to the men were appreciated to the utmost.   Breakfast was timed for half-past six, and at half-past eight, the Battalion moved again, skirting the northern boundary of Lumbres, *via* St. Pierre, Vandringham, Nielles-les-Blequin, to Blequin. The country was hilly and interesting, the weather good, and the men enjoyed it fully.   Again there was no pulling out of the ranks, and at half-past twelve they arrived at their billets, and were warmly welcomed by the inhabitants of the small village.   They rested the whole of the next day, and a march of twelve kilos on the Saturday brought them to Desvres. This town was the centre of a "Rest Area," which was devoted to troops who were having a complete rest, reorganisation and training, and it was here that the men spent many happy hours.

Recreational training and athletic contests kept them happy and fit, and it is pleasing to record that the best of relations were maintained between the villagers and the troops.   The remainder of the Second Brigade were billeted around, and the four regiments soon met in friendly athletic rivalry.

The Fifth were successful in carrying off the honours for recreational training, filled second place in athletics, and shared with the Seventh Battalion the lowest place on the football list.

I

Quite a feature of the French people's daily routine was the morning parade of the Fifth in the market square. Added to the interest always manifested by the French in foreign troops, and particularly in these Australians, was the fact that some of the men were on terms of close friendship with the villagers.

Lieutenant C. Chapman is not likely to forget Desvres. The reason thereof also concerns a stray dog who shared the limelight, until he died. Possibly the dog had the proverbial excitability of the French; at any rate he bit the hand that teased him. This fact would not have been mentioned, in this history at any rate, but that the dog, as has been said, died on the next day. A suspicion of rabies was followed by Chapman being packed off to Paris "at the toot," where he was admitted to a famous hospital, and given specialist treatment for the prevention of the dreaded disease.

There is not much more to the story, except that no symptoms manifested themselves within the six weeks that Lieutenant Chapman attended the Institute as an outpatient; and that he speaks very highly of the hospitality of the Parisians. Suffice it to say that there were many scars to be shown by others of the Fifth during the next few days after the patient's triumphant return, as proof of their unsuccessful tempting of fate.

Baths for the troops were formed in conjunction with the local cement works, and the hot water that was generated in the process of cement making made the bathing pleasant and effective.

The weeks spent in this little town passed very pleasantly, and it was with reluctance that the men got into marching order on the eleventh of December, and turned their backs on the people they had learnt to regard so highly, and whose farewell was obviously so genuinely regretful.

A twelve-kilo march brought them to Ledinghem, where farmhouses billeted them for the night. Next day another march of about the same distance saw the familiar roofs of Elnes again.

The men left their comfortable beds in billets at one o'clock next morning, breakfasted at half-past one, and at three o'clock left in the darkness for Wizernes, where they entrained at a quarter to seven. After three hours of this journeying, they stretched their cramped legs at Zurynebak, and began a short march to huts in Kemmel. As the train had passed through Hazebrouck the enemy were shelling the town again, and down the roads flowed the steady stream of refugees with their household goods on carts or barrows; a familiar sight, this, in poor France.

The Fifth's re-entry into the fighting zone was to be a quiet one, for next day they went into the line near Comines Canal. Here they were to do the routine of four days in reserve, four days in support, and four days in front line, which constituted the tour of duty. The weather was wintry again now, and it was indeed fortunate that nothing but occasional shelling disturbed the quiet. The Hun was some distance away; the country was undulating and uncultivated. Looking over No Man's Land through the criss-cross of the wire, one saw the familiar shell holes that pocked the intervening ground, and beyond, the enemy position. The front was comparatively "quiet," indeed, and the mocking "pom-tiddley-om-pom" rapped out on a machine gun by an expert

Australian, answered by the "pom-pom" of his no-less-expert Hun rival, showed the constrained idleness that enveloped the infantry of both sides.

The regiment's fourth Xmas from home was spent in these surroundings. December twenty-fifth dawned clear and frosty, and the frozen shell holes explained the shivers of the past night. Later the first real snow of the season fell, and in a short while the landscape's scars were softened by Nature's white mantle, making a truly Christmassy scene, one, however, hardly appreciated by the shivering men.

Wherever the Britisher be, he must needs have his Xmas pudding, and in this instance he got an early issue. At four o'clock the morning rations were sent up, including the plum pudding. It was fortunate that the meal was an ample one, as no more food arrived until seven o'clock in the evening. Beyond the usual desultory shelling, the day passed—as far as the Fifth were concerned—in peace and good will.

At this time there were rumours of two Huns in Australian uniform being at large in this sector, and no man was allowed to move about in the rear without being armed.

On December thirtieth, the regiment was relieved and moved back to reserve at "Scott's Farm," a series of dugouts which provided good shelter until they had to evacuate them in favour of the artillery. Four days here, and then back to Lindenhoek, a small village, where they lived in huts until the fifteenth of January. The New Year opened without incident beyond the daily one of training.

Back to the Comines Canal sector again, where each Company did two days front-line duty, which was enlivened with patrol work. Casualties were slight during this time. On the twenty-third, relief came, and the regiment marched back to Wulverghem, where they billeted until the twenty-ninth, then marched to Birr Barracks at Locre.

The officers' mess was arranged in the neighbouring convent buildings, in a room which had echoed to the laughter of many a regimental joke. Numberless British regiments had stayed there awhile before going on to battle, as the panelled walls bore witness with the carvings of regimental crests neatly executed. The Fifth badge and motto, "*Sans Regrets,*" was added to the collection before the Battalion moved on.

The convent was afterwards destroyed during the German advance of 1918, and it is doubtful whether any trace of these carvings now exists. Here, at this time, was to be seen the grave of Major Redmond, the gallant Irish officer who had given his life in the earlier fighting.

Some little excitement was caused among the men one evening by a fire which began in a hut and burned it and two others before the amateur firemen succeeded in making a "save." Chains of buckets, and the forceful smashing down of adjacent huts with duckboards used as battering rams, proved effective.

Paris leave was granted, and those who were lucky enough to have sufficient funds went off to enjoy the hectic pleasures of the Gay City, returning with yarns of happenings so impossible as to bear the strongest imprint of truth.

A football match between the Fifth and Sixth Battalions on the ninth of February evoked intense interest, and many francs were wagered on it. The Fifth were victors by five goals six behinds to two goals three.

On the fourteenth a Battalion route march in "marching order" was held. The triangle of Locre, Bailleul, Meteren was covered, and the roads being in good order, it was not unenjoyable. Subsequently the Fifth met the Eighth at football, but were vanquished by three points, after a willing game.

An order published on the sixteenth of February calls attention to the fact that the men were indulging in the reprehensible practice of pilfering coal from the supply waggons passing through the town. Offenders would in future be arrested and severely dealt with. This threat was seriously regarded by the men of the Fifth, as it entailed meeting the waggons much further up the road than formerly.

After nearly a month of Locre, with the usual and monotonous training, the Battalion left for Lindenhoek on the twenty-second of February, "per boot." About a week here, and they were off again on their endless wanderings, this time to "Curragh Camp." The weather was bleak and very windy, and another seven or eight days passed, enlivened by fatigues of various kinds.

Chapter XXV.

THE GERMAN ADVANCE.

Hazebrouck—La Motte—Moolenacker.

A FURTHER move on March tenth brought the men to "Jamaica Camp," where they settled down in huts for another week or so. Fatigues again employed them, woodcutting being one of the commonest and most arduous forms of work. The weather was fine, and the life generally enjoyable.

Quarters were shifted on the eighteenth, and a march to Tournai Camp, and, next day, to Bois Carrée, supplied a welcome change of scenery, though fresh strenuous woodcutting made the word "fatigue" a descriptive one.

After five days here, the Battalion returned to Tournai Camp, but only for a brief while, as the next day saw their wanderings begin anew. This time a short march of four miles or so brought them to Parrett Camp, where they again had the comfort of huts. Training filled in the days of a week or more till the fourth of April, when they marched to Birr Barracks. These were left behind next day, when the Battalion entrained and travelled to Strazeele. Only the night was spent here, and the men again entrained and went by rail to Hangest, where they expected at least to find a village. A few scattered houses, one estaminet and a railway siding completed the scenery, and this, seen at half-past eleven at night, was not alluring. A march through the darkness of about

four miles brought them to billets in a little village
called Pernois.

On the ninth, a route march of nearly fifteen miles
through Fleselle to Rainneville found the men in good
fettle, and next day another bout of footslogging—
barely five miles this time—brought Pont Noyelles in
sight. This was a small village on the Albert-Amiens
Road, and here General Birdwood had once his headquarters in a chateau in the valley.

Most of the Battalion were billeted in a school. The
village had just been evacuated by the inhabitants,
so hurriedly that they had left most of their belongings behind them.

Here word was received that the Hun had broken
through up North, and that the First Division were
to entrain and proceed to this sector with all haste.

On Friday, 12th, after reveille at 3.45 a.m., the
Regiment marched out through Quierrieu on to the
Albert-Amiens road. Here they were attacked by
German 'planes, but machine-gun fire drove the Huns
off without the Fifth sustaining casualties.

During the series of marches made throughout these
few days past the Battalion had skirted Amiens, but
now, on the twelfth of April, they entered the city
itself. They found it deserted by the populace, and
occupied by troops. Long-distance shells were falling
into the city, and Fritz's 'planes bombed frequently.
While providing working parties for salvage work
and the like, the Fifth sustained some casualties, but
did not lose so heavily as did some of the other regiments.

Entraining at St. Roch, a suburban railway station,
with an occasional shell falling, they left Amiens the
same afternoon.

The remainder of the A.I.F. Divisions, the Second,
Third, Fourth and Fifth, were at this time in the for-

[Copyright by Australian War Museum.]

Some of the 5th at Garter Point, near Zonnebeke, October, 1917.
(The wire indicates where the German Line existed prior to its capture by the Australians.)

ward area, stemming the fierce German advance which threatened to envelop Amiens, among other territory.

At one o'clock on the morning of the thirteenth the Fifth's train journey terminated at Hazebrouck, where, in the shadow of the cathedral, the Battalion padre provided a welcome drink of hot coffee.

At 3.30 a.m. the Regiment marched through Haze-brouck, to a farm on the outskirts of the town, where the men were billeted in barns.

The military position at this stage was a peculiar one. English divisions that had been badly damaged in the heavy fighting down South had been placed in the quieter sectors on this part of the front. A Fifth man bears testimony to the fact that what was osten-sibly a "Battalion" parade of an English regiment had a strength of nine men, but there were possibly other reasons than casualties to account for this.

Portugese troops held a portion of the line in this sector, and it was against these "comic opera" soldiers that the Hun's thrust was primarily directed. How easily he broke through is a matter of history, perhaps as yet unwritten for diplomatic reasons.

Elated, and no doubt greatly surprised at his suc-cess, Fritz streamed through the breach followed in the rear of the fleeing "Pork-and-beans," and soon the grey flood had spread over a salient almost twelve miles deep, and as wide.

Slowly he seemed to advance, as though uncertain whether this was a trap or no. For the time it was reminiscent of early days of the German invasion, for were not the German patrols out cautiously feel-ing their way, while their artillery lumbered on in the rear, in strenuous endeavour to keep pace with the advance? For obvious reasons, there was practically no shelling, with the disposition of the troops on both sides so uncertain, only the usual German long range shelling still continuing on points far in the rear.

Hence it was that ''A'' Company of the Fifth found themselves marching down a road that led out of Hazebrouck towards the advancing tide of Huns, with orders to try to establish contact with the enemy. The remainder of the Battalion breakfasted in a field, and then marched a short distance to La Motte, a village which most of the population had evacuated though some of them still tenaciously stayed on.

Pitiful streams of refugees came down the roads from the villages which the German advance now threatened.   The extremes of age helped each other in this tragic retreat.   Women did men's work in saving the household goods, and the reluctant bellowing calf or the more philosophic cow mingled with wheelbarrows or the occasional horse and cart.   Except the aged, there were no men, and as the column of the Fifth swung along the road singing, the refugees stopped and clustered in little groups to cry, ''Trés bon, Australie,'' to the laughing soldiers.

Looking back as they passed on, the men saw that the retreat of the villagers had received a check, and it appeared that some of them indeed were retracing their steps.

Reaching the deserted village the Fifth found comfortable quarters for the night in the houses, but during the night some of the men found the rightful owners returning, and by morning a considerable number of the population had made their way back.   It was impossible to allow them to stay, however, and they were accordingly told that they must retire from the danger zone, as, apart from the probability of a Hun attack, it was almost certain that the village would soon be shelled. Tearful scenes ensued as the unfortunate people were sent back. If the Australians were here, then it must be all right, and it was quite unnecessary to retire. Which flattering observation did not prevent their removal.

La Motte is an honoured name among the men of the Fifth, who were with the regiment at this period. So hurried had been the flight of some of the peasantry that their little farms were still stocked with poultry and animals. Fresh milk, poultry and pork, eggs and vegetables, now made life pleasant. The nine or ten days' sojourn in this French village was marked by prodigious feats of endurance at the meal table, by these gallant trenchermen.

But to return to "A" Company, whom we left wandering towards an enemy whose dispositions were but vaguely known. Approaching the Nieppe Forest, they were surprised to meet, going the opposite way, confused groups of officers and men of English regiments. When these were questioned, little could be learnt except that "Jerry was coming over in thousands," and had beaten back the English line, but thinly held by these regiments of the Fifth Army Corps (now attached to the Second). Badly hit as we have seen they were down South, they were in ill condition, numerically and physically, to withstand the grey wave that pressed overwhelmingly forward, and it ill becomes one to criticise their defection, serious though it was.

The Australians passed on, richer by some few Lewis guns than before the meeting, and reconnoitred round the outer edge of the wood. Here positions were made for the night, and the small Battalion nucleus next morning joined up and lay in close support to some other units of the Second Brigade, who

were in front, while "A" Company rejoined the remainder of the Battalion back in the comfortable billets of La Motte.

Reluctantly leaving this earthly Paradise, the Fifth
moved again to Thieusouk, near Caestre, another of
the innumerable villages with which France is dotted,
and much like any others of them that the Fifth had
seen. The awkward sounding name was very properly
changed to "Thistlehook," a second distinction for the
place. The other one was the honour of having "the
largest shellhole." Probably there were many such
on the various fighting fronts, but this huge hole was
certainly tremendous enough to inspire pardonable
exaggeration. It made Thieusouk a show place for
Engineers and Artillery officers for many moons.

Here the Fifth found themselves in a position on
the right of the British line where it joined with the
French. A large sugar mill seemed to offer decent
shelter, and here most of the Battalion came, to share
lodgings with a regiment of the famous Alpine Chas-
seurs, more familiarly known as the "Blue Devils."
These dashing troops, with tam-o'-shanter-like caps,
looked askance at the intruders, and relations were,
for a time, not over-cordial. It was not long before
the Australians were sincerely and profanely expressing their admiration of their Allies, the sole basis of
appreciation seemingly being that the Frenchmen were
better foragers than they. High praise indeed from
an Australian!

The shelling was constant, and the mill became a
mark for German gunners before the Fifth moved—
after three days there—by a night march of seven or
eight miles to the Moolenacker sector. Here they relieved the First Brigade.

This sector was in the midst of intensely cultivated country, and the crops looked in good condition to the critical eyes of these men from the land of farms. Warfare had as yet dealt lightly with the landscape, and the little plots made a mosaic of delightful colour to eyes staled with the barren battlefields of the south.

Hereabout the "line" was an irregular length of platoon outposts, constantly changing as the front moved forward. Gas shells were responsible for most of the casualties sutained by the regiment.

Chapter XXVI.

MOSTLY ABOUT RAIDS.

Daylight Raids—Strazeele—Moolenacker—Sercus.

THE sixth of June found our patrols active in No
Man's Land. At night the enemy machine-
guns and snipers were busy, and casualties
were sustained. Lieutenant G. W. P. Kay was
unfortunately, one of those killed. He was a student
for the ministry, and his untimely end was genuinely
lamented by officers and men alike. Three men of
other ranks were wounded, and two gassed.

The next day saw three daylight raids carried out
by members of the Fifth Battalion. These audacious
incidents, which broke new ground in this war of
constant surprises, were originated by the A.I.F. in
the times when little or no big fighting was taking
place. Ever chafing under inaction, and quick to
take advantage, the Australians saw that the enemy
had lost his punch, or, rather, that it lacked "sting."

The conformation of No Man's Land, as yet not
reduced to the blasted pock-marked barrenness, sown
with abdominous and stinking corpses, with no living
occupant save the hideous rats—but green with growing corn and grass and trees, favoured the guerilla
warfare for which the Colonial seemed so happily
suited.

The morning of June the seventh, therefore, brought
swift, unexpected, and daring attacks which must
have brought consternation to the Germans. What

manner of men must these be who crawled like Indians over hundreds of yards of open ground, through wire and past outposts, then jumped in on unoffending soldiery who were peacefully sleeping? Everyone expected activity under the favourable darkness, but it was against all the accepted rules on a quiet sector like this, that the day should be disturbed by unseemly brawling.

This is what the Hun had to complain of.   At five o'clock of this morning, in the broad daylight, 1612 Corporal E. Schwab, 2012 Corporal J. V. Reilly, and 584 Private T. H. Gardiner, having obtained the necessary permission, left the front line and proceeded to a point near Meteren.   Here was a post which had been observed by Gardiner for two days. Armed with a revolver and two bombs apiece, the three crawled and walked stoopingly for the first hundred yards through a sheltering wheat-crop. After that was a potato patch, screened from their objective by wheat shoulder-high.   They rested in a shell hole in the potato field and formulated their plan of action.   Keeping to the right edge of the crop that hid the post, they crawled to the parapet.   Peeping over, Reilly saw two of the enemy asleep in a dugout just below.   He and Schwab sprang down, while Gardiner lay on the parapet keeping watch.   The Germans still lay sleeping, but when they felt their blankets rudely yanked from them. and opened their eyes to see two grim looking Australians threatening them with revolvers—well, it needs little imagination to see their ludicrous surprise and terror.   One of them squealed with fright, and needed little persuasion to accompany them.   The other was inclined to offer resistance—at first.   The raiders returned to their lines with the two prisoners without further incident, having been away twenty minutes, and reported to Captain H. Burke.   Corporal Reilly was subsequently awarded the D.C.M., while Corporal Schwab and Private Gardiner received the M.M.

The second one of these "diversions" was provided later the same morning by another trio of the Fifth— 907 Sergeant A. T. Morrison, 6643 Lance-Corporal W. A. M. Simms, and 5707 Private S. P. Hastings.   The story of their adventure is best told by Sergeant E. H. Barber, who had arranged with Sergeant Morrison to give the latter "covering fire" with a Lewis gun if necessary.

"On 7/6/18 "D" Company was in the line.   I was in charge of No. 7 post.   On my left was Sergeant Morrison in charge of No. 8.   At nine a.m. Morrison told me that he, Hastings and Simms were going to raid a German trench that ran at nearly right angles to ours at a hundred and twenty yards distance.   He asked me to give them covering fire with my L.G. in case there was a fight.   From his post, a wheat crop about two feet six inches high, stretched for some hundred yards to a road which was near the end of the enemy trench.   Wire entanglements screened our outpost and the enemy's.

"Through the wheat the three of them crawled, and at the roadside, stood up and looked around before walking over.   They passed on to the trench, jumped in, and again looked around.   Going on a little way, they stooped down and were out of sight for a few seconds.   Then I saw one, two, three, four Germans with their hands up.   A few yards further along two others surrendered.   Morrison then got up on the parapet and motioned to the prisoners to walk along the trench towards our own line.   They were unwilling, so Morrison threw clods of dirt at them.   Moving along slowly, they climbed out of the trench. Then they wanted to go off at the "double," but Morrison placed himself at their head and brought them back as if on parade. He left the six with some of our boys in the front line and returned to the other two raiders who had rounded up three more Huns, with a machine gun and spare parts complete. By this time the enemy was aroused and began to use revolvers and bombs. Our men came back then, and though a German post on the left fired some shots, they arrived safely."

Sergeant Morrison's account supplements this, but very modestly.

"Went along the trench ten yards. Then saw one Fritz asleep and another round the corner packing his kit. Bailed them up while they kicked like blazes. In a second dugout was a stretcher-bearer, and in the third a sergeant and corporal. The sergeant was nasty, and tried to get the stick bombs and Mills grenades." (Note: these were British ones captured in last offensive.) "The enemy were well provided with blankets and food."

Sergeant Morrison was a better hand at doing things than describing them, as will be seen, and he admitted that he "only went out for a bit of sport."

Three Australians captured nine Germans and a machine gun in broad daylight, and never fired a shot! The God of War surely grinned when Morrison threw clods of dirt at the prisoners to hury them on. This exploit rendered unnecessary a night raid planned by "C" Company, and saved thousands of pounds worth of munitions that would otherwise have been expended in barrage and covering fire. Sergeant Morrison and Lance-Corporal Simms won the D.C.M., and Private Hastings the M.M. for their morning's work.

The third daylight raid of the same morning had but two Australian participants, but these two crammed much incident into the eight minutes or so during which it lasted.

Corporal Reilly and Private Gardiner (the two who at five o'clock had accompanied Corporal Schwab on the first raid), decided that they had not had enough excitement for the day, and agreed to raid another post. Borrowing revolvers from Lieutenant Parker, they left the trench at half-past ten a.m. Under cover of a tall crop they crawled for fifty yards towards the post they had marked down. Lieutenant Parker and Private Duclos remained on watch and saw the two raiders leave the shelter of the crop and crawl into the open towards the enemy. Someone else saw them too; the German sentry. He fired at Reilly at short range, but missed. This was most unfortunate for him, for the two Australians rushed the post, despite the fact that ten or twelve Huns had showed up. Reilly shot the sentry and jumped into the trench. Five Germans ran away screaming, while Reilly emptied his revolver into the remainder. Gardiner shot a Hun who threw a bomb at him, and then accounted for three others. Reilly was down struggling with one whom he at length managed to shoot, and got up in time to face another Hun who fired at him from a distance of ten yards, but missed and took to his heels.

Lieutenant Parker and Duclos threw a bomb at some Huns on the flank who had been alarmed by the shooting, and in a few seconds the whole front line was aroused. German machine guns and bombs seemed to indicate that the enemy had "the wind up." Reilly and Gardiner waited long enough to identify the eight dead as belonging to the 267th Reserve Infantry, 81st Reserve Division, and then crawled back on their hands and knees to their trench, unharmed.

One must admit that they had had all the excitement they craved for, and this must rank as one of the most daring and useful individual stunts that the Australians did. For two men to rush an enemy post in broad daylight, without any preparation, and practically without any assistance; to kill eight of the enemy and to return unharmed, is an achievement that makes one proud of being an Australian.

It followed as a natural consequence that the enemy were busy that night. Shelling and machine-gun fire plastered the Fifth's position, and flares that went up frequently showed that the Hun was now wide awake and ready for anything untoward. One man died from wounds received in the Boche retaliation.

Six days followed of this comparative quietness in the line and then came a move back to Boore, where, in a field shaded by trees the men made little ''humpies,'' and enjoyed a rest in delightfully sunny weather. After six days spent here, their tour of duty in the front area commenced anew.

In the little valley of Boore, prominently placed on a house wall, was a sign that read ''12,000 miles to Griffith's Tea,'' a digger's travesty of the familiar railway signs, that made many a Victorian feel homesick.

On June eleventh, the regiment moved back to Le Peuplier, a small village with a few houses scattered round the cross-roads, and an estaminet or two. It was but a short march, and the weather being fine, the tramp was quite pleasant.

Four days here, and then to reserve at Moolenbacker—two or three miles nearer the line. Here the men remained for seven days, two companies at a time doing front-line duty, and sustaining but few casualties.

Weke Meulin, a small village some seven miles or so behind the line, saw the men with the red and black shoulder patches on the twenty-second. The countryside hereabouts was intensely cultivated, and the green fields, trees and hedges were pleasant to look upon after the desolation the men had left down south.

Hazebrouck was near by, and the Battalion supplied "town picquet" for two days. The town was frequently bombed and shelled, and as a consequence most of the population had evacuated. There were still delectable spots in the shape of wine cellars and abandoned shops, and the picquet, with so many Australians in the vicinity, was a necessary precaution.

On the twenty-eighth, another short march of some four miles brought the men to the small village of Sercus, where, in a pleasant meadow, they were accommodated with tents. The weather was beautiful, with the promise of early summer, and the countryside everywhere showed pleasantly fertile and green.

Here the regiment was treated to a demonstration of model platoon training and aeroplane "contact." The model platoon was composed largely of Tommy N.C.O.'s and some New Zealanders, who had come from a neighbouring school. The parade was held in the Battalion area, and demonstrated with automaton-like precision the new idea of training evolved in the Chelsea school. First of all imitating the usual Australian method of falling in, with helmet askew and chin strap up, rifle slung on shoulder and cigarette depending from lower lip, they demonstrated "how not to do it."

Then a sudden change on the shrill blast of the "Sarn Major's" whistle, and like clockwork they showed how it should be.   As a contrast it was impressive, but it seemed to provide only amusement for the lounging diggers of the Fifth, and they voted it the best stunt they had seen since the last concert party.

On Sunday a Brigade Church Parade was held, which was attended by the Corps Commander, General Beavoir de Lisle, and the Divisional Commander, General Walker. The Fifth's chaplain, Captain C. Neville, gave the address.

On June 6th, Captain-Chaplain C. Neville left for the base, being relieved by Captain-Chaplain E. C. Petherick.   Captain Neville had been with the Battalion since 1916, and by his manly and unassuming demeanour, and his straightforward talks to the men, had gained their confidence and esteem. He had spent much of his time in collecting material for this history.   Some of this related to the period of his association, but he had also, by dint of patiently questioning the original officers and men, gained a great deal of information that extended back to the beginning of the regiment's existence.

Next day the Fifth relieved the Second Battalion, and moved into the support area.   On the night of the following day, they took over the line in front of Moolenacker and Nord Helf, the left boundary being Meteren Becque, a small stream. The occupation was complete by midnight with only two casualties. Lieutenant P. J. O'Farrell and eight "other ranks" went forward and penetrated three hundred yards into No Man's Land without finding trace of the enemy.

At this stage official notice was received of several
decorations awarded officers and men of the Fifth.
Lieutenant-Colonel Luxton, D.S.O., was granted the
C.M.G., while four N.C.O.'s and men gained the M.M.

On the night of the twelfth-thirteenth, they relieved the Seventh Battalion in the front line, completing the operation by 12.24 a.m.   The position
was on the right of the Brigade front, south of Strazeele, with outposts east of Mont de Merris.   The
front-line excitement began straight away when the
enemy counter-attacked on the positions they had lost
the previous night. They were repulsed and left five
prisoners in the hands of the Fifth.

The fourteenth of June was also a day of incident,
and four N.C.O.'s and men of the Fifth gained decorations for gallantry displayed during this day, among
them being 762 Lance-Corporal A. Hall, who won a
second bar to his M.M.

Heavy fighting took place when the enemy attempted to envelope the Fifth posts, and at Mont de
Merris, 3676 Private A. A. Aalto won his M.M. by
staving off a determined enemy attack with his Lewis
gun.   He fired 600 rounds, prevented his platoon
being outflanked, and afterwards withdrew his gun
under heavy fire.

During another attack on a post near Strazeele,
3279 Lance-Corporal E. V. Fowler gained the M.M.
for his bravery in taking his gun out into No Man's
Land during a fierce enemy attack, and doing considerable execution with it.   Twenty Germans were
afterwards counted lying dead in front of his gun.

The Eighty-Eighth Brigade on the right made a raid and the right post of the Fifth co-operated with a Lewis gun, sustaining casualties of three killed, one dead of wounds, one officer and thirteen others wounded, and three missing.

Next day numerous patrols went out and met with opposition. Lieutenant N. S. Maddox (who had just been awarded the M.C.) with five other ranks at five o'clock in the afternoon raided an enemy position. The primary object of the raid was to search for Corporal E. M. Chambers, who was missing; also to secure identification of the enemy.   Sergeant Lucas, Corporal Jacobe, Lance-Corporal Jackson and Privates Merrin and E. Shepherd comprised the party. Minus their identification discs, and armed with revolver and bomb each, they made their way along the Plate Becque to the enemy position. Private Shepherd carried a rifle and bayonet. They reached the spot where Corporal Chambers was supposed to have been taken prisoner, but the post was unoccupied.   Going on, they crossed the Becque, a stream about five feet wide and four feet deep, by means of a plank.   A solitary tree nearby marked their crossing place, should they have to make a hurried return.   On the other side of the stream was a newly-wired barrier.   Negotiating this successfully, Lieutenant Maddox, Sergeant Lucas and Private Merrin advanced through a pea crop, a few inches high, for about sixty yards, when they were fired upon.   They rushed the sentries and beckoned to the rest of the party to advance, but they were already coming ''at the toot.''   The sentries willingly surrendered and threw away their rifles. The raiders found themselves in a nest of eight posts, and had the defenders had any dash, they might easily have overcome the small party. The resolute air of the Australians, backed by the threat of bomb and revolver, quickly emptied the Huns from their nests, however, and the queue of prisoners was started over the parapet towards the stream.   One Hun Sergeant refused to come out of his dugout and persisted in squealing for help till Private Merrin got down and, in the language of the day, "put the boot into him." He proved amenable to this form of reasoning, and joined the others. The prisoners were walked quickly up to the wire, through there and over the stream, and took a sharp turn to the left to reach Lieutenant Maddox's post—the starting point.

At this stage, one of the escort, pointing his revolver at the ground just behind them, fired several shots with remarkable effect. The twelve prisoners unanimously broke into a frenzied run towards the Australian line, and actually reached Company headquarters before their captors. Six N.C.O.'s and six privates formed the "bag," accomplished without casualties to the aggressors.

Lieutenant Maddox gained a bar to his M.C.; Sergeant Lucas the D.C.M., and three others the M.M., for this impudent and successful exploit.

Another raid on the next day was not so successful.   At five o'clock in the morning Lieutenant Davis and three others left the line to locate a new enemy work. They found a machine-gun post and another enemy post in a shell-hole where the enemy were asleep. In the melee that ensued Lieutenant Davis was badly wounded, while three Germans were killed. One man was left with Davis while the others returned for assistance against the resistance that was coming from other quarters.   Later, eight men from Nos. 3 and 12 platoons went out to effect a rescue, but when they were within twenty yards of the post, heavy fire forced them to retire.   Lieutenant Davis and the other man were posted as missing; one other was wounded.

The Ninth Battalion relieved on the seventeenth, and the Fifth moved back to the "Bivouac Area," at L'Hoffard, moving from there on the next day to reserve, and thence to rest area at Sercus.   Here they entered camp and began "training as per syllabus." For seven or eight days they lived the routine of camp life, varied by the Brigade Sports which the Fifth won from the Sixth by three points.

Chapter XXVII.

HARBONNIERES.

Pradelles—Moolenacker-Strazeele—L'Hoffard—
Aubigny—Harbonnières—Cerisy.

ON the twenty-seventh the regiment moved again
to Bivouac Area and then forward to "Support Area" once more. From this date to the
fifth of July, the Fifth occupied the support line at
Pradelles and provided working parties each night,
Trench digging, wiring, and cutting crops in front of
the wire entanglements was diverting and exciting
work at times. Lieutenant A. J. Robinson was
wounded during this period.

American troops were now attached for instruction
with the Fifth, three officers and four other ranks
from the 309th Infantry Regiment and two officers
and fourteen others from the 312th Infantry Regiment.

Patrols were active during the next few days. On
the seventh July, Lieutenant Barber, M.C., and a
party got into touch with the enemy, and after being
absent over an hour, returned. Their casualties were
one killed and seven wounded, one of whom stayed on
duty. Several patrols went out the next day, and
everywhere found the enemy very alert and working
hard on their defences. The next four days saw
similar patrol activity all along the Fifth front, and
the adventures of these little parties must necessarily
be condensed for lack of space, though each in itself
was sufficiently exciting. A note of July tenth mentions that while "B" and "D" Companies were relieving "A" and "C," protective patrols in No Man's

Land had operated, and further remarks that "enemy appears nervous, and on patrols approaching, retires without firing a shot."

Next day Corporal C. Dedman took part in a daylight reconnaissance with Lieutenant D. Robertson. They penetrated four hundred yards and located previously unknown enemy posts, strongly held. They watched these from a distance of thirty yards and Dedman then crawled along in front of the enemy wire and discovered an enemy "listening post" with two men in it. Although covered with a revolver, they refused to surrender, and one of them showed fight. Dedman immediately shot him. The report alarmed the neighbouring post, and as the second man proved recalcitrant, he also was summarily dealt with. The two hurriedly returned with a shoulder strap for identification, under heavy enemy bombing, rifle and machine-gun fire. Some few hours later, Dedman volunteered to proceed again to this post for further information, and with another man, did so. At great personal risk they succeeded and returned with pay-book and papers. Corporal Dedman was recommended for the M.M., and subsequently received that decoration.

On the night of the thirteenth-fourteenth, the Ninth Battalion relieved the Fifth in the left sector of the Brigade sub-sector, and they moved back to reserve at L'Hoffard. Next day the regiment marched to Racquinghem and took over Hurlingham Camp. Four days of "training as per syllabus" now occupied the men, but the work was pleasantly lightened by swimming and cricket matches. Sunday, the twenty-first, saw Church Parade, which General Sir W. Birdwood attended. He subsequently presented the M.C. and bar to Lieutenant N. S. Maddox. He afterwards wrote to Major-General Glasgow expressing his extreme pleasure with the appearance of the Fifth, whom he characterised as "looking extremely well, smartly turned out, and evidently full of spirit."

Two more days of drill and recreational training, and then came the swimming carnival in the Canal, which General Birdwood attended. "C" Company were chosen to represent the Fifth, and after a close and exciting contest, won with a total of two hundred and fifty-five points from the Sixth Battalion with two hundred and fifty. Curiously enough, the Seventh and Eighth followed, thus giving the result the ordinary numerical sequence. The Fifth Cooks were also awarded the prize for the best Field Cooker in the Brigade.

A Brigade review by G.O.C. Second Army (General Plumer) was to have been held on the twenty-seventh, but heavy rain postponed this event. On the thirtieth the Battalion moved from camp and marched to a position in reserve of their former front line (Moolenacker-Strazeele) where they formed a nucleus and the main body went forward to relieve the Ninth Battalion. Casualties of one killed and five wounded attended this operation. Lieut. Garlick was killed by a sniper while on a daylight reconnaissance with Lieut. W. B. Grantham in No Man's Land. A highly popular officer, he evinced a fearlessness and contempt of danger which had made his name a byword among hundreds of men notorious for their daring.

Major J. Hastie returned from leave on the second of August, Lieutenants Maunsell, Corlett, and Kopke having rejoined the day previously. The strength of the Battalion was now twenty-seven officers, six hundred and seventy-eight other ranks. They were relieved this day by the Second Hampshire Regiment, and marched to La Kreule, arriving there at one

o'clock in the morning. At half-past nine next evening they moved on afoot to Lynde about fifteen miles
away, and reached there in good heart at half-past
two in the morning, to go into billets.

Sunday, the fourth of August, had a special significance, for was it not the fourth anniversary of the
declaration of war? Some few of the originals were
left in the ranks, and another two or three months
would see the fourth anniversary of their departure
from Australia. Most of them had been wounded,
some of them two, three and four times, and were still
tempting Providence. Appropriate allusion was made
to this fact during the church parade service.

Lieutenant-General Beavoir de Lisle, commanding
the XV Army Corps, on the occasion of the First
Division leaving this Corps, wrote to Major-General
Glasgow in eulogistic terms. The Division had joined
the XV Army Corps on the twelfth of April, and,
to quote from General Lisle's letter, "a few days
later repulsed two heavy attacks, with severe losses to
the enemy. This action brought the enemy's advance
to a standstill. Since then, the Division has held the
most important sector of the front continuously, and
by skilful raiding and minor operations, has advanced
the line over a mile on a front of five thousand yards,
capturing just short of a thousand prisoners, and causing such damage to the troops of the enemy that nine
divisions have been replaced."

No higher praise than this could be given, and the
fact that *nine* German divisions had been replaced
gauges the fighting power of the Australians in a
striking manner. General de Lisle further adds—
to the eternal confusion, let us hope, of detractors of
the Australia soldier's disciplinary qualities—"Their
high state of training and discipline have elicited the

admiration and envy of all.'' This, from an Imperial officer of such high standing, was praise indeed.

Monday, the fifth, was a "holiday" mostly spent in cleaning up, and next morning at five o'clock Lynde was left behind, and a route march to St. Omer commenced. Arrived there, the men entrained at half-past eleven for Longpré, and after nine hours' train journey, reached a point a short march from Bettencourt, where they finished their day's journeying, a half-hour after midnight.

After resting at Bettencourt some hours, the regiment marched to St. Ouen, and embussed for Fort Camon at half-past ten at night, reaching billets at Camon four hours later, after a half-hour's march from the debussing point. The nucleus of the Battalion remained here, while the majority left by foot at four p.m. for Aubigny, which was entered at eight o'clock in the evening, and found quite deserted by the inhabitants.

Aubigny had been badly wrecked by shelling, and only that morning had been subjected to a further dose.

Leaving Aubigny at 8.30 a.m. on August 9th, the Regiment marched towards Bayonvillers, through Fouilloy, Warfusée, Abancourt, La Motte-en-Sant, reaching their objective at 3.30 p.m. All the villages mentioned had been partially, if not wholly destroyed, and the roads were littered with dead horses and smashed transport. Many German prisoners and captured guns were passed, and armoured cars and tanks were plentiful.

Further along, they came to the old front line, with a few unburied dead lying around. Several disabled tanks were visible, the dead bodies of the crew lying alongside.

The German retreat from Bayonvillers had been a hurried one. Complete batteries of his artillery, arms, ammunition, and equipment, and the indescribable jettison of an army in flight, cumbered the ground.

At two o'clock in the afternoon, the Fifth moved forward in support of the Seventh Battalion to attack and capture the "Red Line," the Eighth Battalion being on the right with the Sixth in support. The Seventh were on the left, supported by the Fifth. This movement was part of the general advance of August eighth. Twenty-seven officers and five hundred and ninety-three other ranks comprised the strength of the Battalion prior to the attack. At half-past three in the afternoon they advanced, keeping Harbonnières on the left flank. A fairly heavy shelling from half-past four inflicted a few casualties during this operation. On reaching their allotted positions, it was found that the left flank of the Seventh Battalion was "in the air," otherwise unsupported, and "C" Company of the Fifth pushed forward to remedy this. The front line of the Seventh was very thin by this time, and "D" Company went forward and reinforced the Seventh Battalion centre positions, leaving their remaining two Companies in support

The fighting by this time was most intense. Well-placed machine gun posts, accurate sharpshooting, and heavy shelling proved the enemy well established and stubborn in defence. At a quarter to five in the afternoon, O.C. "Tanks" reported that all tanks were knocked out, and that there was strong opposition from machine guns in a wood. "C" Company reported at twenty minutes to nine in the evening that they were with "A" Company Seventh Battalion, but were not in touch on the left, and were consequently in the air. Lieutenants Morrison and Hansen were wounded, and there were about twenty other casualties. Machine-gun fire was holding them up and they were in need of ammunition and water. The German machine gunners through the whole of this fighting provided stubborn resistance, and in most cases died at their posts.

Little further progress was made before darkness fell. It had been a day full of strange new incidents. So quickly were the Germans retreating that the pursuing Australians were led by their officers mounted, a quite unique spectacle for France.

Passing far ahead of the objectives that had been fixed, the Fifth experienced but little shelling, and advanced in comparatively close order. Warfusee was passed, a smashed skeleton of roof-timbers and heaped stone, and already full of British guns. The cookers had kept valiantly up with the troops, and before the action had supplied bully beef and mashed potatoes.

The death-roll for the ninth contained the names of Lieutenant Maunsell and Second-Lieutenant Colvin, M.M., while six officers and sixty-two other ranks were wounded, among the former being Lieutenant N. S. Maddox, M.C. and bar, who had figured so remarkably in the daylight raids of some weeks before.

The advance began again the next day under much the same conditions. Isolated bodies of the Germans, whose retreat had been in some way delayed, provided little storm-centres till a rush with the bayonet terminated their resistance. British artillery fire entirely dominated the feeble German gunnery, which must have been conducted under difficult conditions. The casualty list showed twenty men killed in action, Lieutenant H. C. Morrison and one other missing

[Copyright by Australian War Museum.]

Men of the 1st Division Advancing near Harbonnières.

while two officers and seventy-eight other ranks were reported wounded. Lieutenant Morrison, popularly known as ''Rooster,'' was captured, and was the only Fifth officer so unfortunate throughout the whole of the Regiment's active service.

On the eleventh, the Eighth Battalion and a Company of the Seventh moved through the Fifth and successfully assaulted the German position, two companies of the Fifth relieving a like number of the Eighth in the afternoon. Lieutenant P. J. O'Farrell and thirty-six other ranks were killed in action, while twenty-one men were wounded, an unusually high percentage of deaths.

During the night, the Third Battalion relieved, and the Fifth moved back to Harbonnières, having lost exactly twenty-five per cent. of their number in the three days' fighting.

The morning saw them in divisional reserve, where in this comparatively peaceful area, three men were wounded.

Three days were spent here, during which time Lieutenant H. F. Morrison (a brother of the officer previously mentioned) and nine others previously reported ''wounded,'' were now reported ''died of wounds.''

Two battalions of the American 132nd Regiment relieved on the fifteenth, and the Fifth marched to Cerisy, where they arrived at nine o'clock in the evening, and were joined by the nucleus who had been left at Camon.

Cerisy presented the same mournful spectacle as the other villages in this area, and not one house remained intact under the heavy shelling and aerial bombing.

J

Captain E. C. Permezel and four other officers rejoined, the fighting strength of the regiment being increased to thirty-three officers, six hundred and one other ranks.

At this time approval had been given for men enlisted in 1914 to proceed on leave to Australia, and to this end, batches left all regiments of the A.I.F. during September, homeward bound.   By the irony of fate, some of these men who had been apprised of their inclusion in the leave list, were killed a few hours before their time came to leave the forward area, and at least one case occurred where a whole group of the men were wiped out by a shell bursting in the roadside dugout where they had sheltered for the moment.

Bray was chosen as the base for the purpose, and here, in September, about nine hundred men due for leave assembled and entrained for the long rail journey, about twenty-four of the number wearing Fifth colours.

Officers had carriages, men the usual trucks, but these latter were quite clean, and were provided with an abundance of blankets and straw, an average of about twenty-five men being allotted to each truck, and one truck being used as a kitchen. The long and picturesque journey on the first stage of their homeward flight, was keenly enjoyed by all.   Through Amiens, Lyons, the Rhone Valley to Cannes, where they stretched their legs for some hours and bathed in the sea; on through Nice, Monaco, Mentone, skirting Genoa, and turning northwards to Voghera—the whole panoramic beauty of the French and Italian Riviera was enjoyed by these war-worn men who sat dangling their legs in the open doorways of their travelling homes.

At Faienza they spent some hours.   An immense
military camp was the main feature, and the slouch
hat was not unknown.   A barelegged signorita ped-
dling gewgaws surprised a hard-bargaining Anzac
with a reproachful—''Cut it out, Dig! You don't-a
want me to *geev* you the thing, do you?''

Italy was full of interest, and the Aussies left a
trail of bully beef and sardines to gladden the hearts
of the children in every wayside town.   Every stopping place was full of incident, and it would be unfair
to place on record the name of the diarist who, copy-
ing meticulously the lavatory sign on a station, entered
''Passed through 'Donne Uomini' to-day.''

So, with its burden of light-hearted warriors the
train ran through scenery of an ever-changing gran-
deur, till on the eighth day the journey ended at the
seaport town of Taranto, the allied base for all the
theatres of war save the Western Front.   A day or
so here, and the men embarked and sailed next day for
Port Said.   Debarking here, they were taken by train
to Suez, where, after several days in camp, they embarked for Australia and Home.

News of the armistice reached one contingent of
Leave-men while they were in the Indian Ocean, and
was promptly disbelieved till incontrovertibly made
official.   Melbourne gave these Anzacs a royal welcome, and, distinguished by tri-color rosettes below
the colour patches, they carried rifle and web equipment for the last time through cheering crowds.

The usual guard arrangements among the returning leave men were more or less rigorously observed,
according to the character of the orderly officer and
the mood of the men.   As is the practice on troopers,
fresh water for washing purposes was only available

in the early morning, and then only for a brief period. To prevent unseemly jostling, a sentry with a rifle was placed on the hatchway near the wash-house, to preserve order and prevent men encroaching on the hatch.

The sentry on duty one morning, anxious to obtain the much desired fresh-water wash, propped his rifle against the hatchway and got in "before the mob." During his absence the over-zealous officer of the day approached, hid the rifle, and a few minutes later strolled back to complete the discomfiture of the careless guard. He was back at his post, quite unperturbed by the theft of his rifle. Drumming his heels idly against the hatch, he nonchalantly viewed the officer's arrival, smoking the while. "You the sentry?" snapped the officer. "That's me," replied the hero, removing his cigarette. "Where's your rifle?" "Dunno—some thieving —— pinched it." "Well, I'm the thieving ——," was the officer's retort. "What are your duties?" "Oh, to keep the men off the hatch." "Well, what would you do now if you saw a man sitting on it?" "Tell him to get off, a' course." What if he didn't move?" "Tell him again." "But what if he didn't move then?" persisted his questioner. "I'd let him —— well stop there." "But wouldn't you use your rifle if necessary?" "What's the use—I haven't got any ammunition." "But *he* doesn't know that," argued the officer. "What a pity he doesn't—he was on this game himself yesterday." Against such potent reasoning the officer found himself powerless, and left hurriedly to hide his grins.

Chapter XXVIII.

ST. MARTIN'S WOOD.

Proyart—St. Martin's Wood—Tincourt.

THE sixteenth and seventeenth were spent in resting and swimming, delightful weather making the rest a wholly enjoyable one. Next day a move was made to Hamelet, a march of two hours, where the men occupied tents and shelters. A tank demonstration near Hamel was witnessed on the following day.

The Battalion nucleus left on the twenty-first for Corbie, while three officers rejoined the unit Leaving Hamelet at eight o'clock in the evening, the remainder moved forward, and at half-past eleven relieved the Fifty-fifth Battalion in support trenches near Proyart where they found the Seventh Battalion on the right and the Fourth on the left.

Here was a huge British army dump which the Hun had captured and had now lost. Brigade dumps and Divisional dumps are impressively big, but an Army dump gathers round it rolling stock, machinery timber, material, mills and stores of every kind, from big guns to mess tin covers. It is always a long way behind the fighting zone, beyond the reach of the surging tide of war, so that the rapidity and unexpectedness of the German advance may be judged by the fact of their having captured this one.

A curious type of German gun (for the Huns had also lost some of their equipment, as they in turn retreated) was seen here for the first time by the Fifth. They could liken it to nothing better than a gigantic machine-gun, using bullets about an inch and a half in diameter, with brass cases, and evidently fired from a belt in a similar manner to the Vickers-Maxim in use by the British. It evoked much discussion for the time, and it was regarded as being closely related to the "pom-pom" of the South African war.

Unit commanders had reconnoitred the position ahead, against which a Brigade attack was to be launched next day, and had checked the maps and aerial photos. which had been issued at a Brigade conference prior to taking over. As was usual, the different objectives were designated by coloured lines, and the Second Brigade were allotted the "Blue line," the Fifth's share being the "Green line." The attack was timed for a quarter to five in the morning, and every man had been made thoroughly conversant with the terrain to be covered. The "hopping-off" place had been taped, and at two o'clock the Fifth moved forward to their assembly position, "B" Company (Captain Permezel) on the right, "C" Company (Captain Angell) on the left, "A" Company (Captain O'Sullivan) in right support, and "D" Company (Captain Burke, M.C.) left support. The Sixth Battalion were operating on the right of the Fifth, with the Seventh and Eighth in support.

The assembly was covered by patrols from the Fifty-fifth Battalion, and with only four casualties the men were on the mark an hour before time. Some minutes before the zero hour, the anxious watchers in the Australian ranks saw two red lights rise from the German position, and hang bejewelling the darkness.

"Jerry's heard our tanks moving," was the tense whisper that ran along the line, but the minutes passed without further action.

Punctually at zero, the British barrage opened in an inferno of thunder and flame on the German position, and the Battalion moved forward. At zero plus three minutes, the attack commenced, and owing to the tanks being late, companies moved forward without this expected support. Subsequently they came up and took part, but the victorious infantry had swept forward without serious check.

The position was a very difficult one for the whole Brigade, and the Fifth's sector of five or six hundred yards included St. Martin's Wood. Here was an unknown quantity, a dense cover which hid, they knew, many of the enemy, supported with machine-guns. The approach offered little or no cover in the grassy plain, and it was evident that there would be stern resistance encountered here, as obviously no support from the tanks could be expected.

Beyond the wood lay a deep gully, the distant side of which rose steeply to where the crest showed against the sky the bristling horror of barbed wire. Actually this had been the German forward line of many months ago, and the old rusted wire still remained. The enemy now seized the opportunity to strengthen this defence, which was the last strong point that lay between them and a retreat on the open, not-easily-defended country beyond.

Little enemy shelling was experienced, and Stokes mortars effectively dealt with the machine-gun nests that here and there momentarily held up the advance. When the attackers reached St. Martin's Wood, the two support companies were pushed forward to assist in mopping up and clearing the wood. The attackers found the resistance from the Wood, which they had expected, but they overwhelmed it by their sudden dash. This, or the declining morale of the

Huns, was responsible for moderate casualties among the Fifth, and a good bag of prisoners. A corporal found himself separated from his comrades, and ran into a nest of Germans. He admitted afterwards that when he saw a German officer and several men rise up from the undergrowth in front of him, he was so nonplussed that his first impulse was to run. He stood fast, and captured the whole twenty-five of them.

Advancing with irresistible dash through the trees, men disdained to take prisoners, and going right through, left the "supports" to do this part of the job.

Fresh German divisions had been placed on the ridge to stand the shock of the British attack, a most significant manœuvre in face of the demand on German man-power. This, and the contour of the ground. gave the enemy an advantage which proved futile in face of the Australian dash, and the gully was traversed, the height beyond stormed, and the Boche put to flight with the bayonet.

The Battalion took approximately four hundred and fifty prisoners during this action. The death roll showed Captain H. Burke, M.C., killed, Captain B. M. O'Sullivan, died of wounds, and twenty-one others killed in action. Five officers were wounded, with seventy-six other ranks, while there were five gassed and five missing—all this out of a strength of twenty-five officers and five hundred and three other ranks, a slightly lower percentage of casualties than had been suffered in their previous engagement.

The evacuation of the wounded was remarkably expeditious, all cases being completed within three hours from the opening of the attack. Both of the company commanders who were killed had been with the Battalion from the beginning, had risen from the ranks, and were exceedingly popular with their men.   Captain Harold Burke, M.C., an old Melbourne Grammarian, had survived all the fighting of the past years, and his death was very keenly felt both from a military and from a personal point of view. "Ginger" Burke had a fund of sparkling humour that had often cheered his men in the dismal days, and now they deeply mourned the loss of a brave man. He came of a fighting family that sent three sons and a daughter on service.

The tanks, though "late on parade," did excellent work in carrying up ammunition and supplies, but found their duties in other respects usurped by the efficient artillery barrage.   A report of these operations recommended that a section of infantry should closely support each tank to deal with the enemy who remain in the trenches.

Moving back to support on the twenty-sixth, they were again gassed, two officers and thirteen others being added to the casualty list.   That night the Thirty-first Battalion relieved, the operation being completed by five minutes from midnight, and the Battalion embussed for Hamel, and from there marched to Vaire Wood, where bivouacs were erected.   Here the nucleus joined up again.   Lieutenant S. V. Kirwood, M.C., M.M., who was momentarily expecting 1914 leave to Australia, accidentally wounded himself while sitting in a dugout examining a Hun revolver, and was evacuated.   Until the end of the month the regiment rested here, several officers going to training schools or leave.   The strength was now twenty-two officers, four hundred and seven other ranks.

In this action the Fifth had tasted the first fruits of victory in a real sense since their campaigning in

France and Flanders had begun.   The fighting of
August 8-11 had provided the first signs that the
Hun was faltering under the strain, but now they
felt that they were organised for victory.

Since the ninth they had experienced hard times,
had had little food, and had gone through almost continuous and exhausting fighting.   Still their spirit
was undaunted.

From the first to the seventh of September the Battalion rested.   The survivors were in good heart, for
they felt that they had the enemy on the run.   Reorganisation and training filled in the time.   Several
changes took place among the officers, with schools,
English leave, and "1914" leave to Australia.   A demonstration of model platoon work, and of an attack
on a strong point was given on the second, live ammunition and grenades being used for the edification
of the 1st Pioneer Battalion.

On the eight the Battalion embussed at 10 a.m. and
proceeded to the Peronne area near Hamel, marching
a short distance to a point near Mont St. Quentin and
occupying shelters.   Next afternoon a nucleus company proceeded by foot to the 1st Division Reinforcements Camp.

Next day saw the Fifth in the new front line, and
experiencing a quieter time, only having eight casualties.   A heavy gas shell bombardment on the following day proved disastrous.   Two men were killed
and fourteen wounded, while twenty-five were gassed
with the "mustard gas."   Among these latter was
the medical officer, Captain Flook, whose place was
taken by Captain O. J. Ellis.

Moving through Peronne, Flamicourt, Doingt,
Courcelles and Buire, on the morning of the 11th, the
Regiment reached a camping ground close to Tin-

court, where they remained four days. Their quarters were on the site of a burnt-out camp, and the men raking amongst the debris, found the remains of iron huts, which they soon adapted to their needs.

Here was a well-kept German cemetery, where, to do the Hun justice, he had tended the grave of German and Briton impartially. The neat mound was surmounted by a wooden cross, which recorded, "Here rests in God, Private T. Atkins, etc." Nearby was a French civilian cemetery where the Germans, by some strange perversion, had desecrated the dead. Opened graves and smashed coffins showed to what lengths he had gone in his quest for valuable metal.

The First Division A.I.F. took over the sector from the Third Division on the night of the 10th-11th, and the Second Brigade lay in reserve. On the fourteenth Major H. Carter and Lieutenant J. A. Hall proceeded on "1914" leave to Australia with the first batch of men to leave the Fifth. Five N.C.O.'s received commissions, and the strength of the Battalion was given as thirteen officers three hundred and seventy other ranks.

Chapter XXIX.

TRENCH SLANG AND HUMOUR.

AS happens in civil life, bywords and phrases were evolved from daily incident, enjoyed a universal currency, and then, in most cases, died lingeringly, or were supplanted by the newly-coined rival, and so became almost if not entirely forgotten. Some of those that were immortalised in the language of billet and trench were of Egyptian origin, but the majority, as was natural, claimed France as their birth place.

"We've got a nice night for it," survived from the days of Mena, and still solaced the troops under the most frightful circumstances. "His father saw him," was an apparently meaningless phrase that one of the chaplains had fathered on the desert sands. During a sermon, of which the theme was the prodigal son, the padre reiterated the phrase so monotonously that it became a shibboleth with the regiment. Sitting round a brazier in France, enveloped in mud and misery, and steeped in the profoundest melancholy, someone would recite in a deep voice, "And his father saw him!; Not his mother,—not his sister,—not his brother,—but his father! Not the sergeant-major,—not the colonel's batman—" and so on.

"Gutzer," was a descriptive term—not peculiar to the war, of course, but a joyous all-explaining word that aptly fitted the consequence of an unwary step on slippery duckboard or greasy mud, or, more broadly described disappointment in general. "The troops have come a 'gutzer' " intimated cancelled leave, lost rum issue, front line orders and like calamities.

They form a strange, long list, these now forgotten catchwords. "Buckshee stew" was the unused portion of a dixie of stew—something wholly imaginary, "The unexpired portion of the day's ration to be well oiled and returned to store;" "medicine and duty," and "this practice must be discontinued forthwith," are fairly obvious plays on military official language.

A well-known officer of the Fifth was responsible for the creation of a catch-phrase, during the progress of a reconnaissance patrol. Unexcitable and stolid, he led the party out in No Man's Land one dark night, and as they carefully cat-footed towards the enemy line, he stopped and in a penetrating stage whisper said, "Hist! I hear a Hun!" Despite the seriousness of their position, the patrol burst out laughing, and their noise made it necessary for them to return to their own lines. The whole regiment received the new contribution with gusto, and it was long ere it ceased to be a mess joke.

Several strange "chants" were also in vogue, not only in the Fifth, but throughout the whole A.I.F. one of the best known being "The Old Squire." Usually begun in billets or camp when "lights out" had gone, and men were on the second turn to sleep, a deep sepulchral voice from the darkness would aver—"The old squire has been foully murdered," to which a chorus of willing voices made answer a long-drawn-out "Shame." "Yes, and they blame me, his innocent son Jack, for the crime," pursued the interlocutor. A double cry of "Shame!" from the chorus. "But never mind, it is my daughter's wedding day, and a thousand pounds I'll give away!"

"Hooray-Hooray" from the chorus, now full-voiced.
The chanter now wavered in his generosity:—
        "On second thoughts I think it best
        To hide the money in the old oak chest."
    A deep, slow groaning answer from the audience:—
"You lousy old ———"

With slight variations this was enduringly popular
throughout the whole of the A.I.F., and no respectable concert party ever thought of omitting some reference to "The Old Squire."

Every Regiment, whether volunteer or regular, has
its peculiar characters, as indeed every community
has. It would be ridiculous to suppose that every man
in the A.I.F. was true to the type that war correspon-
dents and newspaper men have created. The long,
lean and brown Colonial, with the easy confidence of
look and manner, wonderful daring in battle, and
most astounding intelligence, was not always evident
on a battalion parade. Perhaps this was because the
infantry of the A.I.F., having the most difficult and
dangerous work to perform, received as reinforcement
all the "culls." The man who just squeezed through
the medical barrier at enlistment (and some of them
seemed to have found no one on the gate, so to speak),
and who suffered from hernia, flatfootedness, or
general lack of intelligence, always reached the infantry.

Any other arm of the service demands, perhaps,
some little greater individual efficiency, but that
there should be no method of apportioning physique
in accordance with the physical effort required, was
one of the peculiar anomalies (and there were many
others), characterising the system of recruiting in
Australia.

Hence it was that the weedy, ill-developed man, who had found a kind-hearted or careless medico on duty at the recruiting office, and who had by some wonderful sequence of luck, eventually reached the front line, staggered into action loaded to the back teeth with arms and equipment. He contrasted strangely with the well-set-up, brawny youth who drove a supply waggon, or thrust eighteen-pounder shells into the breech of his gun, neither of these latter worthies carrying anything much heavier than their identification disc while there was a conveyance handy.

All this to explain why certain men were inexhaustible sources of humor in every infantry regiment, owing to their slightly sub-normal intelligence. One such was an excellent butt for the humor of his comrades in the Fifth, in the early Broadmeadows days. After an earnest conversation with some of his tent-mates, he approached the Quartermaster, saluted very properly, and asked for "the paint for 'H' Company, sir!" The worthy Q.M., always impressive to the recruit, became positively ogreish as he bawled, "What paint do you mean, sir!" "To paint the 'First' and 'Last Posts,' sir," was the innocent one's rejoinder. He barely escaped with "the Clink" for this "impudence," but later goaded the Q.M. to another outburst when he arrived at the store—"to be measured for my sentry box, sir!"

Another simple soul was the man who, while on the *Orvieto*, had his fair hair cropped to the scalp, this being fashionable at the time. The comfort of the "convict crop" was very gratifying, but he became alarmed at the suggestion of his comrades that it might not grow to its former luxuriance, unless something was applied to it. He took the bait, and a little

later, was supplied with a plain tin containing a red
paste, which, he was assured, would promote hair
growth if rubbed well into the scalp. Slightly suspicious of the color, he was at length persuaded that
it easily washed off, and used it lavishly. It was
many days before the unfortunate man wholly removed the ox-blood shoe polish which had been supplied him, and much longer ere he lived down the
joke.

But this perhaps gives the reader the impression
that there are many of these simple ones in the Fifth.
Let us hasten his disillusion by recounting some anecdotes of the opposite type. Among an army noted for
the keenness of the gambling instinct, as were the
Australians, it follows that in each Regiment there
were some men who were unusually prominent in this
regard. The Fifth was no exception, for they had,
in the person of one whom we will call Billy East, a
shrewd and inveterate gambler. Let it be clearly
understood that he did not venture *his* money, but
rather did he act as the proprietor of various games
of chance, whereby he amassed considerable fortune.
In the Army, all gambling is prohibited, with the
exception of a game called ''House,'' which is played
with numbered cards and counters. It is the mildest
of gambles, and, except to pass away the monotony
of troopship life, is mostly ignored by the Australian.

Two-up, as a national institution, could never be
eclipsed, but ''crown-and-anchor'' was always a
serious rival. In Egypt, crown-and-anchor was paramount, and around the back of the ''wet'' canteens,
the sand was dotted with interested groups, who put
their money on the painted canvas by the light of
guttering candles. Six symbols were on the canvas.
Crown, anchor, spade, heart, diamond and club made

[Copyright by Australian War Museum.]

5th Division Men Examining German "Pom-Pom" Gun Captured by the 5th Battalion at Proyart.

the total, and three dice, with these symbols repeated on their sides, completed the mechanism of the game. The dice were covered with a cup and rattled furiously, while the proprietor invited all and sundry to play. Certain shibboleths seemed to be universal, and a raucous voice everywhere persuaded customers to—"Come on, me lucky lads! The more you put down, the more you pick up."—"You come here in rags and go away in motor cars."—"What about something on the ole Sargint-Major." (This an obvious allusion to the "crown," that N.C.O.'s badge of rank.)—"What's the ole diamond done?" and the like.

Overhead the purple bowl of night was pierced by the myriad diamond points of stars; the endless leagues of desert sand stretched behind, and silhouetted against the light, was to be seen an interested knot of men bending over the board placed between the gambler's knees. The rattle of the dice, the hoarse cry of the dicer, and the chink of money; all these are fragments of a nightly scene.

At odd times the schools were raided by the picquet. Then ensued a wild scene of confusion as Authority appeared round the corner of the canteen, sometimes without the warning that was always expected. A scattering crowd of onlookers, a dozen hands grabbing at the coins on the gambling boards, sudden extinction of the candles, and a quick disappearance of the implements—all this occurred within a few seconds. Very rarely was there any tangible evidence of misdoing, and immediately after the picquet had vanished, agitated groups might be observed, dredging the sand with their fingers for the spilt money.

Billy East was a battalion pioneer. Mostly the old

soldier sought after this job, as providing less work and more spare time than did the usual training of the foot-soldier. Various matters connected with the sanitation of the Battalion lines occupied the pioneers' time, so they rarely accompanied the Regiment on its daily work, and consequently were more leisured.

East, in the opinion of the men, never did any other work than was necessary to run his ''crown and anchor'' board, and he was never without this. Nor was he ever known to refuse the invitation to begin the game, but, selecting a suitable spot, would spread the canvas, and, rattling the dice, begin the stereotyped cry peculiar to the occasion.

As a South African veteran, East was properly contemptuous of these ''new-chum'' soldiers he was amongst, though unkind rumor had it that in this former campaign, he had been guiltless of firing a shot. East's scathing remarks as to how the recruits would behave when they got under fire were many and frequent, and he always opposed prideful comments on the day's work by crude sarcasm. The ''new-chums'' were silenced, but the sting remained until it was assuaged by happenings in the first few days of action.

Then it was that the boaster was silent—with fear, and it became the turn of the younger soldiers to jeer at the seasoned veteran. He comported himself on the day of the landing in such a manner that they were glad to leave him in a gully in charge of some packs which had been dropped as the men went over the ridge beyond, and here East dug in.

Snugly hidden in the side of the hill, his dug-out barricaded with the packs, East spent the first few precarious days in a welter of fear. His only means

of knowing how the battle went was to ask men coming down from the front line wounded, or on fatigue
work. Even strangers guessed his fears, and added
to them by highly imaginative tales of how the day
went against the Australians. A dozen times did
East gird himself together to start hot-footed for the
beach, when these black reports were shouted from
the path below, but as often he delayed the movement
that might bring him into the hands of the beach
police, who would doubtless escort him to the dreaded
front line.

So in his dug-out he remained for the eight or nine
days the Regiment was in the line. When they mustered on Shell Green for the first roll-call after the
Landing, the sadly-thinned Companies gave a great
shout of contempt as Billy East appeared from the
gully below. No whit abashed by the fierce comment
that played about his hoary head, he sought his position in the ranks, and not much later, produced his
crown and anchor board for the amusement of those
who deigned to acknowledge his existence.

His very impudence assured the breakdown of the
ostracism that surrounded him for a little while, and
while the Battalion waited in general reserve at Cape
Helles, before the fateful advance, East was seen, the
centre of a small group, endeavouring to win a few
shillings before the men should go forward, and perhaps lose everything.

It is a relief to turn from the contemplation of this
shrewd rascal to more humorous characters. One
other of the Pioneers deserves mention. As has been
noted, it was very seldom that they went on parade, so
when this infrequently did occur, they were considerably fluttered. On one such occasion, when they
had been instructed to get into full marching order,

the Pioneer's hut was the scene of turmoil and strife. Their long-disused equipment was in a hopeless tangle and partly buried in the sand of the floor. Bayonets stuck in the walls served as candlesticks, rifles were choked with sand, and various parts of their web equipment littered the untidy quarters.

At length, some semblance of military order was obtained in each man's kit. Rifles were cleaned, to such an extent at least, that the bolts could be moved. Bayonets were swapped until they found the rifle they properly belonged to, and the Pioneers were on their way to be ready for parade. Now came the problem of packing the various articles, including the greatcoat, into the pack. Properly folded, the greatcoat slips neatly into the pack and leaves the latter, when filled, with an unwrinkled, flat surface.

Very few soldiers ever mastered the art, and it took much squeezing and squashing after the pack was filled before the average platoon was at all presentable. Imagine then the plight of the Pioneers, untrained in this particular branch of soldiering. In an atmosphere of profanity, they rolled their clothing into shapeless bundles and rammed them into the packs, whose sides yielded in ungraceful contours to this rough handling.

On parade at last, the Cooks and Pioneers presented an appearance calculated to drive a Sergeant raving mad. He had started on the third cycle of cursing when the Quarter-Master appeared to look over his details before they joined the Battalion parade. In a more gentlemanly, but none the less effective, fashion, he proceeded to inform them of their many deficiences, irritated beyond measure by the sight of the packs of varying size and shape. In the midst of his tirade, his eye was pleasantly assailed by a pack of such wondrous symmetry and neatness that he stopped, and ordered the fortunate possessor to the front.   Undoubtedly it was perfect.   Unwrinkled and square-cornered, it was aggressively perfect, contrasted with the others, whose sides bulged out as if they were packed with boulders.

The Q.M. turned the paragon round so that the pack faced the untidy ones.   "Now that's what I call a pack!" he thundered at them.   "There you are!   Greatcoat folded neatly; everything in its place; everything neat and soldierly!"   To emphasise his remarks, he struck the pack approvingly with the flat of his hand.   Alas for enterprise!   From the corners of the pack, at the impact of the blow, came little jets of chaff with which the wily Pioneer had filled it!

Speaking of Pioneers brings the conversation naturally to Cooks or "Babblers."   (Cooks—Babbling Brooks—Babblers).   One such worthy, who for many months presided over the dixies of a company of the Fifth was a universal favorite.

Let us call him "Joe."   The advantages of education withheld from him in his youth, Joe endeavoured to improve his conversation by attention to the speech of those, scholastically, more favoured.   Unfortunately, his memory proved a poor assistant, and it was responsible for Joe's strange excursions into philology. Joe is popularly credited with having described an evening walk with a French girl as being—"a promenade with a nice little 'bint' up that there revenue of popular trees."   Acting for the sergeant cook one day, he gave the mess orderlies their order to advance on the tea dixies in a stentorian voice—"On your respectable dixies—Quick March!"   This movement executed, he was asked by one whether he was to take this particular dixie or no, whereupon Joe waved a lordly hand and said, "It's imperial to me which one you take, my boy!"

Later, when the troops were in the front line, cooking was performed under greater difficulties, which were explained by Joe to the Major as being due to "the congestion from the big guns knocking the debreese into my cooking reptacles." It was good old Joe who translated an order prohibiting men from loitering in the vicinity of the cooks' lines. "Hey, youse blokes!" he called out to some trespassers, "Didn't yer hear the orders?" "What orders were those, Joe?" queried one of the offenders. "Why, yer not allowed to hang round in the virginity of the Cooks' lines," explained Joe. And wasn't it Joe, who explained to an enquirer that the Q.M. was not in his tent, but had "gone down to Audience"? This, Joe's method of indicating the Ordnance Stores.

It was at Suez that the whole Battalion witnessed a highly humorous incident. A water barge, escorted by a fussy tug, had been brought over to the *Orvieto*, to replenish the fresh water supply of the trooper. The tug edged the deeply-laden barge near to the side of the huge steamer, a cable was made fast, and then a large squad of "Gyppos" laid hold and began to haul in.

The operations were watched by a large and interested crowd of the Fifth on the decks above. Amid tremendous jabbering, the native gang gradually hauled the barge nearer the sides of the *Orvieto*, with the minimum of personal effort, despite the yelling of the foreman in charge to put their backs into it. At length, after much clamorous and unmusical yodelling, the job was almost completed, and the energy for the last pull was about to be applied to the rope, when, in view of the gang, who had never taken their eyes from the decks above, a penny clattered down on the water-barge.

The effect was electrical. Every hauler dropped the rope and dived for the coin. The quickest there was buried in a mass of struggling grabbers and in the excitement, two were pushed overboard. Meanwhile the rope slackened and the barge drifted away. By dint of superhuman muscular and vocal energy, the foreman at last got the gang back on to the rope, and proceeded to recover the lost momentum.

Again the barge was slowly hauled to the steamer's sides, the natives' eyes rolling wildly upward in readiness for other coins, if they came. They did. Just as the last pull was reached, more coins came chinking down from above, producing exactly the same result. By this time, the captain of the tug, the native foreman, and the officer on duty on the *Orvieto,* were in a fine frenzy, but before the job could be completed, all the troops had to be cleared from the decks, and the barge was then, and only then, made fast without further incident.

Chapter XXX.

ROISEL—THE ARMISTICE.

*Roisel—Tincourt—Ailly-le-haut Clocher—Bazuel—
The Armistice—Marching Towards Germany.*

THE Second Brigade relieved the First Brigade in the line near Roisel on the night of September 14th-15th, the Fifth Battalion relieving the Third Battalion in the support left position. Captain E. de T. Permezel commanded temporarily, and the operation was completed by ten o'clock in the evening. The neighbouring village was being constantly shelled by the Hun, but the Fifth suffered no casualties.

On the 15th, a Sunday, heavy aerial bombing from the Huns was experienced in this sector, but the men had the satisfaction of seeing three enemy 'planes shot down in the evening. For the whole time the Fifth were here, they suffered the attention of the night bombers, but without loss of any of the Regiment.

Here the Fifth remained in support for some days. Lieutenant-Colonel Luxton returned from leave, and resumed command, while three officers returned and joined the nucleus.

On the eighteenth, at five o'clock in the morning, the First and Third Brigade attacked, the Second remaining in reserve, with the Fifth and Sixth Battalions prepared to move as soon as the attack was launched. All objectives being gained, the Second Brigade had no occasion to move. Five tanks operated on the Divisional sector. A gas shell was responsible for Captain F. Angel being evacuated to hospital. Until the twenty-first, when the Battalion moved into the front line, the casualties in reserve had been eleven wounded, four of these being gassed, leaving the strength at twenty-one officers three hundred and ninety-eight others.

During the night of the 21st-22nd, the Second Brigade relieved the First Brigade in the Divisional left sub-sector, the Fifth relieving part of the First and Third Battalions by eleven o'clock in the evening. This was in the vicinity of Harlicourt. The nucleus rejoined, and a new nucleus of "1914" men was formed. Lieut.-Colonel Luxton handed over the command of the Battalion to Major T. Hastie, M.C., and proceeded on leave to Australia with the second batch of "1914" leave men, twenty-four other ranks also completing the party.

There were now many American troops arriving in this area, and on the night of 23rd-24th, the Fifth were relieved by three platoons of No. 1 Batt. 59th American Brigade, and moved back to their old place in the Tincourt area, having suffered the loss of one killed and five wounded whilst in the line.

The difference in the strength of the two Battalions is well illustrated by this, and the Americans found that there was little room in the trenches when they had occupied them. They subsequently were shelled by the enemy here and sustained heavy casualties.

As the Fifth were marching through Roisel en route to the billeting area at half-past one on the morning of the twenty-fourth, a long range shell landed in the roadway among the column with disastrous effect. Headquarters of "B" Company and No. 13 Platoon "D" Company suffered mostly, fourteen men being killed, and another two subsequently dying of their wounds. Second-Lieutenant Felton and fourteen others were wounded. Two officers and

four N.C.O.'s left on the twenty-fourth to take up
duty with the 30th American Division, while the Battalion, together with the remainder of the Brigade,
rested until the afternoon of the twenty-sixth.   At
half-past four in the afternoon the Fifth entrained at
Tincourt, and travelling all night detrained at Longpré les Corps Saints at half-past four the next morning. From this detraining point they were to proceed to a small village near Abbeville, named Ailly
le Haut Clocher, a combination of names which proved
too much for the average digger.

Ailly, "etc.," was reached in time for an early
breakfast after a route march of two hours, and the
men enjoyed a loaf for the remainder of the day.

News was now received that Lieutenant G. L.
Makin, an original member of the Fifth, had died of
wounds.   Previously he had been listed as wounded.
He had risen from the ranks, and had done sterling
work through all the recent fighting.

Next day, Company Commanders inspected and reorganised their commands. Ten per cent. leave was
granted the men to visit Abbeville, a fairly large town
on the Somme. On Sunday, the twenty-ninth, a Brigade Church Parade was addressed by Bishop Long,
who was in France on the A.I.F. Educational Scheme
work.   Next day the Battalion paraded at nine
o'clock in the morning and marched to a concert hall
where the Bishop explained the working of the excellent proposal, whereby the authorities purposed to
begin the educational repatriation of the Australians
while yet the war was in progress.

The Battalion was destined to remain at Ailly le
Haut Clocher for some weeks, during which time they
underwent a rigorous course of training in every
branch of infantry work. Musketry, bayonet fight-

ing, Lewis and German machine-gun practice, bombing—all these, with the necessary leavening of sport and recreational training, filled in the days until the eighth of November.

Billets were comfortable, and the men rapidly regained the physical perfection which had been sapped by the experiences of the preceding weeks.   More "1914 men" left for Australian leave, and many decorations were awarded to officers and men.   Five M.C.'s, eight D.C.M.'s, and seventeen M.M.'s made an honourable total for the Fifth. On October fourteenth Major J. C. M. Traill, D.S.O., M.C., was promoted Lieutenant-Colonel, and came over from the Eighth Battalion to assume command of the Fifth, *vice* Lieutenant-Colonel Luxton, C.M.G., D.S.O., on leave to Australia.

During this time a gas inspection by the Divisional Gas Officer tested the efficacy of the anti-gas appliances, while the N.C.O.'s absorbed military legal technique from the Divisional Courts Martial Officer.

The first of November was marked by the Fifth winning a football match from a neighbouring regiment, and by the receipt of a message from Brigade H.Q.:—"The Brigade will probably move to the forward area on the 5th or 6th inst." This was not surprising to the men, as they had known only too well what their strenuous training of the last few weeks had portended. Their morale was excellent, and the officers rightly felt that they were leading men who could repeat—even if they could never excel—their fighting feats of the past. They were, indeed, in the mass anxious to attack again, feeling that they were the superiors of the Boche in every way.

Next day a muster parade was held, and simultaneously the woods and billets throughout the corps were combed out for absentees.

Sunday, the third, brought three events of note. Church Parade was held in the morning, and in the afternoon the Fifth's football team asserted their superiority over the Third Army Brigade, Australian Field Artillery, the battle ground being in the neighbouring village of Bussus. Thirdly, came another message from Brigade H.Q.:—"Batt. will hold itself in readiness to move to forward area at 12 hours' notice."

On the fourth a Divisional R.C. Parade was held at Longpré, at which the Bishop of Amiens officiated.

Later, Brigade issued another communiqué:—"It is believed the move has been cancelled 24 hours."

Wet and stormy weather next day prevented training, but did not prevent Brigade from speaking again. The lectures and specialist training proceeding in the billets were interrupted sufficiently long to enable all ranks to be informed that "The Battalion will entrain at 7.16 a.m. on the 7th inst."

The sixth dawned stormily, and all outdoor parades were cancelled. Midday brought further news from Brigade H.Q.:—"Battalion will stand fast until instructed," but at 2 p.m., it was added that "arrangements have been postponed 24 hours."

"D" Company left the Battalion next day and marched to Longpré to act as entraining company for the Brigade, who had issued the order that "entraining hour is 12.16 p.m. on 8th inst." The doubters jeered at this, fully expecting that by the army's familiar method, several more changes of plans would be made. They grumbled mightily when reveille at a quarter to six aroused them on the morning of the eighth, and were almost silenced when the regiment moved at eight o'clock and began the two hours' march to Longpré.

A quarter hour sufficed for the Fifth's entraining process, and they kicked their heels in the trucks until they moved at ten minutes past twelve en route for the front line and renewed fighting. They were fit and well, as has been already said, and they sang as the train moved off.

The long journey ended next morning at half-past six, and the men stretched their cramped limbs in Roisel once again. Breakfast done, they began the next stage in motor 'buses at half-past eleven, and bumped their way along until Bazuel was reached at half-past three. The convoy of 'buses was a remarkable one, seventy-six being allotted to the Fifth and Sixth Battalions. A prodigious number of Head Quarters details, Veterinary Section, Trench Mortar Battery, Machine Gun Company and incidentals occupied a corresponding space. Rations for forty-eight hours filled four 'buses. The Battalion transport proceeded along the same route, but "under their own power."

Reveille for next day was generously delayed until ten o'clock, and the men rested. A voluntary Church Parade in the evening attracted a goodly number, impressed to seriousness by the danger they expected again to face in a few more hours.

Monday, the eleventh of November, 1918, brought a fateful message from Brigade at a quarter past eight in the morning. It read, in the terse army style: "Hostilities will cease at 11.00 today a.a.a. No alterations will be made in our arrangements a.a.a. V.E." It might be reasonably supposed that a riotous enthusiasm and rejoicing would mark the receipt of news that meant the war had ended. In March, 1915, the Regiment—and the same Regiment in soul, though only a sprinkling of its original personnel re-

mained—had received from the lips of their beloved
colonel the news that they were to leave for the
Front.   Astonished natives at the foot of the Pyramids heard the mighty shout of exultation that rose.
Men gripped their comrades by the hand and looked
their sober joy, or more mercurial, flung hats and
dignity to the the wind and danced insanely on the
sand.

And now?   The note for the day's movements
reads:—"Message received quietly."   It may be
assumed that the men were not on the whole disposed
to accept the message as being quite final.   You who
have read the preceding messages from the same
source as this one, can perhaps understand their feeling.   Then they had in mind the duplicity of the
Boche, and were inclined to discredit it for that reason alone.   And, lastly, you are to believe that there
was some disappointment. Remember that these men
had tasted of victory, had felt that physically, mentally and morally they were better—individually and
collectively—than the Hun.   Remember, too, that
they had been schooled and trained, rested and reorganised, until their very fitness of mind and body
urged them on to follow up the blows they had dealt
their enemy in these last stages of the German retreat.   Therefore there was no enthusiasm; only the
feeling that they were weary of war for war's sake,
but that soon the Regiment they had helped to make
would dissolve and never cohere again.   All the fine
comradeship and the sacrifice—and the jollity—that
made the Regiment what it was, would be dispersed
soon—for ever.   It was a sad thought for the men
who had endured till now; who had looked Death in
his grisly face, and had hid their fear beneath the
grim joke or grimmer profanity.

So they thought as they marched along the cobbled road to Sambreton at ten o'clock, the doubters uttering their opinion that they were still due for fighting. "Yes, yer silly cow, there's half an hour to go!" rejoined a voice from the rear. Sambreton was reached at a quarter to one, after a cold, rough march.

Brigade orders issued in the evening instructed the Brigade not to move next day. It was a quiet, cold evening; the ground was snow-covered, and what little food there was, was unappetising. The Brigade rested next day, a warning order apprising them that they would move to the Catillon and Ste. Souplet area next day, preparatory to moving on the fourteenth to the Bohain area.

Nine o'clock on the morning of the thirteenth saw the Battalion beginning their marching anew, three hours of it bringing them to now familiar Bazuel. The weather was clear and sunny, and the men's spirits rose with the thermometer, so that the sound of their voices raised in singing was heard along the country road.

The march next morning, from Bazuel to Bohain, though it lasted more than twelve miles, found them still cheerful. An atrocious cobbled road for most of the distance made slow time and hard work, but no one fell out, and comfortable billets at the journey's end made their very tiredness enjoyable.

The weather was still fine and frosty for the next two days, and the overhauling of clothing and boots and the issue of pay was all that troubled the men.

On Sunday, the seventeenth, Brigade Church Parade was held, at which Captain-Chaplain Petherick, the Fifth padre, gave a thanksgiving for

the cessation of hostilities.   The Brigade massed
bands played the *Marseillaise;* it was only the second
time that the Fifth had played this tune.   The first
time was in compliment to the French warships at
Port Said, before the regiment was blooded.

A slight fall of snow next day made the exercise
of a route march welcome, and on the Tuesday a
bathing parade at Meteren Baths was only rendered
bearable by the fact that the water was heated.   Medical inspection for fitness then followed, in view of
the march into German territory, which was proposed.

Two football matches were played in the afternoon,
the Fifth defeating the Fourteenth Battalion by seven
points, under Australian rules, but suffering defeat
in a soccer game against the Third M.G. Company.
The football team was in fine fettle, and two days
later defeated the Sixth Battalion.

Then followed a period during which, as regard
the finer and more spectacular points of drill, the
Fifth were never more proficient.   On the twenty-
second, Bohain was left behind at seven o'clock in the
morning, and *via* Vaux Andiant, Ste. Martin's, the
Battalion reached Mazinghien at a quarter-past
eleven.   Fine and frosty weather made this and the
next day's march *via* Cotillon and La Groise to
Prisches most enjoyable.   Eight o'clock on the
twenty-fourth saw the Regiment on the road again,
and at twenty minutes past eleven they arrived at
Avesnes, the furthest point—reckoning   Germany
as the objective—that they had reached.   The roads
here had been blown up by the retreating Hun, and
the constant stream of motor transport waggons that
were taking food up to the semi-starved population,
almost bumped to death the hapless refugees they

were bringing back to happier times—and peace. Although the roads and railways had been destroyed, the infrequency of actual fighting had left the countryside comparatively unharmed.

The Regiment found comfortable billets in Avesnes, where lately the Germans had lorded it over the conquered people.   The poorly-fed inhabitants were rich with anecdotes of the German High Command and their satellites.   Hindenburg, they averred, was less hated by them than was the average Hun officer. He proved to be affable and kindly, if not officially, at least personally, and would stop to talk to a little child.   On the other hand, Ludendorff displayed all the arrogance and hateful qualities of manner that gave the German his well-deserved epithet of "Boche."

Avesnes was left at twenty minutes to eleven next morning, and a five hours' march commenced through Avesnelles and Flaumont Felleries to Sars Potteries, where the Battalion found quarters in a large factory. Here there was a tremendous German dump, with its attendant railways, rolling stock and machinery. Millions of shells, bombs and fuses were stacked, and loaded trains lay in the siding just as the fleeing Hun had left them.

The men rested on the day after their arrival, and while they were having their boots repaired and their ragged uniforms patched, the Battalion resolved itself into a number of fatigue parties who were set to work to clear up the town and destroy bombs and other explosives.   It is a remarkable fact, considering the carelessness of the individual soldiers, that no casualties occurred during their dangerous task.   An incident related by one of the company commanders well illustrates the men's indifference to

the violent death they handled so nonchalantly.
Searching for some of his men, he found them snugly
ensconced in a railway truck from which they had
dislodged shells to make the necessary room, and he
was deeply concerned to discover that the "steps"
leading to the doorway from the ground were composed of "106" German fuses.   These "106" fuses
were the remarkably effective ones that occupied the
business end of the German shells knows as "Daisy
Cutters." So delicately adjusted were they, that on the
shell hitting the ground, the explosion took place in
such a fractional part of a second that the burst was
distributed laterally along the surface of the ground,
without expending any of its force in excavation.
Remarkably deadly when used against troops in open
ground, they had the curious effect of leaving the
ground practically undamaged, so that there were
no shell-holes left for the men to shelter in.

Impromptu and unofficial firework displays amused
the troops at night, and the firing of bombs and
coloured lights showed that the men had conserved
for their peaceful amusements some of the materials
of war they should have destroyed in the regulation
manner.   Several barns were accidentally or otherwise fired, and added to the many coloured glares
around the village when evening fell.

Next day, the Eighth Battalion inflicted a football
defeat on the Fifth, the first that had befallen the
Regiment in this part for some time.

The C.O.'s report for the past month mentioned
the health of the troops as being excellent. Despite
their having been billeted among civilians whilst the
influenza scourge was at its height, only five cases
had been evacuated. The number of men suffering
from sore feet, after all the heavy marching, was

practically nil. Fresh vegetables were scarce, owing
to the lack of motor transport, but the Comforts Fund
had atoned for this by its generous distribution of
foodstuffs, tobacco and cigarettes.

It would be pleasant to record the final parade of
the Fifth as a Regiment, just as has been described
their first parade in Victoria Barracks Square, in
August, 1914. One could imagine the formal assembly
of the Battalion on some historic battlefield of France
where so many of their gallant dead, too, would be
present, or perhaps in the same Australian barrack
square, where the Regiment first came together; with
the disabled ones—repatriated long before—swelling
the ranks for the last time. For the last time to hear
the company sergeant-major's "Steady! Eyes—
Front!" and then the tense silence as the Battalion
"clicked up" to be handed over to their commanding
officer. To hear some few words of passionate farewell to the Regiment that had seen and suffered and
achieved so much; that had forged a soul for itself
from the raw material of untrained men; that had
made history and written large its historic deeds on
the sacred fields of France, the barren hills of Gallipoli; and then to hear the sharp, clear order—"Battalion—dismiss!", and the scrape and click of heels
as the men turned to the right to halt a second—and
then disperse—for ever!

Never again to meet in its entirety. Its survivors
busy at bench and counter and desk; in the lonely
islands of the North; ploughing the flat Mallee lands,
or clearing the Gippsland timbers: scattered broadcast in their peaceful pursuits, with the memory of
dark days of misery, and suffering, and danger dim-
ming with every year of home, but with ever a keen

recollection of the jest and gaiety of some long-dead comrade.

It would be a pleasant thing to write of this formal dismissal of a Regiment, but it was not so. Instead, the Regiment disappeared gradually under the slow process of attrition, as men were repatriated from France, according to length of service. No date can be recorded on which the Regiment ceased to exist. When the number became too small to form a Battalion, the Fifth and Sixth Battalions amalgamated, as later did the Seventh and Eighth. When still more men had left for Australia, the remainder of the Fifth were only sufficient to make one Company of a Battalion, the other Companies being formed by three Battalions of the Second Brigade.

At length only a skeleton for administration was left, and about March, 1919, these few officers and men left Charleroi for Australia. Some few of the men still remained to help with the work of the Graves Commission, but the Regiment, as a Regiment, dribbled away in unromantic fashion, and never the commemoration parades in the after days will gather it together again.

No tattered flags hang in misty cathedrals, honoured standards of its glorious memory. Perhaps in some little country town square, in some grassy suburban park, will be seen the field gun or trench mortar captured by the Regiment. In quiet fields in France and Flanders, the peasant swerves his plough to skirt the little group of white-crossed mounds that juts into his holding. Under the wild olive the Turkish goatherd looks across the gully, dotted with the scattered graves of the invaders, to the blue Asian shore. There are the Regiment's only tangible honours.

To have known the fear of sudden death, or the keener horror of fearful, lingering agony; to have thirsted and hungered; to have known pain, and sickness, and uncleanness; and the loss of the comrade who had laughed and cursed and shared all with you; to posses the quiet knowledge of duty well done—is to have sounded the deepest wells of misery and gained the laurelled heights of happiness. The men of the years here recorded have known all this; but we are apt to forget in the soft days of Peace. Even the pain, the fear, and excitement will be erased with the passing years. But above the recalling of this, if the memory of the deathless dead who lie in alien fields is kept green in their comrades' hearts, then this book has justified the writing of it.

THE RETURN.

Now they come back to the winds and the stars they
    know,
  Now the ship lifts to the lift of the Southern foam,
From the fields of Troy, from the desert sands and the
    snow,
  Wounded and blind, they have set their faces home.

But who are those among them whom no man sees?
  Whose are the feet that pace the deck unheard?
When the ship draws in and in to the shouting quays,
  Is there no word for those shining ranks, no word?

There's a prayer breathed low, and a tear that's inly
    shed
  And a light in the soul for the coming years to
    prove—
Ye too return, O beloved, O gallant dead,
  Ye too return—there is no death in love!
               —Enid Derham.